Praise for *Once I Was a Princess* by Jacqueline Pascarl
'All parents tucking their infants safely into bed at night can only begin to imagine the torment Jacqueline has endured. Her excellent book will do much to increase public awareness of and sympathy for the wicked realities of child abduction'

— *Daily Mail*

'I read it at a gallop, like a thriller, sometimes forgetting that it is all horrifyingly autobiographical'

— Helen Osborne, *The Spectator*

'Jacqueline Pascarl's life is like the blockbuster movie it will probably become'

— *Mail on Sunday*

'...the literary equivalent of Edvard Munch – one long scream of unbearable grief and pain'

— *The Australian*

'...a vivid picture of a stifling, enclosed world, where women are neglected or abused, and kept in a state of ignorance which robs them of all initiative'

— *Sydney Morning Herald*

Abducted

The Fourteen-Year Fight
to Find My Children

Jacqueline Pascarl

MAINSTREAM
PUBLISHING

EDINBURGH AND LONDON

First published (under the title *Since I Was a Princess*)
in Great Britain in 2007 by
MAINSTREAM PUBLISHING COMPANY
(EDINBURGH) LTD
7 Albany Street
Edinburgh EH1 3UG

ISBN 9781845963033

This book is a work of non-fiction based on the life, experiences
and recollections of Jacqueline Pascarl. In some cases, names of
people and places, dates, sequences or the detail of events have been
changed to protect the privacy of others. The author has stated to the
publishers that, except in such respects, not affecting the substantial
accuracy of the work, the contents of this book are true

A catalogue record for this book is available
from the British Library.

Typeset in Bembo and DearJoe

Printed in Great Britain by
Cox & Wyman Ltd, Reading

For my four amazing, uniquely individual and fascinating children. Know that wherever life's journey takes you, I hold you close and proudly in my heart. Never give up on what you know to be just and truthful, or those you love and respect.

Author's Note

I was married to a Malaysian prince for five years and came to learn that princess is a state of mind, not a state of royal grace. Every child living on the globe has a right to a childhood, and to have a place in someone's heart as their prince or princess. Parental protection, nurturing, innocence and self-esteem contribute greatly to a young person's expectations, self-image and sense of place in the world – without them we all have the potential to founder.

'Always live in hope . . .'

Prologue

May 1999

The wailing permeated my gut and travelled to that plateau just above the breasts where pain and empathy reside so closely.

Even before I could pinpoint its location, I recognised the cry as the timeless sound of great loss and grief. I knew its origins well; I was familiar with its resonance and acquainted with its depth. In my past, I had, myself, been the originator of many such cries. It was a call to which there was no answer and no panacea – nor did it expect one. Its vibrations spread to my temples and the back of my skull, finally settling as a great, unyielding lump in the back of my throat. As I stumbled across the rock-strewn terrain of the refugee camp, I thought how strange, and yet somehow comforting, that the sounds of tragedy do not differ from one section of humanity to another.

High-pitched screams now punctuated the wails of grief, competing with the dull 'thump, thump' emitted by the rotors of a passing armoured helicopter. The chopper, probably carrying missiles, a reconnaissance team or some other NATO cargo, was visible only as a blackened presence against the night sky. This tract of land over which it passed was wedged between the battle zone of Kosovo and the bright lights of the Macedonian capital, Skopje, thirty kilometres down the unlit road. Our small sanctuary, just eleven minutes within the Macedonian border, provided a meagre haven for 27,000 displaced souls – women, children and men who had fled the armed conflict of Kosovo and the relentless pursuit of the Serbian military forces.

Stenkovec II was one of the three major processing and refugee camps in Macedonia set up under the protection of the United Nations High Commission for Refugees (UNHCR) and run on a day-to-day basis by CARE International, the global humanitarian aid and development agency. The camp was bleak and unforgiving, occupying a series of high-walled rabbit-warren gullies, interconnected by excavated cuttings just wide enough for a tank to pass through. At its core was a vantage point, a small hill up which children scrambled during the daylight hours and where an effort had been made by the United Nations International Children's Emergency Fund (UNICEF) to cobble together the semblance of a school and kindergarten. Formerly a stone quarry that had served, until recently, as a heavy artillery and weapons range, the locale was devoid of trees, running water, electricity and sewerage.

The moon reflected off the battered face of my watch – 3.27 a.m. We had been processing and unloading these latest busloads of refugees (or 'internally displaced people', as the politically correct amongst us insisted on saying) since just after 1 a.m. The initial headcounts suggested about 800 souls had been crammed aboard six buses, each normally intended to carry fifty-five passengers.

Closing in on the weeping, I picked my way around the

rear of the huge khaki-coloured 'horse tents' – so named, I assumed, because the military arm that had donated them to the relief effort was a cavalry regiment. It was here that our new arrivals were to be sheltered. Each human being would be allotted a one-metre-wide space which would have to serve as sleeping quarters, living room and storage for whatever possessions they had managed to carry on their back or shove into plastic shopping bags as they began their escape to safety. A requisite two metres separating the rows served as a central walkway between the two sides of the tent. These were the minimum allowances under World Health Organisation (WHO) and UNHCR guidelines during a time of emergency. This was the theory; but that night, in a tent meant to accommodate thirty, nearly one hundred weary people would sleep cheek by jowl with complete strangers in utter darkness. This was just one of the frustrating realities we faced as aid workers: we witnessed humanity at its lowest ebb forced to masquerade as sardines.

I checked each canvas, trying to pinpoint the grieving woman. The torch on my head bounced light off startled faces peering back at me from the darkness. There was quiet sobbing in every shelter I visited, whispering, groaning and sometimes the whimpering of babies and children, but the sound I sought was on a different level – it had a different intensity. Tangles of guy ropes and tent pegs running off our makeshift town hampered my path; I tripped and broke my fall by making a grab for the cyclone wire perimeter fence, and that is how I found her.

My torch illuminated her feet, shod in battered tan high-heeled shoes. Knees drawn tightly up to her chest, she sat on the ground oblivious to my approach. Her brown gabardine skirt was heavily stained, that much I could see, and she now emitted guttural howls as she repeatedly banged her forehead with the heel of her hand. To witness such grief, and then to be capable of identifying it from the outside looking in, is an unspeakable invasion of a person. Even now as I write, my chest compresses hard against my lungs and my eyes are drawn out of their sockets by the insight it affords.

Her brown hair was short and streaked with blonde, her hands and nails grubby and torn. The blouse she wore had once been white – a teacher's or secretary's garb, I guessed – but was marred now by a few missing buttons and what appeared to be dried blood. Thirty-plus, I estimated, around my own age – young enough, yet ancient, too, if life has imploded all normality.

Grasping her pounding fist, I dragged it downwards as she threw back her head. Her jaw slackened with a huge expulsion of air and wailing from the back of her throat. Another woman emerged from the shadows, a grandmother, judging from the little girl clutching at her long cardigan. She spoke to me in Albanian, a tumble of words I couldn't understand. I tried a few words in Bosnian and there was a flicker of comprehension. The grandmother called to a teenage boy who had hung back against the tent wall.

Selma was the distressed woman's name, according to the boy, translating the grandmother's words. Two days earlier, at a pre-border check by the Serbian paramilitary, she had been subjected to a body cavity search. The soldiers had found a roll of cash secreted on her person. Her punishment for attempting to smuggle cash out of Kosovo was the murder of her child.

Apparently, she was on her knees as she struggled to stop the thugs from tearing her seven-year-old son from her arms. One military type grabbed her by the hair while another wrenched the small child's arms above his head, put a pistol to the base of his skull and pulled the trigger.

'His eyes, his eyes,' was what I now understood Selma sobbed as I held her tightly in my arms, her head against my shoulder. The last image of her terrorised child had seared itself into her mind with the efficiency of a precision laser and marked her as a mother shattered by its final brutality.

It was then, for the first and only time ever, that I broke the cardinal rule of aid work: never cry in front of your charges. Fuck that; I was crying *with* her not *for* her, and some of my tears were for the awfulness of our fellow human beings and the deeds of which they were capable.

The incongruity of my journey to that point in time was not entirely lost on me. How had I come to be wading through such violence, poverty, desperation and shining hope? I've often thought it bizarre that an Australian mother of two had become the common denominator linking a refugee camp in the foothills of the Balkans, a child literacy project amid the Maasai of Kenya, heavy-duty army boots and an international furore over parental child abduction.

But the straight truth of the matter is that nothing surprises me much any more; I now just accept the vagaries of life as a natural progression towards some distant point in the future.

Years ago I had to make a choice: either to shut down my faculties, my heartbeat, my potential for joy and wallow in unassuageable grief and torment, or to survive and create a new life for myself by harnessing all my negative experiences into one positive and stubborn force and following the direction in which it led me. That was *the* single most important decision I have made since my children were abducted.

One

From Palace to Pension

It was an ill-conceived compulsion – dangerous, and one I knew I'd regret even as my hand ferreted in the bottom of my duffle bag and shakily withdrew the small album of family photographs. The images contained within flung me onto a roller-coaster ride of emotion. They buoyed and mocked me with their simplicity and happiness and reminded me of a life that was no longer mine, of children who were no longer embraceable and a time so long past. The small album I held in my hands was my private talisman of determination, my future and my past. Sleep would now be unattainable, but the reminder of what had once been allowed, the normality of mundane life and of a sanity I once knew, was worth it.

I lay still and quiet in my bed, waiting for dawn to release me from my unwelcome thoughts. I contemplated how the years following a tragedy can pass in the blink of an eye or with the protracted and torturous ache of an unhealed and suppurating amputation. It depends entirely on the mindset of the person counting the minutes. For me, that experience of time passed through both dimensions depending on my relationships, surroundings and activities. Losing both my children had devastated and galvanised me on the most unpredictable levels of pain and survival. Manic activity meant little time to think when the pain was too excruciating to analyse. I came to understand that the human mind remembers moments or days, but the overriding psychological imprint is that of emotions and milestones – missed and shredded.

Decisions I had made as a seventeen year old, when I was swept off my feet by a seemingly mild-mannered foreign architecture student, who had attended Prince Charles's alma mater, Geelong Grammar, would haunt me decades later and leave me and my children dealing with the consequences of my wilfulness.

The quiet young man I had met and fallen in love with was the clichéd tall, dark and handsome gallant; he also turned out to be the grandson of the late Sultan of Terengganu and a royal prince in his own right. I see now why Bahrin was attracted to me – he had been married (and divorced) once already to a fellow student of the same age who had left him for an Aussie gardener. In me, as a fairly damaged teenager from a dysfunctional home who just wanted a family to love, he had found a girl he could mould into the sort of princess he wanted. Fresh enough in terms of genealogy, parentless in terms of interference, and always an outsider in Australia because of my mixed racial background (Australian born of French, Irish, English and Chinese decent) in a then xenophobic country, I longed to fit in, and that is what he offered – complete acceptance under Islam and a firm place in his family.

We settled down to a strange married life within Bahrin's family, a branch of the Malaysian royals in Terengganu – quite a wealthy state where the royals benefited from its gas, oil and mining reserves, as well as the logging of rainforest timbers. I was a breeder and he took a punt that my bloodlines would enhance his. Our ten-year age difference seemed inconsequential at the time of our union but, like many hopeful fairy tales, the gilt wore off the marriage fairly quickly when our cultural differences became apparent. I objected to his philandering and physical poundings and he disliked my objections. The other problem was that once I became a mother, even though I was a teenager, my malleability dissolved and I grew a brain – a very Westernised brain – which provoked my husband's blue blood to the point of boiling.

My erstwhile prince became increasingly abusive towards me, but the straw that broke this camel's back was his polygamous marriage to a scantily clad nightclub singer a couple of weeks after the birth of our youngest child. Subsequently, when Iddin was just two years old and our daughter, Shahirah, five months, we returned to my home town of Melbourne.

Following a protracted legal battle regarding the correct forum for a hearing (the prince had wanted me deported from my own birthplace to stand before an Islamic Syariah court in Malaysia), Bahrin voluntarily signed over full custody of our children to me, allowing me to forge a new life with my children in Australia.

Contrary to various media reports at the time, the prince was not hard done by legally or emotionally and had liberal, although conditional, access to our little ones. But unfortunately it wasn't all plain sailing after the custody orders were ratified in the courts – that would have been a far too rational outcome from a highly controlling man such as my erstwhile prince charming.

The prince's contact with our children was sporadic and draining, for them as well as for me. Although arrangements had been put in place at my instigation during court proceedings for their father to telephone once every second Sunday, the children would usually wait in vain for the call to come through at the appointed hour. It soon became an onerous chore for them to sit inside waiting all day whilst their friends gambolled in the sunshine. Eventually I decided that if we had waited for more than two hours on any given Sunday, we would just continue with normal family activities and give up on the call. Access visits in situ had also been arranged very rationally to ensure that 'double bookings' didn't occur and that I could organise the children's holiday activities without a clash. I believe it very important that a child knows both parents and really hoped that Bahrin would avail himself of this quite liberal access arrangement. Given that he had declared in open court that it was his 'Islamic jihad' to retrieve his son from an infidel country, my nerves at this contact had to be put aside ahead of what I considered a fundamental right for my children to have contact with their father. The prince agreed in court that he would give one month's written notice prior to him coming to Australia to see the children and that, upon arrival, he would surrender his passport, ticket and credit cards to my solicitor to circumvent any risk of abduction. Although I was well aware that he could have any number of credit cards on his person, only two were mentioned in court proceedings and logged – I didn't want to push things too far.

Instead of regular visits, my former husband chose to come to Australia less than once a year and simply refused to abide by the legal orders directing notice of his arrival. It was not unusual for Bahrin to sweep into town unannounced on an early morning flight and demand that the Family Courts convene a special session at an hour's notice. One Easter

17

Thursday, six years after our divorce, he pulled this stunt, having decided on the spur of the moment that he wanted to see the children over the Easter Bank Holiday weekend – notwithstanding that a vacation at a holiday farm had been planned and booked months earlier and the children were looking forward to the jaunt. What was a normal and completely innocent holiday was declared a snub against Islam by the prince: he insisted that he take the children to a mosque the next day for Friday prayers and that all our vacation plans be set aside by the court to allow him to do this.

The judge pointed out to a very angry Bahrin that this was impossible and, as the prince had not, on numerous occasions, abided by previous legal rulings to give due notice of his intention to exercise access to the children, he would have to wait. His Honour pointed out with the utmost courtesy that whilst Friday prayers were obviously important to the prince, Easter was a traditional school holiday in Australia and our vacation had been booked many months in advance. The judge offered access for the following Friday instead, to allow for Muslim prayer services, but Bahrin was not placated in any way and stormed out of the proceedings in high royal dudgeon. He seemed to relish protesting this singular and supposed religious prejudice far and wide afterwards and used it to justify his future actions.

All this kerfuffle meant a lot of expensive legal fees for me and for him, simply because he had refused to write a letter and give advance warning of his plans. Bahrin bowed to no one unless it was a senior royal, and he detested having to fit into anyone's schedule.

I quashed my frustrations with a fair amount of difficulty, always feeling that the children came first, but I drew a line in the sand when my young son, Iddin, complained to me that during overnight stays at his father's hotel no bed was provided for Shahirah; my daughter was expected to sleep on the floor. It took the verbal intervention of a male friend to elicit some equitable and responsible treatment of our children not based on gender.

As time went on, I dealt with the upheavals of their father's vagaries as best I could, mustering all my confidence and suppressing my fears that he would try to snatch the children back in a vengeful vendetta. Those around me, especially my then solicitor, told me to water down my apprehension that Bahrin would carry through on his threat of a jihad. Perhaps the sheer normalcy of our lives lulled me into believing that, as the prince had taken other wives and had more children, my offspring would hold less significance – after all, Bahrin was not at the head of the line to any throne and neither were my children.

The life I tried to build for our little family unit was glaringly simple. We were happy and self-contained, a marked contrast to my turbulent life in the royal Islamic household. I worked in the years following our divorce as a waitress, typist, ballet teacher and later a public relations consultant, always juggling childcare and income, with the priority being the children and our time together. Money was tight, but the children and I lived happily in a rambling old house that I had renovated with my own hands. Each night, as I read Iddin and Shahirah a bedtime story, or watched them play mud pies in the garden, I smothered my acorn of alarm and wariness, buried it deep, and just allowed myself the indulgence of loving them, and being loved, without the constraints of royalty or foreign protocols. Registering the echoes of their laughter as my own lullaby as I lay in bed at night, I told myself that physically and emotionally we had put down roots a million miles from the violent and hollow existence I had led in Malaysia.

There was what I can only describe as a lightness in my children's existence then – they were shiny and joyous and giggling. I remember climbing the old apricot tree in the garden with them and dangling from its branches, and teddy bears' picnics in the park. I suppose, at that time, we were growing up together, as I was a single mother at the age of twenty-two. There were raucous afternoons spent quite literally rolling in the mud and snorkelling in the bathtub and making cereal boxes into hats and spaceships. But most of all, we were together, and however modest my income, my children were never hungry and never dirty and there was always plenty of love and cuddles. I think that is what, even after all the years of separation from Iddin and Shah, I missed the most – the cuddles: the heart-wrenching and primal instinct to softly sniff your child's scent as they snuggle in, and the knowledge that the heartbeats you can faintly feel as they press against you first began in your own body.

Two

Exquisite Torture

I often wonder how many other people in this world can pinpoint the exact moment that their lives were changed irrevocably: smashed, redefined, uncategorised and forever divorced from the normal comprehension of their peers.

I had known, even before I steeled myself to walk into that hotel at the appointed hour, that its doorway was more than the entrance to a nondescript building – it was the gateway to hell. I caught my reflection in the mirrors that lined the lobby and noted with detached satisfaction that my face appeared calm and gave no indication of the turmoil I was masking beneath its shell as I walked to the house phones and dialled Bahrin's room. No answer, but then I knew there wouldn't be. They were gone . . .

*　*　*

If I try to recreate the chronology of events and the feelings of general disquiet leading up to July 1992, I must start with the telephone call that came from Bahrin in February. His unexpected contact with the children around Iddin's birthday was not what triggered the uneasy sense that all was not as it seemed; rather it was something about the nature of the call itself that had me pondering its significance for hours afterwards. In the rush of receiving what I assumed to be an expensive international call, I had hurried the children to the telephone. It was only later that I realised that the normal 'international pips' had not sounded when I picked up the receiver. I had instead heard the distinctive 'beep, beep, beep', signalling connection of a long-distance call within Australia. When I mentioned this strange anomaly to a couple of friends, they assured me that I must have been mistaken or had confused the international call sign with the Australian one. I wasn't entirely convinced, but I opted to go with the status quo as it was the easiest course to take and the least likely to prompt raised eyebrows and insinuations about overprotectiveness or jokes about paranoia.

To write this portion of my story is to verbalise the scenes, nightmares and ineptitudes that coloured my life for the interminable time that has gone by.

'If only I had . . .' is the phrase that I scourged myself with throughout every waking and sleeping moment that I drew breath. If only I had . . . what? If only I had listened to my gut instincts, if only I hadn't listened to other people, if only I hadn't wanted to behave like a mature adult, if only I had listened to Iddin and Shah and taken heed of their wishes. But the futility of hindsight and what-ifs won't change any of our lives now.

July in that long past year of 1992 was to mark a return to normal family life, starting with our traditional birthday bashes, for Shahirah, who would be seven, and myself. I had remarried two years earlier, five years after leaving Bahrin. By contrast, Iain Gillespie was light and laughter, the quintessential Pied Piper/Peter Pan I had missed in my childhood. He came as a package deal with teenage children and worked as a documentary film-maker and journalist. Our children fell in love with each other and we lived a happy, busy suburban life in a leafy Melbourne suburb. Bike rides, weekends at Iain's family farm, loud dinner parties and a frenzy of domestic activity – what more could anyone expect with five children often residing in the house together and the occasional foster child or sleepover.

Iain and I had dreamed of adding to the family but were left shattered when I miscarried twin boys. As a result my health had taken quite a blow. But after the forthcoming term break, I would surprise Iddin with the saxophone lessons he'd been hankering after and Shah and I would begin the construction of the prefabricated doll's house I had ordered. All the children in the family would be back in school and life would settle down to its regular schedule of parents' committees, ballet classes and long bike rides.

Bahrin telephoned after a silence of almost six months to confirm the details for his impending visit the following week. It did strike me as strange that he telephoned during the school day to speak ostensibly with Iddin when he knew that both children would be at school. But, as his tone was more than conciliatory and his voice devoid of its usual belligerence, I did my best to be friendly. He was so charming, in fact, that I wondered why. When I reminded him that the children were never home at that time, he settled down to have a long chat with me, commiserating over the recent loss of the babies, hoping that I was keeping well and politely enquiring after the health of my beloved grandmother. It was only later that I realised I had never told him about my recent miscarriage.

What followed was an astounding backflip in attitude: one that I had always hoped for but never expected. 'Look, Yasmin

– sorry, Jacqueline – this time when I come to see the children, I'd like it if things could be more friendly between the two of us. For the sake of the children, we should let bygones be bygones and concentrate on making them happy. What do you think?' (Yasmin was the name Bahrin had chosen for me to use on official documents after our marriage.)

I was stunned. I could not equate the cordial voice I was hearing with Bahrin. I was dumbfounded. 'That's all I ever wanted, Bahrin,' I replied. 'I just want to make things easy for Iddin and Shah, and so does Iain.'

'Fine then, I'll see you next week. Please send my best to Iain and your nanna,' he said, and the line went dead.

I was left bemused and off-balance, staring at the receiver I still held in my hand and wondering if, after all the years of backbiting, threats, abuse and grandstanding, Bahrin had finally grown up.

To try and make sense of this turn of events, I rang Iain at his office and my lawyer, Lillian Webb, and repeated verbatim what had just passed. Iain was very pleased, telling me to take it as a sign that Bahrin had finally accepted what was best for the children and was behaving rationally and maturely for once. Lillian's reaction was identical to Iain's and she dismissed my 'what's his angle' question with an impatient groan. For some intangible reason, the hairs on my neck were standing on end and my stomach felt queer long after I had replaced the telephone onto its cradle.

But at that point in time it was the least of my worries: I had a seventh birthday party to organise and fifteen children to transport to the Plaster Fun House, where Shah had decided to hold her celebration. Her present from me was a much-wanted Minnie Mouse doll that she had not so discreetly angled for over a number of months; just seeing her face as she opened her present that morning confirmed that we couldn't have chosen anything better. Long after that day had passed, I could remember with relief that I was able to give Shah the type of party she wanted and could be thankful that I had encouraged Iddin to bring along his two closest friends to be his companions.

Sunday, 5 July 1992 was a good day, a happy day, a day when all of our closest friends and family descended on our house for my birthday. They stayed until the evening, laughing and joking, as hoards of unruly and excited children played hide-and-seek and chasey through the house and around the garden as the sun went down. At this new milestone, I was finally happy, safe and looking forward to many more birthdays like this one: children and friends everywhere, a blossoming career as a television journalist, a caring husband and the hope of a new baby at some stage to anchor us all even more firmly together. The only thing that marred my thoughts was the impending arrival of Bahrin and the fact that Iddin and Shah would be spending the following night with him at his hotel.

Monday dawned bleak and rainy, the children protesting that they didn't want to go to a hotel, that they'd rather spend their term holiday at the farm with Iain's parents and their fourteen-year-old stepsister, Skye. Iain lectured Iddin on the positive sides of the impending access period and also forbade him to write our telephone number on his leg in felt pen, as he had secretly been doing for a couple of years. Iain told him that it wasn't necessary, that there was no danger from Bahrin and that it was going to be a wonderful treat for Shah and him to stay with Bahrin at the hotel. Iddin's facial expression showed how dubious he felt this advice was.

The prince arrived in the middle of the afternoon to collect the children. Studiously cordial and polite, he turned down

Iain's offer of coffee and requested the use of a telephone to book a taxi for the return trip to his hotel. Shahirah began to complain in a loud voice that she didn't want to go with Abah (the name for father in Malay), and Iddin echoed her sentiments as Bahrin stood poised by the kitchen bench with the telephone receiver clenched in one hand. I noticed the whiteness of his knuckles and the stiffness of his neck, a sure sign of his displeasure and of the undercurrent of tension that ran beneath his blank face. I put his reactions down to the fact that our dog, Muckle, was sniffing around his ankles, having earlier greeted him with growls and furious barking. Bahrin loathed dogs and had always been intimidated by their presence at close proximity. I took secret delight at his discomfort and hoped that he noted our children's love of their pet and their nonchalance when around her. To me it illustrated just how different from him, how normal and natural, they were. Animals had always figured in our family life – cows, rabbits, dogs, cats, horses, kangaroos; neither of the children could ever abide a 'sook' around the creatures they loved. Looking back now, I truly think that Muckle had the measure of the situation and I kick myself for restraining her when she nuzzled in the general direction of Bahrin's crotch. I wish now she had taken a piece out of him then and there, or had leapt straight at his jugular. Instead, I ordered her to sit and drop on her belly at my feet, where she continued to eye my ex-husband balefully and follow his slightest movement with great intensity.

In the new spirit of cooperation that both Bahrin and I were exuding, I persuaded him to let me drive them back into the city, citing the inconvenience of taxis and the rain but not daring to voice the opinion that the children's transition from one environment to another might be eased by this show of unity and harmony. So I found myself shepherding Bahrin, Skye, Iddin and Shah into Arnold, our sturdy red four-wheel drive, for the trip into town. Bahrin and Iain shook hands at our front door and the children kissed him goodbye, with Shah, as usual, throwing her arms around Iain's neck and saying in a loud voice, 'I love you.'

Iddin and Shah were less than enthusiastic about this overnight stay with Bahrin and made no bones about letting their father know it. Shah also insisted on taking Whitey, her white fluffy goat, which had been her first Christmas present from Iain, to keep her company at night.

The conversation between Bahrin and me was painfully polite throughout the drive and I found myself groping desperately for some topic or common ground. I had tried the children, their schooling and hobbies, but this subject seemed to hold minimal interest for him so I turned to architecture, pointing out one particular building I thought would interest him – a beautifully renovated and deconsecrated church which now accommodated a successful advertising agency. His reply, with its venomous contempt, stunned me.

'That's disgusting, only *mat sallehs* [white men] would use a holy place as an office.'

I heard myself begin to try and justify the restoration, not demolition, of a gracious building but, realising the futility of this, my voice trailed off and we lapsed into silence, all attempts at conversation abandoned. Mercifully, we soon arrived at the hotel and, as the rain was pouring down, there was a mad scramble of half-mouthed protests from Iddin and Shah, goodbye hugs and kisses, and shouted messages between Skye and the children as Bahrin, with an audible sigh of relief, carefully opened his door and alighted. I told the children firmly that they had to stay with Abah and that I would see them again on Wednesday, reminding them that Bahrin and I had agreed that they were allowed to telephone whenever they wanted and to say goodnight. This reminder mollified them somewhat and I quickly jumped back into the car, with a wave and kiss blown into the air, leaving them on the footpath beside Bahrin – their father but little more than a stranger to them.

The front gate clanged shut, announcing Iddin and Shah's homecoming to the accompaniment of frantic barking from Muckle and the ringing of the doorbell. As I swung the heavy white door open, I could hear Shah on the other side crying.

'Mummy, he wouldn't let me bring Whitey home. I can't get to sleep without him,' she sobbed, as I took her into my arms. I looked enquiringly over her head at Iddin.

'Abah wouldn't let us bring anything home with us. He even made us leave our toothbrushes. He said it didn't matter,' Iddin explained.

Quickly, I looked towards the gate and saw Bahrin lift his hand in greeting to me as he slid into the back seat of the waiting taxi.

'Wait,' I yelled, in time to catch the car before it drove away. Leaving the children standing on the verandah, I ran to the gate. 'Why didn't you let her bring her goat home? She can't get to sleep without him.'

'She doesn't need it.'

'But I told you about her, how—'

Before I could go on, he interrupted me. 'Look, I don't care, Yasmin, it doesn't matter,' he said, clearly trying hard to control his anger. 'She can get it when I take them back to the hotel tomorrow.' And with that he slammed the door, effectively cutting off the conversation, and the taxi drove away.

How I wished I could simply cancel the access arrangements then and there, but I dared not risk another court battle. At least the children would be with Bahrin for only two nights. I mentally thanked my foresight for the stipulation that, as Iddin and Shahirah were not that familiar with their father, his access was to be broken up throughout the week.

After we went inside, Shah threw herself on her bed, sobbing for Whitey, and I sat on its edge stroking her hair and trying to convince her that Whitey would be all right for one night alone at the hotel. I told her that we were going out to have dinner with some of our favourite friends that evening, but nothing made any difference. She was still sobbing as I closed her bedroom door and went to talk with Iddin. I felt so utterly infuriated with Bahrin: why was he so callous and uncaring? What was so difficult about packing up two small overnight bags and a fluffy goat?

Dinner that night was alternately relaxing and tense. Our friends went out of their way to make it an enjoyable interlude in the midst of a difficult time, but the evening was punctuated with Iddin and Shah using any excuse to tell anyone who would listen that they didn't want to go back to the hotel and Abah. Around 8.30 p.m., just as we were sitting down to port and coffees, Shah announced that she felt tired and wanted to have a lie down until we were ready to go home. Minutes after she had snuggled down, she began to cry for Whitey. She begged me to drive to the hotel and collect him; she said that she never wanted to go back there and she asked Iain and me not to send her back with her father the next day. She kept crying until her nose was running and her shoulders heaved with sobs as I rocked her in my lap. Iddin edged into the room with our friends' son, Nicholas, who was carrying a small white teddy. 'Here, Shah,' he said, 'this is my favourite teddy, maybe he'll make you feel better,' and he pressed the small bear into Shah's hands.

'Thank you.' Her bottom lip wobbled as she struggled to catch her breath.

During the drive home that night, Shah dozed next to her brother in the back seat as Iain and I talked in quiet tones about the children and Bahrin.

'Don't worry,' Iain told me. 'He'll be gone by next week and it will all be over until next year.'

'But I don't want to go back tomorrow,' came Iddin's voice from the rear of the car. We had assumed that he, like his sister, was asleep. 'It's so boring there and he doesn't understand anything about anything and there's nothing to do. He's trying to suck up to us with presents and toys and stuff . . . I want to be with Skye at Nanna's land for the holidays.'

'Look,' Iain told him, 'it's only for a few more days. Just try to have a good time and we'll go down to the land next weekend to see Nanna. It's not like these are the only holidays you're going to have to go and visit Nanna and Grandad.'

Thursday. 9 July

After the phone call came at 5.10 a.m., telling me that Kelvin was dead, I lay beside Iain and watched the night change into a grey day. It hadn't felt real hearing that Kelvin was gone; after all, the children and I had been to see him only the day before. Shah had drawn him a picture of a unicorn and brought it with her; she had kissed him gently on the forehead as she laid it on his bed and walked quietly from the room. Iddin and Shah had both known that Kelvin was dying from AIDS and that he was getting weaker by the hour, but they had insisted on following me upstairs when I went to check on him. I myself had kissed him goodbye as he slept, tiptoeing from the room not knowing that it would be the last time I would see him. I was glad that he had died in his own home surrounded and cared for by a roster of his close friends and visited by a constant stream of former students, colleagues and ballet partners. He had his dignity and he had love; those were the most important things to him.

Kelvin Coe was a former principal dancer with the Australian Ballet. We'd been nothing more than casual acquaintances during my ballet years; Kelvin was a virtuoso performer, an internationally respected artist and ballet master, and a much more senior dancer than I was. He was someone I'd worshipped from afar for many years when I was growing up, and even when we were teaching at the same school and sharing the same friends I was too much in awe to do anything more than take his direction in pas de deux class and mumble affirmative replies.

More recently, though, I had become very close to both Kelvin and his partner. I had been working for a couple of years as a TV presenter and interviewer and I had profiled their relationship for a special report months earlier then joined Kel's care team, ferrying casseroles and chocolate cakes from my kitchen to theirs. So when the phone rang again some time after 7 a.m., I knew what it would be. I was being called into work to put together his obituary for the evening news, just as I had promised him all those months ago. It was rare for me to work flat out when the children were on holidays – my job on a radio programme and the special reports I did for television were tailored around the children's school hours and allowed me the flexibility of being able to drop them off and collect them from school every day, which was just as important to Iddin, Shah and Skye as it was to me. This one time would be an exception and I knew they would accept it as the right thing for me to do.

I was already up and dressed when the children arrived at the breakfast table. They took the news of Kelvin's death with sadness and understanding, and Iddin's comment was particularly insightful: 'At least he won't be so sick and hurting any more. He didn't look happy for a long time, Mum.' I kissed his head in agreement and gave him a hug.

The film crew arrived at the house to collect me at 11.30 a.m. amidst the children's protests about the second instalment of access time with their father. I remember being very firm with them both and explaining in no uncertain terms that they did have to go and that I would be speaking to them by telephone throughout the day and to say goodnight before they went to sleep. After kissing and hugging everyone goodbye, I turned to Iain, promising to ring home during the day to see how everything was going. Iain would be staying home to be with Iddin and Shah and to effect the official handover when Bahrin arrived at 5 p.m. that afternoon. We always covered each other; our work usually enabled one of us to be home for the children and we juggled our respective schedules to accommodate the hiccoughs of family life.

'It'll be all right, Jack,' he told me reassuringly with a concerned smile. 'The kids and I will have some fun together. Elizabeth [our housekeeper] and I will get their bags ready and packed for when he comes.'

Turning to wave one last time before I drove off with the crew, I saw my family standing on the front verandah blowing kisses and clowning around for my benefit by pulling funny faces. And then I gave full attention to the questions I would ask at my first interview that day.

I checked in with the children around 4 p.m. and told

them that I loved them 'billions, trillions and infinities' and that I would speak to them later that night at the hotel. I will always remember that Iddin asked me one last time for a reprieve from the impending visit with his father and that I, in the midst of editing problems and the rush to have my story on Kelvin completed for the five o'clock news, cut him short with a definite 'no'.

'All right, Mum,' Iddin dragged out in a resigned tone and a heavy sigh. 'I love you. Here's Shah.'

'Hello, Mummy, I love you, love you, love you. Bye bye, bye bye,' she sang down the phone.

That was the last time I spoke to my children.

I arrived home quite late that evening, thoroughly depressed and exhausted. Iain had organised dinner for us both and reiterated that the children had been collected exactly on time by their father. I missed the children's presence that night; somehow their happy voices and sticky fingers would have helped to reaffirm the positive sides of life after having dealt with death and bereavement all day. I suppose most of all I wanted to tell them how much I loved them. So it was with this thought in mind that I reached for the telephone and dialled the number of the Victoria Hotel, where Bahrin and the children were staying.

Over the following seventy-two hours, I tried at regular intervals to contact Iddin and Shah by telephone. The first call I made was answered by Bahrin at the hotel. He refused to allow me to speak to either of the children, telling me firmly that both were asleep and would call me in the morning. I waited all of Friday for their call, but it never came. I tried to turn my mind to the weekend radio show I was meant to be preparing, but I couldn't quite seem to keep a focused train of thought. By evening, I began to telephone their room at hourly intervals, comforting myself by rationalising the situation, telling myself that they were off on a day trip to the zoo or somewhere equally as logical and that they would be back in their room soon – but with little conviction and all the while driven by this strange and prickly sense of urgency. I left message after message at the hotel reception until the operator there began to recognise my voice.

Saturday was worse. I had to complete all the pre-production work for my radio programme, but I found that I couldn't concentrate. I found it even harder to refrain from charging straight over to the hotel and sitting there until Bahrin and the children returned. If I intruded on the scheduled access time that I had voluntarily agreed upon, I risked sanctioning from the court and a resumption of the hostilities between Bahrin and me. I also knew that it would be ludicrous to seek the assistance of the police until there was tangible evidence that something was amiss. By 5 p.m. my hand had gravitated towards the telephone again and I was ringing on the hour, leaving what had degenerated to perfunctory messages with the hotel telephonist. Each time she heard my voice she would kindly assure me that none of the staff had seen Iddin and Shahirah enter or leave since my last call but that she would pass on my message when she could.

My stomach was a ball of knots, my ribcage constricted my lungs like an iron corset and all I could do was mentally pray that the worst possible scenario, the one that kept running through my mind, was an overreaction. Iain tried hard to calm my fears and reminded me that Bahrin and the children were probably out somewhere having a terrific time, but his reassurances did little to convince me or quell my uneasiness.

'Everything's okay. Everything – will – be – okay,' I stressed to myself over and over again to stem the rising panic I felt. 'He couldn't have done it, not after all this time, he couldn't have,' I reasoned. Kidnap after seven years was ridiculous, insane, far-fetched – but deep down inside, in the very core of my being, I knew that was exactly what Bahrin had done, even though I refused to verbalise what I knew was true.

By 8 p.m. I began to wonder if my behaviour was becoming irrational. I put myself on a strict quota of one phone call to the hotel every half-hour. I only hoped that the staff there wouldn't become exasperated with this frequency and cut off my only tangible pinpoint on the children's location.

Every fibre in my body told me that something was seriously wrong. I couldn't wait for the access period to expire at 12.30 p.m. the next day – I had to do something.

I rang the Family Law Squad of the Federal Police. The officer I spoke to understood my distress and agreed that the situation as it stood did point to something suspicious, and his explanation about procedures and the need for tangible evidence of the children's disappearance was nothing more than I had expected. There was little more I could do but wait until the official expiry of the agreed deadline for Iddin and Shah's return. Prior to that, all the officer could do was make an unofficial note of my call and concerns and hope for the best.

Minutes ticked by like hours and by the time the clock showed 11 p.m. I knew that I had to try to enlist the help of the hotel staff. The duty manager understood immediately the seriousness of the situation and told me to wait by the phone; he would call me back after checking with his staff. In fact, he did more than that – when his call finally came he painted an ominous picture that left me climbing the walls in despair. The adjoining rooms shared by Bahrin and the children had not been slept in for two nights and none of his staff seemed to have seen them come or go since Thursday night. Only the luggage and toys that peppered the rooms made me clutch at the hope that it was all a huge misunderstanding and that Bahrin was merely attempting to twist the knife. I thanked the hotel manager profusely for his help and put down the phone, steeling myself for the longest wait of my life: it would be thirteen and a half hours before I would know the truth. My emotional control was almost non-existent by this stage; it was everything I could do not to lash out at Iain as he continually assured me that I would see the children the next day and that I was getting far too overwrought about the whole thing. But I knew. It was as if Iddin and Shah had a pulse beat within my body that I had never recognised before and that pulse was weakening, leaving me with a dull ache and a feeling that my soul was teetering on the brink of a precipice.

Sunday, 12 July

Somehow I got through the radio programme, glancing at the clock continually, willing its hands to reach 12 p.m. and signal my release. Iain and I then drove directly to the Victoria Hotel to collect the children. We were fifteen minutes early, so Iain insisted that we wait in the car until the designated time. We were playing this game of Bahrin's strictly by the book. As we sat together outside the hotel, rain began to drizzle down the car windows, falling in murky puddles on the street. People laughing strolled beneath hastily unfurled umbrellas and the aroma of freshly made coffee filtered through the car from the Italian café nearby. Finally 12.30 p.m. came around, signalling that it was time for me to confront my greatest fear. Iain squeezed my hand reassuringly before I swung open the hotel's door and placed one foot in front of the other to get me to the bank of house phones at the reception desk. Before lifting the receiver, I mumbled a tangle of words. I prayed that I was wrong or that I would spin around and catch sight of Iddin and Shah running towards me across the foyer – anything but my worst fear.

I dialled. No reply. I tried again in case I had misdialled, even though I knew I hadn't. Careful to keep my tone even and squashing the hysterical note that broke through my voice, I turned away from the phones and I made a request to see the duty manager. She immediately swung into action, leading me towards the elevators and speaking rapidly about security, privacy and legalities. Her words tangled in my mind. I found myself nodding dumbly in acknowledgement of whatever she had just said. At this point I would have colluded with the devil just to get some information about Iddin and Shah. Eventually, after scurrying down a dimly lit corridor, we stood before the door that held my children's future behind it.

'Remember, you have to agree not to touch anything, madam,' she admonished as the key was inserted in the lock and the door swung open. Behind her the room was deserted, but the scene presented something more haunting and terrifying to me than any scene from a horror film. I looked down, only dimly aware that I was treading on more than a dozen messages from me that had been slipped beneath the door during the preceding twenty-four hours. The first room was obviously Bahrin's. A suitcase lay open on the floor to the right, its contents spilling out onto the floor. The bed was unslept in – a bad sign. Continuing through the communicating door to the adjoining room, I noticed that Bahrin had finally given Shah her own bed, except that it too was empty, as was Iddin's. In this room I could almost imagine the echoes of the children's voices still hanging in the air. Balloons and streamers hung from the central light fixture, a piece of glossy gift-wrap paper was affixed to the wall and a giant birthday card hung crookedly beside it.

My gut twisted as I realised that the room had been left by Bahrin for me to find, its messages clear only to me. Atop Shah's bed sat Whitey and Minnie Mouse, silent witnesses to what had transpired there. Near the foot of the bed lay Shah's red cloche hat, the one that we had chosen together weeks earlier to match her new winter coat, but it was what Bahrin had done to the hat that made my stomach heave and the room begin to rock: the small bright object had been crushed and twisted in such a rage of vindictiveness that it was irreparably destroyed. Iddin's pride and joy, his oversized Reebok sports shoes, the ones that he had nagged me for months and months to buy, stood pidgeon-toed and discarded by the bureau, his baseball cap flung on the bed as if he had just tossed it there. It was as if time had stood still in this cheap hotel room. It was a vacuum created by a twisted mind bent on the ultimate revenge. The scene brought to mind the ghost ship Marie Celeste, deserted mid-ocean, meals half-eaten and the radio on full blast; only this was not the Bermuda Triangle and this was no unexplained mystery to titillate the tabloid press: it involved my babies and they were gone.

I stumbled from the room and managed to rejoin Iain in the lobby. I blurted out what I had seen upstairs, holding back the sobs that were rising in the back of my throat and fighting to keep control so I could summon the only help that was available, the only chance that my children had.

There followed a whirlwind of fear and anxiety. The next minutes, hours and days flashed by in a jumble of despair, anger, rage, hopelessness and battle that suffocated me in their intensity and remained with me in every millisecond of my existence. A frantic phone call to the Federal Police from the lobby of the hotel, a barely coherent conversation with Lillian and garbled messages left for John Udorovic, my friend and Queen's Counsel, alerting him to what had happened, and a hastily arranged formal interview at Federal Police headquarters.

Questions, questions and more questions; the officers from the Family Law Squad were kind and to the point as I struggled to remain coherent against the catch in my throat that rose every time I spoke Iddin's and Shah's names. Details requested and given – ages, birthdates, clothing, possible destinations; I spewed forth all these answers with machine-like rapidity. Anything, anything to raise the chances that my children would be found. Although I volunteered much, no one asked me about their weight and height. And then came the request that brought the reality of the situation home to me, that made me realise that this whole experience was indeed real and not some disjointed dream from which I would soon wake: one of the officers asked if I had a recent photograph of Iddin and Shahirah to put out on the police alert computer and all points of exit from Australia. I groped for my handbag and rifled through its contents, searching for my wallet. Only days before I had inserted Iddin, Shah and Skye's new school photographs into the plastic window reserved for maternal pride. Only the day before I had flipped my purse open to proudly display how much the three children had grown. Now I was fumbling as I withdrew their faces and handed my babies over to the policewoman, a stranger. From just a single frozen moment in time, how could a stranger comprehend that these children were living, breathing human beings? 'These are my babies,' I wanted to scream. 'Please find them, help them, bring them home.'

I fought the urge to grab the officer's sleeve and demand that she listen to me. I wanted to tell her about the children, about their personalities, their likes and dislikes, about how terrified they'd be feeling in the midst of all this mess; but I correctly gauged that the officers weren't interested in my hysterics and that I had to keep myself under control for the sake of the children. When the tears did come, I quickly curbed my desire to dissolve into a blissful sobbing escape. I knew that there would be many more questions I would need to answer coherently. I had to keep myself together for the children's sake. They were counting on me, they would know that I would move heaven and earth to find them. I couldn't let them down, I had to hold on: I had to try and stay one step ahead of Bahrin's thinking.

When finally I had exhausted all of the police questions with my answers, Iain led me from the building and out into the cold, grey Melbourne street just as my stomach began to heave. I lurched towards a marble pillar and began to dry retch, wave after wave of nausea engulfing me until I felt as if my stomach had been turned inside out, until my body began to shake uncontrollably. Iain half-dragged, half-carried me to our car and bundled me into the front seat for the journey home to an empty house.

It took ages to locate John Udorovic that Sunday – I needed John's logic and his legal expertise. He would know what else I should be doing and, foremost, he had known my children since they were babies. It seemed as if I spent hours by the phone, my fingers dialling and redialling his various numbers, until one of my messages found him and he telephoned our home. A line of action was quickly decided upon following

John's call. We needed to obtain a warrant for Bahrin's arrest and the return of Iddin and Shah and, more importantly, it was urgent that I receive formal permission from the Family Court to publicise the children's kidnap in the hope that someone, somewhere, had a vital clue about their whereabouts and would come forward with the information.

A planned three-pronged attack to try and prevent Bahrin leaving the country evolved. John contacted the registrar of the Family Court to organise an immediate hearing before a judge as a matter of urgency. This was eventually obtained during an 'in-chambers' session conducted in the Family Court building in the presence of the registrar, with the judge at home several kilometres away making orders via speaker phone.

The first set of warrants obtained were very specific in wording: they ordered that officers of the Federal Police and all police forces across Australia search for Iddin and Shah, that they search all vessels, ships and planes for the children, and use force, if required, to take custody of the children and return them to me, their legal custodian.

I waited at home, with John's two teenage children watching over me with great intensity and care. It was an agonising time. I kept glancing at the telephone, willing it to ring, hoping that at any moment the children's voices would come down the line and into my ear. I did nonsensical things to fill the oppressive silence in the house. I prayed that the whole thing was a misunderstanding. I couldn't sit still, I couldn't cry either. I tried to fill the hours by cooking one of the children's favourite meals of fruit and veal curry. I made two huge steaming pots of it. I tried to believe that we would all be sitting down together as a family the next evening and laughing about this ridiculous kerfuffle as we ate our meal. The curry was later eaten by the scores of police, helpers and journalists who filled the house the next day. I cleaned the bathroom and walked the dog up and down the hallway, but none of it really helped; nothing could erase the growing reality of what was happening to our lives.

At 10.30 p.m., finally armed with the necessary court documents allowing publication and identification of myself and the children in the media, Iain and a friend burst into the two major newspaper offices in the city and laid before the respective news chiefs our private life stripped bare. It was hoped that all the attendant publicity would aid in the search. I, in turn, telephoned the acting news director of my own television network to beg for help and to let him know what would be splashed across the daily papers the next morning. I raised him at home, dragging him from his comfortable bed. When I told him that Iddin and Shah had been kidnapped by their biological father, he laughed at me, obviously interpreting what I had blurted out as a joke. 'Yeah, yeah, sure Jack,' he said and put down the phone in my ear. Subsequently, my own network missed the story.

Associated Press were notified as well, flashing the news by telex across the country in order to cover the broadest possible area. I knew that our only chance of finding them before Bahrin managed to spirit them out of Australia was to get the children's faces and names plastered across every paper, television screen and radio wave possible. I prayed with every fibre in my body that we weren't too late.

John's children had fallen asleep on the couch by the time I had finished my phone calls. For one brief split second, I would have given anything for their sleeping forms to be replaced by the compact shapes of Iddin and Shah: 'Dear God, where are they, what are they thinking, are they safe?' But no answering sign came. My close friend Deb Gribble arrived within minutes of my call. She was to hover and help for many hours that night as I alternately retched and rocked.

At some point, a sobbing noise, raw, ragged and barely controlled, came to me from the direction of the family room at the back of the house. I opened the door slowly to find Iain leaning into Deb's shoulder, crying and whispering hoarsely to her. 'She'll never be the same after this. She'll change, Deb. What am I going to do for her? She'll turn hard and bitter and she won't be the Jack that I love so much, I—'

Iain hurriedly pushed Deb away as he became aware of my presence behind him. He rose from the sofa and threw himself towards the bathroom and closed the door, avoiding all eye contact with me as he did so. I looked to Deb for some explanation, but all she did was hug me and say, 'He blames himself and now he's overwrought with worry for you and the children.'

Sliding back the bathroom door, I joined Iain in the room where only days ago I had bundled four squirming children – Iddin, Shah and their two cousins – into the bath, soaking and scraping off the remnants of birthday cake, paint and glue, evidence of a happy day spent partying as a family. I struggled to bring my eyes back to Iain. I murmured something like, 'Tell me it'll be all right,' and moved a step closer to him. As I did so, Iain turned, grabbed me by the shoulders, talking determinedly all the while. 'I'll show you what I'll do if I get my hands on him. I'll shake him till his head snaps off.' He could have been talking to a stranger for all the recognition of my identity I saw in his eyes.

'Stop it, darling. You're hurting me, Iain,' I gasped, as my head was thrown back and forth like a rag doll's. Releasing me immediately with a curse of recognition, he spun rapidly and punched the left wall of the bathroom and then the right, leaving two gaping holes in the plasterboard, which were like mouths open in a silent scream. Then he began to apologise, rocking me in his arms – but I couldn't banish the image of a triumphant and smirking Bahrin from my mind as I pressed my head into Iain's chest.

We lay in our bed that night for an hour, barely touching, two shell-shocked people too afraid to say anything else lest we fall into the pit of despair that we were both teetering on.

I was numb all over on the outside and terribly cold, the type of cold that cuts through your bones and makes them ache. Every few minutes I ran to the bathroom to retch up the bile left in my stomach. All food had long since been disposed of either by this non-stop vomiting or the diarrhoea that had gripped my stomach with monotonous regularity. The world had changed, nothing balanced any more and somewhere out there Iddin and Shah were terrified of what tomorrow would bring. What would Bahrin do when Shah demanded her goat Whitey? Would Iddin manage to get to a telephone? Had they eaten? Who was comforting them when they cried for me, were they being hit to make them stop crying? Were they warm enough? Shah had a bad rash that needed cream, had Bahrin even cared or remembered? Where, oh God, were they?

The questions went on and on in my head, as did my fears for them. I curled myself up into a foetal position and imagined every angle of their faces, every smile, every hair, how it grew around their hairlines and how good their arms felt around my neck. When would I feel them again? When could I tell them that it was all over and that nothing and nobody would hurt them again? But, most of all, when would I be able to rock them in my arms and tell them how very much I loved them? When?

Three

Freefalling Down a Rabbit Hole

Monday, 13 July

I was strangely relieved when the telephone rang at 5.30 a.m. Sleep had eluded me entirely during the hour I had spent in bed. I had lain there, willing my mind to fathom Bahrin's next move and tormented by fears for the children. The ringing of the phone gave me an excuse to get up. Anything was preferable to remaining inert and sick with worry. The call was from the media with a request for an interview, the first of the thousands that were to engulf us for the next days, weeks and months. News of what had happened to our family was plastered on the front page of the Monday morning newspapers. HUNT FOR PRINCE, CHILDREN; KIDNAP AUSSIE KIDS and POLICE TOLD TO FIND CHILDREN were the headlines, accompanied by copies of Iddin and Shah's school photographs. I had never before allowed Iddin and Shahirah to be identified publicly as members of the Malaysian royal family; I had always shielded them from the media and never used their titles openly. Privacy was a very precious element

45

in their lives and one which I felt was intrinsic to their being able to grow up as normal children with a good set of values, undisturbed by media intrusion; however, now all that was about to go out of the window. Our anonymnity would be no more and my children's heritage would make them objects of curiousity. It all seemed so surreal to me. It was other people's children who disappeared, with whom I commiserated from afar and for whom I felt concern – not mine.

Within twelve hours, I had gone from reporting the news to being the news, and it was a side of the camera that I did not relish at all. I steeled myself the best I could before the first television crew arrived at 7 a.m., dragging cables, lights, monitors and microphones into our home and setting up a large broadcast van on the street outside, topped by a satellite dish and television logo. Nausea still controlled my stomach, leaving me no choice but to continually run to the bathroom. I fought very hard to halt the shaking that had gripped my hands since reality had hit me; my right hand was the worst, jiggling so much that it was difficult to guide a glass to my mouth without the support of my left. I was a mess, but self-pity was a luxury I could ill afford; a complete collapse wasn't going to help me get my children back. I needed to fight, I told myself. I had no choice, other than to dissolve into a puddle of tears and give up then and there. So I did the only thing that my soggy brain could think of: I resolved to pretend as much as was practical that the media barrage I was about to face was part of my job, that it was work and that my 'job' was to get a message out there about my children, to reach people that I had never known before and to ask strangers for help.

I think my attitude initially threw the various media off-balance. Here was a 'victim', but the victim was known to them already, she worked in the industry, she knew how to fasten her own microphone to her collar and was comfortable in front of a camera. But I had neither the time nor the inclination to bother about how my demeanour affected their perception of me during a time of personal crisis. Iddin and Shah were my only priority and it was imperative that I do my best for them.

I did thirty-six interviews that first day: eight television interviews, radio from all around Australia and newspapers as well. The strangest part of it all was the scenario that unfolded that first morning as the TV crews began to trail into the house. Many of the cameramen and their assistants knew me either socially or because I had worked with them in the past. Some of them gave me an encouraging hug or pat before the interviews began. That personal contact, and the sight of familiar faces, made me feel less vulnerable as the questioning started. Over and over again I explained the same details to the various journalists, patiently outlining the history of the case and spelling and respelling my babies' names. I refused to weep on camera and repeatedly begged the viewers who would eventually watch the reports during their comfortable evening meal to contact the Federal Police if they had any information about where Iddin and Shahirah could be.

As a result of the kidnap I got to see the uglier side of journalism as well: the cold calculation involved in coming up with a fresh angle, the drive to bring back the emotion-charged picture that would label the story as tragic, and the outright manipulation that one journalist was willing to perpetrate to snatch an image of me weeping uncontrollably in Iain's arms. The particular man in question used every trick in the book to trigger my tears, phrasing questions in the most dramatic fashion and asking the same thing over and over with a slight variation each time.

'How will you feel if you never see your children again, Jacqueline? Do you blame yourself for not being careful enough? How much do you love your children?' Eventually he had me so distraught that I could feel myself losing control: my throat began to close and a terrible pain overwhelmed my body, a mixture of howling grief and utter despair. I could feel myself drowning in it, unable to go on with the interview. I requested that they switch their camera off, telling them I needed a respite and some privacy, and I was assured earnestly by the journalist that the camera was no longer filming. I succumbed to tears, sobbing wildly as Iain comforted me, blaming myself for listening to others and rambling about how I had forced the children on the access visit and now they were gone. Needless to say, and regardless of the assurances that I had been given, excerpts of that private grief-stricken moment were broadcast nationally that night, laying me open and naked for increased ratings points.

Friends. Friends are what kept me semi-sane throughout this entire nightmare; I will never be able to repay them for their support and understanding, their protectiveness and selflessness. It is amazing, too, how quickly it is that one discovers who one's true friends are. From the moment that they heard the news my real friends were there to support me in every way imaginable. At 8.30 a.m. in the middle of the first press conference, our doorbell rang, announcing the arrival of our closest friends. This team of amazing people swept in and took over the phones and the door, made endless cups of coffee, cleaned, cooked, comforted me and stayed with us in what was to become twenty-hour shifts of endurance over the next fourteen days. And they were truly needed. A control centre eventually evolved in our living room, four incoming telephone lines, two borrowed mobile phones and a fax machine which whirred and shrieked every few minutes. At the height of the media frenzy surrounding us, one of the telephones rang every ninety seconds. The telephone would begin ringing at 5 a.m. every morning with requests for updates. It was utter madness and remained that way until the last phone call came in around midnight. Without the support of our true friends, I would have turned up my toes and crumbled.

That first day I didn't eat a thing, drinking only orange juice when it was placed in my hand by someone. I wasn't able to cope with the thought of food; I could only think about the children. I was desperate for news, anything to ease the total silence that surrounded their whereabouts. I prayed that Bahrin hadn't managed to get them out of Australia and that he was lying low somewhere waiting for his opportunity to flee.

My solicitors had been approached in October the previous year by Bahrin's lawyers who suggested that their client wished to sign over full custody of Iddin and Shahirah to me. This would settle, once and for all, the uncertainties of future litigation and ratify the status quo as it had stood for the past seven years. All he asked in return was two weeks' access per annum, of which I knew he would never avail himself, and a relaxation of the conditions I had placed upon his access to his credit cards and documents. At the time it had seemed like an offer too good to be true, but whenever I voiced my reservations to either Lillian or Iain, I was reprimanded. I was accused by Bahrin's lawyers of being too severe, too extreme, paranoid and neurotic. For the sake of harmony and balance, I ceased to question and caved in to his demands.

On 1 November 1991, Bahrin signed full custody of the children over to me in Australia by way of court orders made by consent. It was stipulated in the orders that the children be able to telephone me a minimum of once a day during the time they were with their father and that Bahrin's passport be held, not by my solicitor as in the past but by his. There had been absolutely no request by Bahrin for anything else to be included in the terms and conditions of access. Too good to be true? It was.

The knock at the door came at 11.55 p.m. on the first day of the kidnap. It caused everyone in the house to freeze in mid-motion, to hold their breath and will the children to be on the other side of that door. Hurling myself at the front door, ignoring all admonishments, I flung it open wide only to find a man and a woman brandishing police identifications. They told me they were the officers assigned to our case and that they needed to run through some details. They indicated that they wished to speak to me in private and then, with little preamble, presented me with a list of phone numbers that Bahrin had dialled from his hotel, along with duplicates of faxes which Bahrin had had transmitted from there as well. I was asked to identify any numbers which appeared familiar to me and to provide further information about Bahrin's Australian friends or business acquaintances. I did the best I could, on the sketchy information I had gathered over the years, but they had to remember, I told them, I hadn't been his wife for seven years so any information I could give them would be woefully outdated. But I told them what I could, mentioning that the Sultan of Terengganu owned a mansion in an exclusive suburb of Perth in Western Australia and that certain members of the family had access to both light aircraft and boats. Having told them this, I then asked if the coastguard had been alerted to the search. The sergeant assured me this had been done and, further, added that they had already told Iain this.

A photocopy of another fax was also shown to me: it was the text of a handwritten letter which had been sent by Bahrin to his solicitors advising them in emotional terms that he intended to take matters into his own hands and would be holidaying with the children until he decided he had had enough. This fax was dated and sent Thursday evening, but his firm of solicitors maintains that they didn't receive it until he had already kidnapped the children. I was later to learn that this was not the case.

The conversation then turned to information volunteered by the public. The police officers assured me that, as a direct result of the media coverage, a valuable public response was still flooding in. I questioned how valuable and asked them if they had any idea where my children were. In reply to my query the officers adopted a conspiratorial demeanour and spent a number of minutes warning me of the dire consequences should we divulge any of the information they were about to 'share' with me. Both Iain and I had to swear to keep what they were about to tell us in inviolate confidence or it was likely that we would never see the children again, they warned. Neither of us had any intention of hindering the police in the search for Iddin and Shah; we both would have done anything to ensure their safety. Finally convinced, they gave us something to cling to.

I was told that there had been two definite sightings of the children and Bahrin: the first at 8.30 a.m. on the Shepparton Benalla Highway, a major country thoroughfare, where a fellow motorist had stopped to give assistance with a flat tyre. The witness told police that the children had been in the back of the car and that they were also accompanied by a tall, red-headed man. This man had been aggressive in behaviour and had told the concerned motorist to leave, that they didn't need any help. The second 'positive' sighting was in a toy store in the township of Griffith in the neighbouring state of New South Wales. There, they told me, the children had been hurried from the store and into a car. My hopes rose, of course, and, like a lifebuoy in a choppy ocean, I hugged the possibility that the children hadn't left Australia. Nothing would get me to break that confidence.

When I made enquiries about the abandoned hotel room and the children's possessions, the officers told me that the room had been 'sealed' and had been thoroughly 'looked at' by members of the force. With that, and a promise that they would be staying in close contact, the police officers departed, leaving me with a faint glimmer of hope to nurture.

I continued to pace and retch and pace and retch. Sleep held no appeal for me and every sound grated on my nerves like fingernails down a blackboard. During the first twenty-four hours of the kidnap, I had been offered Valium and various other tranquillisers to calm me down, but I had adamantly refused all. I had no desire to go through this nightmare in a drug-induced stupor that would only leave me to deal with the realities and the horrors at another time. I needed to be as clear-headed as possible and as in charge of my faculties as the trauma allowed. I owed that to Shah and Iddin – they were counting on me to bring them home. So I spent another night lying rigidly in bed on the pretence that I was actually attempting to get some sleep. Eventually I gave up even that and crept down to Iddin's bedroom, collecting Muckle on the way down the hall. I didn't reach for the light switch as there was a direct shaft of moonlight coming through the open drapes. It bounced off the white marble fireplace and spread itself across the foot of Iddin's bed like a splash of fluorescent paint. I huddled on Iddin's quilt with the dog, burrowing my head against Iddin's pillow to catch the scent of him there. I inhaled it deeply and with such longing that I thought my heart would break. I conjured up fleeting images of them both and heard snatches of conversations long gone. Until they came home, this was all that I had and it would have to do.

Tuesday, 14 July

I woke up cold and stiff in Iddin's bed the next morning, my whole body primed to relax from a very bad nightmare. Instead the realisation that this was my new reality gripped me and offered nothing but shaking and the now familiar onset of diarrhoea and retching. As I showered and dressed I was careful to avoid looking at myself in the mirror. I brushed my hair and cleaned my teeth; the only thought in my mind as I did so was what the children were doing at that precise moment.

I was just scraping my hair into an elastic band when Iain entered the bathroom. Peering over my shoulder at my reflection in the mirror, he appeared to examine me minutely. 'Put some make-up on, Jack,' he said. 'The public is more supportive of pretty women and more sympathetic.'

'I can't. And what does it matter?' I replied, as another wave of nausea began its ascent from the pit of my stomach.

'It does, trust me. I've been in the media game long enough to know what's needed, and right now pretty is better than plain,' Iain pronounced with such certainty that I didn't dare equivocate. But with every stroke of the make-up brush and every sweep of powder, I was disgusted and numbed: it felt as if it were a secret betrayal of the children and I railed at the shallowness of a world which apparently demanded that victims appear spruced up and photogenically ready in order to garner public support and network coverage.

The day limped into its pattern of phone calls, questions, television crews, photographers and journalists. I jumped when a call from the Federal Police came in, but it was merely a formality, a courtesy to let us know they were on the job. The waiting was endless and hollow.

At some stage I talked with a close friend who works as a forensic psychologist. He tried his best to comfort me, but he knew as well as I did the implications something like this has on children and that normal platitudes would do nothing to still my fears.

My two children had suddenly become nothing more than two very small needles in an extremely large haystack.

Somehow I remembered to telephone Nanna's nursing home and warned them to keep the news from her until we knew something further and concrete. At ninety-two years of age, my grandmother was too frail to deal with this trauma.

Wednesday, 15 July

There was still no definite news. Phone calls kept pouring in: sightings, information; so many people were absolutely sure that they had seen the children or Bahrin. One man told a television journalist that he had spotted the children at an air show 150 kilometres from Melbourne and that they were boarding an aircraft. Another caller phoned to tell the authorities that she had seen the prince travelling in a convoy of BMW cars in the direction of Melbourne International Airport.

We were still on every front page around the country. I saw it as our only hope that someone, somewhere would turn Bahrin in. The Federal Police rang to tell me that they were certain that Bahrin and the children hadn't left the country. They were so positive that I believed them without question.

So many things flashed through my mind as I sat inside what had once been our happy family home. Would it ever be again? I asked myself repeatedly. Would Iddin and Shahirah ever bounce through the family room on the way to a refrigerator foray? Would any of us ever recover enough to return to normality?

I decided to telephone the only member of the Malaysian royal family I trusted and loved, HRH Tengku Ampuan Bariah, known as Endah to me, the Sultan of Terengganu's consort, and appeal to her for help.

I replaced the receiver in its cradle with an overwhelming mixture of despair and dread. If Endah, a woman to whom Bahrin owed fealty and respect, knew nothing, what was I to do? What I had heard in her voice was the incredible shock and dismay at Bahrin's very public actions. She promised to do what she could but, as she reminded me, she was virtually powerless unless she had the Sultan's support.

Thursday, 16 July

I seemed trapped in what had become my morning routine: arise, vomit, retch, run to the toilet yet again with another bout of diarrhoea, be reminded to put on lipstick, give interviews. The children were so much in my mind that I was incapable of focusing on anything else. Everyone wasted a lot of energy trying to coax me to eat, but I simply had no appetite. Friends never stopped ringing and I was far too nervous and jittery to allow anyone to switch on the answering machine, even at night, just in case somehow Iddin or Shahirah managed to contact us. I knew I was irritating Iain by leaping for the phone whenever it rang, but I was unable to restrain myself. Every time I heard the phone I'd hold my breath and pray for news of the children before I lifted the receiver. I felt a frantic dependency on the lines of communication into the house and, as irrational as it was, I felt that if I wasn't the one to answer the phone the children wouldn't ring.

Iain shared my anxieties and deep anger over Bahrin's actions, but I had no sage words to comfort him. Perhaps in all honesty I had to grapple with biting off the futile words to Iain: 'I told you so.' This would have served none of us in any way.

At midnight, as I surveyed the city skyline from the living-room window, I looked up and caught the stars in my peripheral vision. I was so furious and depressed at the same time that I didn't know whether to open the front door and run out into the night, smashing windows, or curl up into a ball and will myself to disintegrate.

I found it difficult to comprehend that the Australian Federal Police were really bumbling incompetents. One of the officers had rung earlier that afternoon to inform me that the staff at the Victoria Hotel had packed up Iddin and Shah's belongings. She requested that I go to the hotel to pick them up. But it was something I cringed away from; it seemed so final, as though a chapter had been closed tightly, never to be opened again. I asked a friend to collect them for me.

He arrived at our home at 11 p.m. carrying four green plastic garbage bags into which had been bundled everything that had been left at the hotel by Shah and Iddin. I couldn't stop crying as I emptied the contents of the bags onto the floor. We sat alone in an empty room with the remnants of my children scattered across the floor. Suddenly I had a flash of understanding that stopped my breath and shredded my optimism. Bahrin wanted to obliterate anything that could remind the children of home. Every single item of clothing, socks and underwear, even their shoes, had been discarded by their father when they left. It explained why Whitey had been left behind, along with the things that the children treasured most. As far as Bahrin was concerned, they were to believe that they had no other life before he kidnapped them. He intended to reshape their personalities, their very selves, into what he desired, like clay dolls without minds or feelings. Iddin and Shah he considered his possessions, his belongings, 'things' he owned and had lost once but was now determined to reinvent to suit his ego and his desire for revenge on me.

Digging further through Iddin's overnight bag, I found evidence that he was worried about what was happening around him before the kidnap. As I emptied all the contents I discovered secreted tags and receipts beneath the hardboard lining in the base of the bag for the new clothes that Bahrin had dressed them in. These bits of paper were my link to the David Jones department stores; they itemised and described the purchases in minute detail. It meant that we finally had an accurate idea of what the children were now wearing. I felt so proud of Iddin at that moment. He was so clever, so quick-witted and resourceful to think of leaving behind some clues.

Further into the things I found a pair of Iddin's dirty socks balled up. When I rolled the socks out I found a strand of reddish brown hair that tallied with one of the sightings of an accomplice the police had mentioned. As Iddin loathed wearing shoes inside, the only way that sock could have picked up that hair was if the man had been in the hotel room. Here was DNA material to test. There were also several glossy books across which I could see large adult size fingerprints. These I also laid to one side. The sheet of birthday paper I had seen stuck to the wall in the abandoned room had been folded and included amongst the children's things; it also had large fingerprints on it. All of this the Federal Police should have found; there was no excuse for this omission. Even the hotel staff had rifled through the children's possessions – how much forensic evidence had been discarded as rubbish by their untrained minds?

The police sounded very sheepish when I rang to tell them about my discoveries. It was so obvious that they had given the hotel room nothing more than a perfunctory look. A forensic officer would be around to collect the various items in the morning, the voice on the phone told me; in the meantime, they asked me to be very careful not to damage the forensic evidence in any way. I assured them that I had already placed all the items in separate plastic bags and had scrupulously avoided touching anything more than necessary. I told the officer that I had learned that from a detective novel and asked if they used the same book in their training. I hope he understood my sarcasm.

Friday, 17 July

Eventually I did sleep for about two hours, but I wished I hadn't. Nightmares held me fast in terror. In the dream I could hear Shah and Iddin crying for me, but I was blind, I couldn't help them, I couldn't even see them, all I could hear was them asking me to come to them over and over again. I woke up crying out their names.

Scanning the headlines of the morning papers, I read about Iddin and Shahirah's kidnap with as much detachment as I could: CLASSMATES SHARE ANGUISH; PRINCE IN HIDING IN AUSTRALIA; TOYS, BUT NO CHILDREN COME HOME.

Taking it upon themselves to offer us some form of support, the parents from Canterbury Primary, Iddin and Shah's school, began to drop in casseroles and prepared food.

I was very grateful for this kindness because although I had a house full of people to feed I found it impossible to cook. Children from the school also started to deliver letters to us and drop posies of flowers at our front gate with small notes and drawings attached; their juvenile handwriting and misspelt words reminded me how small my own children were and also how trusting, kind and vulnerable. How would Iddin and Shah ever cope without the support of everyone who cared for them?

I'd never realised before the kidnap how loved by their friends Iddin and Shahirah were and how much a part of our local community they had become. It came out in all the letters we received, which I folded away and filed carefully for future reference. I planned to show the children these notes of love and support when they came home, thinking that it would be good for them to know how many people had cared about their disappearance. I tried to focus on the positive and ignore the negative as much as possible, but it was a huge internal battle.

One cold-blooded and rhetorical newspaper commentary did very little to uplift my frame of mind. I can summarise this thirty-centimetre column in a few words: a sacrifice of two small Australian children on the altar of international trade is worth it for the export dollars. It called for compromise. Perhaps the writer saw it in simplistic terms, such as slicing the children into pieces or, better still, rescinding their legal Australian citizenship. After all, the trade dollar must be gathered at all costs.

An official from the Ministry of Foreign Affairs placed a courtesy call to me. He was polite, if noncommittal, but it was quite obvious that they were expecting the worst. With the Federal Police still assuring me that the children hadn't left the country, I really found it hard to keep a perspective on what was real and what was useless, but I resolved to keep fighting.

Muckle insisted on following me everywhere; she refused to let me out of her sight. Dogs have a way of offering comfort just by their presence and it also seemed to make her pine less if I allowed her to stay at my heels.

I believed intensely that it was all my fault that the children were going through this ordeal. I felt that I should never have trusted anyone else's opinion when my instincts were screaming no. I had promised Shahirah and Iddin that everything would be all right, that Bahrin would never try to take them away. Now they knew I had lied.

There was, by this time, an almost hysterical drive within me to ensure that I said exactly the right things to the media. If the children were still in Australia, this continuing pressure and attention would, I prayed, flush Bahrin out. All the journalists kept requesting new 'vision' – after so many days, the story had begun to go a little 'stale'. They wanted to photograph Iddin and Shah's rooms, but I refused; the children would have little enough privacy left when all this was over and I was not about to let people poke around their belongings unless it was absolutely necessary. In the course of the huge media interest, several women's magazines began leaving messages every hour on the hour. They all wanted to do stories on the kidnap, but I wasn't interested. The children, I promised myself, would be home by the time any of the magazines were published and a feature in them wouldn't help locate Iddin and Shah. We needed the type of immediacy that only the daily press, TV and radio gave, I decided, with Iain's backing.

That dismal afternoon I reluctantly agreed to speak to a nightly current affairs programme. The outside broadcast unit arrived to set up their satellite dish as I was finishing my eighth trip to the toilet that day. I was coming close to deciding that it was much simpler not to eat anything at all in an effort to control at least one of my bodily functions. I felt so ill that I didn't know how I was going to get through the interview with any semblance of intelligence or dignity. I was, by now, so physically and emotionally run down that I was unable to control the shaking of my right hand and continually teetered on the brink of passing out.

It had been agreed in the pre-interview negotiations that before I spoke to the host of the programme I would first watch an interview conducted earlier in the day via satellite with Bahrin's uncle, Prince Ibrahim. It was further agreed by the producers that I would not be put into an adversarial position against the uncle but would be free to comment on his statements. What in fact happened was that without warning I was hooked up to a three-way exchange via satellite between the host, the uncle and myself. I was devastated and absolutely furious by the time the pre-record was over: I had had to sit through Ibrahim's callous comments about female circumcision, during which he admitted that if Shah did end up in Malaysia with her father then of course she would be circumcised. 'What's the big deal?' he said. 'We all go through it. Millions of girls go through circumcision and it's no big deal. It's a minor operation.'

This particular procedure, where the clitoris is cut away from the genitals of female children, is generally considered worldwide as sexual mutilation and is recognised in civilised societies as a total invasion of human rights. The concept of this form of mutilation being inflicted on my daughter completely snapped whatever reserves I had left and caused me to lose control. I began to sob openly as I leant against Iain's shoulder for support. It wasn't for several seconds that

I realised that I was doing so in the full hearing of Ibrahim, who was still on the line and not, as the producers of the programme had promised, disconnected. The television movers and shakers got what they wanted: increased pathos that without doubt upped their ratings points. Far be it from me to point out that their little stunt may have jeopardised both my children's safety and any future contact for me with the royal family.

Iain and I circled each other, afraid that our individual pain would explode if we collided. We weren't talking very much by this stage, except about Iddin and Shah — words just hurt too much.

Saturday, 18 July

Nine days had passed since I'd last held Shah and Iddin in my arms and I still had no definitive lead on their whereabouts. The newspaper headlines still carried the story and screamed across their pages: MALAYSIAN KIDNAP MUM TELLS. One journalist even managed to dredge up a story that was three years old and included quotes from a former lover about our past relationship. To be fair, there was nothing wrong with the article, but I failed to see what that relationship had to do with my children.

No matter where I looked in the house, I was reminded that our normal lives had perhaps been destroyed forever. The family bikes were in their usual places, lined up along the hallway. I tried to avert my eyes whenever I passed them — it hurt too much. They conjured up vivid images of other Saturdays long past, days when we cycled twenty kilometres in a family convoy, laughing and singing as the dog ran to catch up. Would we ever do that again?

Small things now had the ability to make me furious. The

feeling that the children were being mauled over and were having their humanity chipped away tormented me more than anything, so when I noticed that the two photographs of them which sat on the mantelpiece were being ruined and smudged with journalists' fingerprints I couldn't cope. It forced me to venture outside the house for the first time in seven days to buy proper silver frames for my babies' images. Rationally or irrationally, it became a burning compulsion, almost symbolically so, to protect anything associated with them.

This spur of the moment shopping trip was a real disaster. I refused to have anyone come with me: this was a mother's duty. It was horrible being recognised on the street, everyone pointing, whispering and staring. This was something I wasn't used to and it was hardly flattering to become recognisable because of something as terrible as the loss of my children. When the shop assistant held my hand and squeezed it, telling me that she was praying for us, I broke down and left as fast as possible.

Sunday, 19 July

One week exactly had now passed since we plummeted into this abyss, although it felt more like an eternity emotionally.

Every morning I would scan the newspaper headlines trying to pinpoint anything that would bring the children closer and to double-check that Iain and I were doing the best job we could. Indications had begun to appear in the news that the Malaysian royals were beginning to rally around Bahrin to present a united front in public. With headlines such as ABDUCTION OR RESCUE? A QUESTION OF RELIGION. I realised that many avenues of potential information were about to close to me.

This particular article exasperated me. It quoted the royals as saying that Bahrin hadn't known that the children were christened in an Anglican church – this was quite untrue. Bahrin knew that the children attended normal kindergarten and school in Australia and he also knew that they took part in Christmas pageants and all the other things that are part and parcel of Aussie life. Furthermore, he was formally notified that the children had been christened nine months before he offered to sign permanent custody of the children over to me. He was never denied the right to have a say in the children's upbringing, he just never concerned himself with it. If he hadn't been happy with the way Iain and I were raising the children, he should have said so in court, not kidnapped them.

What makes me very angry about this article was that the journalist used, I believe, every means available to cultivate me, giving me assurances that she would try to find out anything she could about the children for me. This was not just another story; this was a story that involved two innocent children, my children. I wish I'd never given her the information she was after, let alone the protocol and etiquette procedures for dealing with Terengganu royalty. I felt misled in the worst possible way, and it made me physically ill to find that my children had become caught up in what I viewed as a journalist's self-interest to secure an exclusive story.

My diary entry for that day read: 'I love Iddin and Shah so much. They've never spent this long away from me since the day they were born. I feel like I am functioning minus a limb, or both limbs. Where are they?'

It was a question no one could answer for me.

Friday, 24 July

Despite our situation, or because of it, the Australian government of the day was less than forthcoming in its support of our family. Indications came out of Canberra, the federal capital, that they would be very pleased if the children were indeed found to be in Malaysia, especially if I could be backed into a situation whereby I agreed to fight for Shah and Iddin in the courts there. The government hardly seemed perturbed that Australian Federal Law had been flouted by a member of the Malaysian royal family. This attitude appeared to be the malaise that this government exhibited whenever any touchy issue came up between the two nations, especially in the sphere of human rights. It's called 'placate at all costs and sacrifice the lambs'. They would rather back down over moral issues than risk offence. The then Foreign Minister continually insisted in the media that my children's kidnap was a private domestic matter and nothing to do with governments. My only question was: if the breaking of a major Federal Law wasn't an intrinsic government issue, what was?

As a result of the less-than-supportive stance which my own government took, a friend began a public petition urging the Foreign Minister to take action to effect the return of the children and the apprehension of Bahrin and his accomplices. Thousands of people signed the petition and I was told by journalist friends in other states that similar documents started to circulate in their cities as well. The idea seemed to snowball. I hoped that, with other people behind us demanding definitive action, the government would fight for Iddin and Shah. Without them standing firm and insisting that the children were Australians, we were lost.

* * *

The second week of the kidnap was far worse than the first. As the hours went by, my hopes faded that we'd find the children in Australia, no matter how many times I was reassured by the Federal Police. My confidence in them began to ebb away – particularly when they admitted to me that they had not checked on the Sultan's house in Perth and had neglected to search a departing cargo vessel, the *Bunga Delima*, before it had steamed out of Perth only a few days earlier. There was no centralised taskforce searching for the children; the Federal Police considered the abduction a purely domestic spat. With very few avenues left open to me, and because ultimately I realised that by their own admission the police didn't have the manpower or the resources to follow up the most basic leads, I began to jump up and down in the media.

Some sixth sense also prompted me to personally contact the owner of the Griffith toy store. As this was the sighting that the Federal Police continued to work on as the only lead, I was desperate to know more. It was like clutching at straws, but I had to know. The bottom fell away from the basis of all my hopes when the proprietor began to apologise profusely, telling me that he had been mistaken, that the children he had seen in his store were new arrivals to the community and not Iddin and Shah. He also went on to add that when he had realised his mistake he had left a message for police, which had never been returned; furthermore, he had never been interviewed by officers nor had he been asked to identify the children from photographs.

As a result of my criticism of the Federal Police in the media, I rceived a call from the assistant commissioner. He assured me that every possible resource had been applied to the search. I asked him if the coastguard had definitely been alerted and he reiterated that it had been. It was easy to pick up on the fact that he didn't like me; I can only assume he'd taken offence at my telling the truth in the newspapers about the police force's incompetence. I didn't give a damn – I was now convinced that if I sat around smiling and witless twenty-four hours a day I might please the media and the government but I wouldn't be helping the children. If they didn't like what I had to say, they could bloody well handle the situation properly. I was determined to do whatever was necessary to protect Iddin and Shah; everyone else could go to hell. My children's lives were at stake and no one was going to tell me to sit on my hands.

Now that it was drawing near to the close of the second week, a number of Australian journalists travelled to Terengganu to cover the story. None of them had any doubts that the children were either on their way to Malaysia or in hiding in that country. One TV crew from the network I worked for was arrested by Malaysian police for coming a bit too close to the royal family; fortunately they were released unharmed several hours later. The only consolation I could now draw on was that with journalists I personally knew and trusted covering the story, the truth would be told to me with brutal honesty.

Some sections of the media had started to conclude that, victim or not, fellow journo or not, I had shown myself ready to fight doggedly for my children, therefore I didn't hurt. How wrong they were. I hurt like hell. My soul had been ripped out. But, yes, I was still capable of fighting: there simply wasn't any other option.

Four

Empty Arms – Broken Heart

11.15 p.m. Saturday, 25 July

This was the moment when my soul was amputated from my existence and I was left both afraid and fatalistic that it would never return. The only way I am able to convey this part of the story is by including my diary entries from those days.

Sunday, 26 July

I haven't tried to sleep now for more than forty-two hours. My stomach is riddled with knots and my brain is screaming for respite, my hands shake uncontrollably and I've just noticed that my hair is beginning to fall out in clumps when I brush it. My pulse is beating so rapidly, I feel as if my chest is going to explode. I'm so worried about the children; neither of them like really hot weather and Shah's rash will probably get worse in the Indonesian heat and humidity. God, I'd sell my soul to the highest bidder if it would mean the children were safe in my arms. Iain looks like death as he dozes from exhaustion in the armchair. All around me I see our friends, sitting or leaning dejectedly against doors and furniture – none of them have slept in the past thirty-six hours; all of them have been fighting for the children. Lillian left an hour ago, she'll be back in the morning. Until then all I have to do is make some sense of what has transpired in the last twenty-four hours.

At 11.15 p.m. last night, Lillian received a call from the Foreign Affairs Department to notify her that the children 'are in Indonesia travelling towards Malaysia'. She immediately contacted John and told him to meet her at our house. When they arrived without warning close to midnight, I knew that the news was bad. One look at their faces was all I needed and from there it's been one long turmoil of anxiety, fear and absolute rage.

I spoke to the Foreign Affairs representative around midnight. He refused to elaborate on what he had already told Lillian and kept repeating that the children 'are in Indonesia travelling towards Malaysia'. I asked who had sighted them, on what island and what condition were they in, but he maintained his distance, refusing to answer any of my questions. I was so distraught and furious by this stage that I told him exactly what I thought of him and his department. How could I fight for Iddin and Shah if my own government refused me the information I needed to do so? My legal team continued the conversation with him and were told that the Foreign Minister, who was attending an ASEAN conference in Manila, had only hours ago been apprised of the situation and had had a meeting with the Indonesian Foreign Minister about my children. We were told he was also seeking to meet with Malaysia's Foreign Minister, who was also present at the conference.

On hearing this, I leapt to my feet and snatched

the phone away, dictating in no uncertain terms that under no condition were they to agree to any deals with the Malaysian government, such as trading one child for the other. I really feared that Bahrin being Bahrin, the value he placed on his son would far outweigh the value he placed on a daughter and that it was likely that he would offer Shahirah in exchange for his own safe passage. 'Don't you dare do any deals without my consent, don't you dare,' I screamed down the phone. 'Please tell me where my babies are.'

After the phone was replaced in its cradle, we all stood around looking shell-shocked for several minutes before even contemplating what was ahead. That was that. The children were definitely out of the country, despite assurances from the Federal Police that they had not left.

We need to know exactly where in Indonesia they are so that we can try to obtain an Indonesian court order restraining Bahrin from leaving, but I can only do this if I have an idea of their location. Indonesia is a country made up of hundreds of islands. Without my own government's cooperation, it will be like looking for a needle in a haystack. Foreign Affairs obviously know far more than they're telling us and I simply fail to understand why they aren't making a more concerted effort to assist us. Surely the government's first duty is towards its citizens. I'm very proud to be an Australian, but it's got to mean more than carrying a passport with an Australian crest; it should mean that my government will do everything within its power to protect its citizens, especially when the citizens in question are defenceless young children. I really feel that my children and I are being sold down the river for the sake of a trade agreement.

The rest of last night passed in a blur of phone calls. I woke politicians, unionists, diplomats and journalists across the country; Lillian and John drafted legal documents at the computer, with Deb providing the back-up.

Phoning, phoning and more phoning. I refuse to give up on my children. I'll bloody well keep phoning and pestering and demanding and begging and calling in favours until I get what I need for Shah and Iddin. They are my babies, my whole life, I love them with all my heart and all my soul, they deserve better than this and I won't give up until this government acknowledges the fact that two tiny Aussies have been kidnapped by a member of a neighbouring country's royal family in flagrant breach of an Australian judicial ruling. I thought that one of the most basic oaths that a sitting government makes is to uphold the laws of Australia. Faxed off a plea for help to the United Nations Committee on the Rights of the Child. I hope they reply quickly.

Cutting off Bahrin's escape from Indonesia is imperative; it's our last chance to save the children. With Malaysia and Indonesia being so close geographically, time is of the essence. Once he gets them to Malaysia our chances of extricating Iddin and Shah plummet. I've spread out all the maps and Skye's school atlas on the floor. I don't know what the use is really. I keep staring at the maps of Indonesia and Malaysia, trying to get some sort of telepathic location on the children. On the map, the distance between Indonesia and Malaysia is only one and a half centimetres – a couple of hundred kilometres, nothing by plane.

I am trying to imagine what Iddin is thinking. I know what his personality is like: he's very cautious and careful, he avoids taking risks and doesn't like to embark on important ventures without first making sure he'll succeed. I have spent a lot of time trying to encourage his self-confidence, building up his faith in himself. I know that Iddin will have been looking for a way to escape, but that he won't contemplate it unless he is certain that he can get Shah away as well. Iddin would never risk his sister's safety, of that I'm sure. He'll watch and listen and try to get away when the time is right. I can almost hear his voice asking me what to do, if only I could tell him.

I've spent hours telephoning Indonesia trying to retain a lawyer to act for us there; eventually, through a friend of a friend's cousin, I managed to track down that country's top family lawyer. He had no hesitation in accepting the case but pointed out that he was powerless to file documents or even attempt to mount a case when he did not know where in Indonesia Bahrin and the children were. Even the name of the island: Bali, Java, Sumatra, Sulawesi or any of the hundreds of others would be enough to start with. He can't understand how the Australian government could be so wilfully obtuse in a matter involving two small kids. Left him awaiting further instructions while I try to move heaven and earth to get more information. Dear God, why won't anyone tell us where the children are?

Heard today that the fax machines in the Foreign Minister's offices in Canberra and Melbourne are being jammed by the thousands of petitions demanding Iddin and Shah's return. Good.

The house looks like some kind of military command centre: maps, logs, phones and constant activity. I suppose that's what it's turned into — we conduct our battles from here.

Goodnight darlings, sweet dreams, God bless. Mummy loves you very much. Just be brave, we'll get you home.

Thursday, 30 July

My deepest fear has come true. Shah and Iddin are in Malaysia. I feel as if my body has been hacked to shreds with a blunt knife. There is an enormous void at the core of my being, so desolate and inconsolable that I know that I will never be whole again. With every pore of my body, I long to hold them. Oh God, what will happen to us all; nothing will ever be the same again.

The first warning we received was a call from Ministry of Foreign Affairs, just after 1 p.m., informing us that the embassy in Kuala Lumpur had notified them that Bahrin was in Malaysia and had called a press conference at a major hotel for 4 p.m. Melbourne time.

That was the longest three hours of my life as I attempted to balance what was left of my composure and fight to keep a hold of the hysteria that was rising in my throat. I had so many questions. Did the children understand what had happened? What had Bahrin told them? Were they frightened? How were they sleeping? Were they eating? Was Shah's rash hurting her? Were Iddin and Shah separated or together? Most of all, how were we going to get them back without the government's help?

At 4.30 p.m. confirmation came through from journalists that the children were in Kuala Lumpur and presumed to be staying at the Terengganu palace in the capital. Bahrin announced at the press conference that he had kidnapped the children in the name of Allah.

From that moment on, life ceased to hold much value to me.

Many of the hours following the official confirmation were lost to me in a haze of hysteria, anguish and semi-consciousness. I collapsed after hearing the news, my carefully maintained shell disintegrating at last. I was drowning, falling,

dy g while still alive. When I didn't stop crying, someone
ra? the doctor. I had lost the sight in my left eye, which was
bulgin out of its socket, and my head felt as if it was ready to
explod They put me to bed when I couldn't cease my tears.
I ember hearing wailing somewhere, as though an animal
was being tortured: long racked sobs and moans, primitive
and lost I'm told that it was me. I was given an injection of
pethidine, but it made no difference; this was a pain that no
drug could ever hope to alleviate. I was told to stay in bed and
everyone conspired to make sure that I followed the doctor's
orders. I was unable to argue as my head ached. I was half-
carried, half-dragged to the toilet sometime later. I had no
vision by this time, but I could hear the voices all around me
that immediately stopped when I entered the family room.
When I asked what was going on I was told that the house
was full to overflowing with the media and lawyers. No one
expected me to talk to them, someone whispered in my ear,
they understood my distress. I think I eventually passed out.
I don't know and I don't really care. Nothing and no one
mattered except Iddin and Shah.

Friday, 31 July

I got up and began fighting again today. I was terrified
of what I would have to do, terrified of what the media
would ask. As I have not been fighting for the children
for the past few days, I am nervous about starting again.
Lillian and John have been covering for me all week,
but today it is unavoidable: I have to speak. The press
agreed to an 'all-in' presser [en masse interview] at law
offices in the city, focusing on the legal issues and the
government's response to the situation.

The headlines go on and on. So too does the public
debate and comment about our situation: letters to the

74

papers, talkback radio comment and letters – letters to us that flood into our mailbox. Letters written personally to me are full of encouragement, love and support, for which I am very grateful. I hope to eventually answer these kind people, but I don't know when.

By way of contradiction, the revelation that we are now public property, that our personal traumas are discussed and debated in offices and factories, or as lurid accompaniment to dinner party chitchat, is an anathema to me. It seems to demean the very existence of Iddin and Shah as individual human beings and strips them of their humanity.

I need public pressure for the children yet I find that total strangers have a proprietorial attitude to us. It is very much a double-edged sword.

Then that terrible beast, racial prejudice, reared its ugly head: comments made by one Sydney radio personality that I was a 'slitty eyed whinger' and should be sent back where I belonged. This stance was adopted by some of my fellow Australians, too. I suppose I should have expected this to happen. I guess I've been too naive – forgetting to look in the mirror and see what some ignorant people judge me by.

One journalist rang wanting to do a story on my racial heritage. I told him that my family had been in Australia since 1801, that they came as administrators and explorers. If I'm honest, I have to admit that the perception that I'm foreign hurts a lot. Are Iddin and Shah less valuable because they are a product of a cross-cultural marriage? Show me the person who says that and I'll scratch their eyes out. How dare anyone evaluate the worth of my children by their racial mix?

Later that day, during the drive to the press conference, something really horrifying occurred. One minute we were driving down one of Melbourne's main streets and the next

Iain was being held in a headlock by a screaming man wearing a motorcycle helmet. As the car had stopped at traffic lights, a man had suddenly leapt off his motorcycle, which had pulled up beside our car, reached in through Iain's open window and started punching him and screaming unintelligible abuse. Panic-stricken, I tried to prise his arms from around Iain's neck. At one stage, the man's eyes locked with mine and he screamed, 'You bitch, you deserved to lose your children!' Iain swung a punch at him in return. Unfortunately Iain's knuckles only made contact with the man's helmet before we drove off. We arrived very shaken, with Iain's hand pouring blood from where his knuckles had split on impact with the helmet.

The press conference was a terrible ordeal. I felt dizzy and overwhelmed by the packed room full of people and I kept fighting back the tears. Questions about the children, about the future, about the government, about how I felt now were fired at me from every direction. I answered them as best I could. I told them that I wanted the children home where they belonged, but that if I couldn't get them back immediately, at the very least I needed to speak to them by telephone. I wanted, and needed, the opportunity to reassure Iddin and Shah, and tell them that I loved them.

During the press conference I also had the opportunity to deny all the false stories going around the media that I had kidnapped the children in the first place. Bahrin had hired a professional public relations firm, purportedly called Damage Control, to handle all his media and to disseminate lies about me.

Lillian tried unsuccessfully for days to obtain a Malaysian lawyer to act on our behalf. No one in that country wanted to become embroiled in a battle against the wealthy and powerful royal family. I can't say that I blame them.

We made many requests to Bahrin's Melbourne solicitors for a single telephone conversation with the children, but the pleas fell on deaf ears.

How could the government not act when it was revealed by the press that Iddin and Shah were taken out of the country via boat from Queensland, in Australia's far north? The Federal Police had failed to notify the coastguard, which had since announced that it heard distress signals from a boat, purporting to be an Indonesian fishing vessel, *Pencheroboh*, which had drifted out of control for four days in the Torres Strait, the body of water which separates Australia from Indonesia. Furthermore, the coastguard had been aware of the boat while it was still in Australian waters and had coordinated a full search and rescue operation from Canberra. They abandoned it at the very last minute. After monitoring distress calls mentioning that two children were aboard, a coastguard aircraft had circled the vessel and a navy boat, HMAS *Dubbo*, had even been dispatched to intercept the drifting craft. It had come within hailing distance when it was suddenly ordered to break off the rescue and return to base because the *Pencheroboh* was refusing assistance from Australian authorities and had requested Indonesian military intervention instead. The radio request, which was monitored and made in English, demanded that a specific Indonesian Army colonel, the Indonesian Military Forces commander-in-chief for the territory of Irian Jaya (the Indonesian half of Papua New Guinea), be contacted. The disabled motor cruiser, with the children and Bahrin aboard, was subsequently towed into Merauke, in Irian Jaya, by the Indonesian military.

The Federal Police also finally admitted in the media that they had not informed the coastguard or other similar authorities: it was an oversight, they said. They had also failed to follow the terms of the warrants issued by the Family Court: they 'forgot' to formally notify the Queensland Police of the case. With such blatant Indonesian interference, how could the Australian government still maintain that Iddin and Shah's kidnap was a 'private matter'?

When I learned about the method used to spirit the children from the country, I could have cheerfully, and without compunction, castrated Bahrin with my bare hands. God only knows what sort of conditions my babies had had to endure adrift in a tiny motor cruiser in the middle of the ocean. Bahrin can't even swim; he's afraid of the water. If there had been an emergency, he would have been totally incapable of saving the children. Iddin is a fairly capable swimmer – I had made sure of that by spending months taking him to a regular swim class; but Shah was terrified of putting her face in the water and loathed having her hair washed for that reason. Bahrin was willing to put all their lives in danger in his quest to punish me.

Another startling event had come to light which the government were trying to ignore. On 20 or 21 July, the same day that the Indonesian military towed the disabled motor cruiser into the port of Merauke, two planeloads of Australian government officials were inexplicably detained by the Indonesian military, placed under house arrest in Merauke, forbidden access to their aircraft and surrounded by armed guards. Coincidence? The Australian government have declined to elaborate further on the matter.

Other facts were also beginning to surface. A Melbourne helicopter pilot seconded to work in the Indonesian territories abutting the nation of Papua New Guinea arrived back in Australia and was shocked to discover that he had travelled with Bahrin and the children on a small domestic aircraft between Irian Jaya and the island of Sulawesi. At the time, it struck him as strange that two children of Malaysian appearance had been annoying their father by playing word games in a broad Aussie accent. The children were not allowed to leave the aircraft during the numerous stop-offs it had made on the journey; they were also confined individually and not allowed to sit next to each other. Bahrin was accompanied by a bodyguard, who was in charge of Iddin and sat beside him for the entire journey. Shah was placed next to her father in the seat in front.

This man was very kind and took the time to telephone me after news of his experience hit the press. I took a small amount of comfort in what he told me. He was very specific about the type of game the children were playing: they were reciting tongue twisters such as 'Round the Ragged Rock' and 'Betty Bought a Bit of Butter' over and over again until their father had become very angry with them. Those tongue twisters held a very significant message for us. Iddin and Shah were copying a game that Iain and I often played when we took long family drives. He and I would compete, reciting those particular rhymes faster and faster as the children egged us on and chose the winner of the game. To me, it was a secret message that Shah and Iddin remembered the game and chose it to annoy Bahrin, knowing that he would never know the significance.

The chief commissioner of Malaysia's police force announced publicly that he was extending every courtesy to Bahrin along with full twenty-four hour police protection. It was tantamount to thumbing his nose at Australian laws. Several Malaysian government ministers also held press conferences to show their support for Bahrin's actions. Bahrin was using the children as some sort of staging platform to becoming a national hero: he cunningly turned his self-serving and vile actions into some sort of statement about the Islamic religion and Christianity. Religion was never an issue, and it certainly didn't have anything to do with his kidnapping Iddin and Shah, yet he succeeded in duping the populace of his own country; I suspected too that before long there would be an announcement that he was standing for political office. He had always had aspirations in that arena.

The datelines on the newspapers reminded me every day of the passage of time since I'd last held the children and swamped me with memories and wrenching emotions. I wrote in my diary:

> I've spent the last hour lying on Iddin's bed holding Whitey to my chest and crying. The children's presence is everywhere; my nostrils drink in their scent and I imagine I catch snippets of voices in the hallway. I remember how I used to kiss them both goodnight, brushing the hair back from their foreheads and settling the quilts beneath their chins. I remember Shah's pleas for one last story and the way that she devoured books just the way I do. I remember hearing her voice singing in Italian at 10.30 p.m. at night and her footsteps as she crept down the hallway towards the living-room door.
>
> Sidling in, she announced, 'Mummy, I can't get to sleep.'
>
> 'Why not?' I asked.
>
> 'Because my brain keeps talking to me.'
>
> 'Well, tell it to be quiet,' I replied, trying to keep my face straight.
>
> 'I have, but it doesn't listen to me.'
>
> I remember the look of concentration on Iddin's face as we worked together on his most recent school project on the solar system and his exasperated comment about what he had learned. 'All I know about Venus is that its

atmosphere is made of pneumonia.' I don't know when I'll be able to tell him that that project earned him his very first A.

I remember, I remember, I remember — everything. Surely Bahrin can't expect to obliterate any trace of me from their memories. Oh God, help me get them back.

Nothing is certain any more, the only constant I can count on is the ache that consumes my whole body with longing for them and the nightmares that come at night.

Sunday, 2 August

Television news reported that Bahrin and the children had arrived back in Kuala Terengganu by car. Apparently Bahrin stopped at mosques several times en route to join in thanksgiving prayers for the children's successful kidnap. Iddin and Shah were surrounded by armed police officers and secreted in my old house behind a new, specially built three-metre-high fence. They were treated like caged animals, being aired for public showings and photo sessions. One picture released by the Malaysian media had Shahirah brandishing a Malaysian flag while Iddin sat nearby, a detached and pensive expression on his face. Bahrin assured the press that the children were assimilating into Malaysian life with absolutely no problems and had no longings for Australia. I wanted to know what happens when they cry for me at night, or when they ask to come home. I wanted to know what they're told when they cry for me. Had he told them that I'm dead? Had he told them that I gave them away? Did they know how hard I'm fighting for them?

Three different child psychiatrists and two forensic psychologists have explained the emotional impact this sort of situation has on children: they would be experiencing post-traumatic stress syndrome, which encompasses insomnia, anxiety and emotional distress, coupled with the Stockholm syndrome, a phenomenon peculiar to kidnapped hostages. With the Stockholm syndrome, the hostage begins to relate to their captors as a means of survival. The hostage may even begin to take on the mannerisms and ideals of the captors and, as in the case of kidnapped American heiress, Patty Hearst, join in the abductors' activities from sheer necessity. The experts say that it is totally impossible for two children to be kidnapped from the only home and people they've known and transplanted to a foreign country without becoming severely traumatised.

How could the government sacrifice two small children in the name of harmonious diplomatic relations? Bahrin told the press that I would not be allowed to speak to the children under any circumstances. What had become of Iddin and Shah's basic human rights?

The headlines kept coming: LOVE-TUG PRINCE SLAPS BAN ON MUM; FEMINIST AND MULTICULTURAL VALUES CLASH. The former was truly ridiculous: 'love' had nothing to do with Bahrin's motivation to kidnap the children. In all his interviews, not once did he say he loved the children. He talked about religion, never well-being or emotional welfare.

Australia finally requested that the Malaysian government allow Australian Consular officials access to Iddin and Shah and we waited on tenterhooks for a response. Their reply was ambiguous and non-committal.

I discussed the feasibility of going to Malaysia to see the children, only to discover that I had been refused a visa to travel there. I was persona non grata in Malaysia; not only that, Bahrin had managed to have me charged with various offences so there was, and still is, a Malaysian warrant out for my arrest. If I attempt to set foot in that country to see my children, I would be arrested on sight. He managed to have court orders backdated to March 1984, the period prior to my return home to Australia and more than eighteen months before our marriage broke up. These orders gave him sole custody of 'both the children of the marriage'. An amazing feat, considering that Shahirah hadn't even been conceived then; perhaps he got custody of my left ovary.

At this time, I began to receive disturbing letters from a man offering to kidnap the children back for me. His letters were full of hints and statements about his prowess with weapons. We found out that he was known to the police. I wouldn't let a person like that within a hundred miles of my children. I wanted them home alive, not dead. His was not the only letter of this kind we received from would-be Rambos. They suddenly seemed to be coming out of the woodwork, offering their services – for a fee.

Another who reared his ugly head was a private investigator based in Queensland who purported to specialise in re-abducting children. This man was interviewed on national television and intimated to the reporter that not only was I his client but that he had put a foolproof plan to us to get the children back using force and we had rejected it. He also made similar claims in a major women's magazine. I had never spoken to this man in my life, nor would I ever, considering how he touted for business and lied about me.

Sleep stopped coming to me without nightmares; no matter how hard I tried to make it through the night without one, they proved to be unavoidable. I wished I could find someone to talk to about the kidnap, someone who had been through it. I felt I was losing my mind. The lack of sleep and the weight loss didn't help: my weight plummeted from 53 to 40 kilograms. I ceased to care. I tried to cook, but I burst into tears when I went into the kitchen, remembering the pot of curry I made the night I knew the children were gone. Iain and Skye existed on takeaway food and neighbours' food parcels. My hair was still falling out by the handful in the shower and it began to recede at the front. I wondered what I'd look like bald.

On the evening of Wednesday, 5 August 1992, I saw Iddin and Shahirah on television for the first time since they were taken. It was a carefully staged photo opportunity. Iddin looked solemn and angry about being on show and Shah was just Shah – very aware of the photographers and journalists. The children appeared to be fighting. The commentary covered most of the natural sound, making it difficult to decipher, but later, when we boosted the background sound, we were able to hear Iddin telling Shah to behave or they'd get into trouble.

To enhance the atmosphere, they were surrounded by rabbits, mice and guinea pigs in cages; they both concentrated on the animals and tried to ignore the cameras, except when directed to smile by someone standing out of the shot. Shah's legs were covered in insect bites.

I replayed the videotape dozens of times just to see their images. Iain was upset when he found me resting my head against the television screen and crying against their frozen faces. I couldn't help myself. It was the nearest I could get to holding them.

Friday, 21 August

As time passed, I found it harder and harder to live with the reality of what life was like without Iddin and Shah. I lost my identity just as I lost them. The things that used to be important to me, the ways I defined myself, had been excised from my existence with surgical precision. Our family limped along but the pretence was difficult to maintain; two members were gone, two small individuals around whom we tailored our balance and our optimism. Just to hear their voices would have been an immense joy and relief but those hopes remained futile. Every day I sat beside the telephone and tried any gambit that could give me some form of contact with them. I rang and rang the various phone numbers belonging to Bahrin's family, but with no success: they had all changed their numbers. I rang the switchboard at the main royal palace, Istana Badariah, in Terengganu over and over again and begged to speak to Endah in the hope she could give me news of the children. Each time I was either refused point blank or if the line was answered by the telephonist, Kasim, who was once a friend, I was fed lame excuses. I used a Malaysian accent, and threw in a dialect for good measure, but nothing broke through the barrier. Occasionally I managed to draw Kasim out and extract a promise that he would relay my message verbatim to Endah. 'If she won't or can't speak to me,' I pleaded, 'please tell her I have no intention of causing her any disturbance,' and then I phrased my plea in 'high Malay', mindful of etiquette and social niceties:

'With great respect and love I remember Her Highness and hope that she is well. With respect I beg that she will take my children's best interests to heart and for their sake watch over them and protect them. With respect and not with any desire to disturb the harmony of her life, I also humbly beg her to consider whether or not she will tell Their Highnesses, Tengku (Prince) Iddin and Tengku (Princess) Shahirah that their mummy loves them very much. For this consideration I do respectfully and humbly thank Her Royal Highness.'

Then I would hang up the phone gasping for breath, sobs escaping as my shoulders heaved and I cried for my babies. I knew that if she had the chance, Endah would watch over them from a distance; it was the best I could hope for – even though I would never get any indication that she had received my message. That door was now closed to me.

On other occasions when I tried the palace, unfamiliar servants answered the phone. They played games with me, tormenting me, adamantly insisting that the entire royal family of Terengganu were residing indefinitely in Singapore, or that none of the family now had a telephone. Sometimes they simply put down the phone for long periods of time and I could hear them laughing and planning what sort of verbal games they would play, or arguing about whose turn it was to say something cutting to me about my race, before hanging up in my ear. They called me *kaffir* and Satan but I no longer cared; all that mattered was that I tried every avenue to get a message to Iddin and Shahirah. The fight for them was the only thing that kept me going; they must know that I would never give up trying.

We continued, with monotonous regularity, to appear in articles in the media. Our story was fast becoming unnervingly like the Lindy Chamberlain saga, or the Lord Lucan one: public debate, questioning and opinions flew around us. I became the unwilling rallying point for disgruntled non-custodial fathers and the target for spiteful Malaysian students studying in Australia. Our car tyres were slashed; one night an old man started banging on my car window when I stopped at an intersection.

Bahrin began citing the one-off Easter court order made in March 1991 as the reason that he kidnapped the children. He claimed that he was prohibited by the Family Court from taking Iddin and Shahirah to a mosque and he inferred to journalists that this was a permanent ban. It made me so angry that he was able to manipulate the facts and make them sound plausible. The circumstances had in fact been vastly different.

So many people who didn't know us jumped on the bandwagon, proffering opinions and analysis to the media on the merits of cross-cultural marriages. We became a rhetorical debate on Islam versus Christianity, and I was transformed in one fell swoop from who I am into some kind of born-again, Bible-bashing Christian. These commentators dissected our lives as though they had some inner knowledge of us, projecting their own preconceptions and prejudices onto me and the children. I would become enraged and offended and it was up to friends to constantly remind me that these opinions had no bearing on our case. It was difficult to agree. I felt violated and used. I worried about the public perception. I viewed the people who supported Iddin and Shah's return as important and intrinsic to forcing the government to take action for the children; without this type of backing I couldn't help them.

My chief goal was to force the government into taking criminal action against Bahrin and to file extradition papers with the Malaysians. I felt Australia owed Iddin and Shah at least that much: an acknowledgement of their rights as Australian citizens.

In the meantime I functioned as best I could, one day at a time, one foot in front of the other.

Five

Life Limps On

Running away from all the turmoil and the grief of Iddin and Shahirah's abduction was not an option for me. I could attempt to numb the pain for fleeting nano-seconds of respite, but the puncture in my existence was unpatchable. It permeated every element of my existence – it peered over the shoulder of any intimacy with my husband, Iain, and mocked me as I carried out the most routine chores. Loading the washing machine was like a slap in the face: the absence of the children's clothing screamed at me that life should stand still. But it wouldn't, no matter how hard I tried to push it away. Life – real everyday, mundane functioning – felt like a betrayal and a divorce from the pain and confusion my children, I knew, would be experiencing.

Were they bewildered and frightened? Were they trying to comfort each other? Were they crying themselves to sleep every night? If I am very honest and delve downwards to the darker, most painful elements of self-analysis, I know I began to shrink back into an emotional life where an estrangement from the familiar phrases of living equated themselves to utter loneliness – even though surrounded by others. My shopping list was now devoid of reminders like 'must buy cornflakes' or 'pick up Vicks for Iddin's chest', and I pined for the mundanity. Too hard to maintain the normality of relationships from within the context of the family lost, I began to redraw boundaries, to re-contextualise the format of my intimacies. Parts of me hardened like grapes withering on a maternal vine. Other parts began to awaken to the pressure of the invisible band of copper wire entwining my torso and constricting my capacity to be who I had been in the *other* life, and so disallowing me the ability to move entirely outside of its deceptive malleability as a metal. It was a restrictor nonetheless that allowed me growth only in *its* chosen direction, and that direction compelled me to search out other parents who had a parity of grief and isolation to my own.

Knowledge, I felt, would arm and sustain me, and the repository of this knowledge, must, I had reasoned, be other parents of abducted children.

With a resigned wisdom very uncommon in my personality in those days, and after some urging from an insightful friend I realised it was time for me to speak to an independent professional who could help me with the seemingly bottomless well of grief into which I had plunged. Instinctively I had begun to realise, too, that I needed help to 'age' my stolen children in my mind – to accept the passing of time and to better comprehend the manifestations of the traumas they would be going through. If I was to fulfil my role as their mother in the future, I would need to understand their developmental phases.

But the bottom line was that I was teetering on the brink of my own emotional implosion, spreading myself so thinly my nerve endings were transparent. I was skeltering through life at a frenetic pace. I was doing anything I could put my hand to so I didn't have a spare moment to think and could fall into bed every night exhausted. It was also becoming harder to ignore the obvious fissures in my marriage – random and oddly placed, the cracks were beginning to resemble the plasterwork in an earthquake-shattered building. Forces (some of which I had manufactured to cope after the abduction) were pushing me over a brink I felt I could never rescale if I didn't take definitive action.

As a child, I had suffered sexual abuse at the hands of my mother and stepfather and, as a result of this, I had always been pretty skittish about baring my naked anguish more than necessary.

I had been raised by my beloved nanna and my godparents, Auntie Connie and Uncle Kevin, almost from birth after my mother had suffered a nervous breakdown, so Mum had only ever figured in my life as a shadowy figure shrouded in illness. When I was two years old, my mother had begun taking a surfeit of prescription drugs, some of which were only on clinical trial. As a direct result of this cocktail of medication, she suffered adverse reactions which resulted in an embolism (a blood clot and air bubbles to the brain) and was at one point pronounced clinically dead for eight minutes. Ultimately revived by a stubborn young doctor who refused to give up, she was to be left with temporal lobe epilepsy and mental issues that estranged us more effectively than a dozen oceans. Some of my earliest memories are of my mother's Grand Mal seizures and, later, my subsequent instruction by a doctor (when I was five) on how to deal with her fits and offer assistance in terms of straightening her limbs and getting her down onto the floor to avoid further injury. My early childhood was full of dark shadows and whispered voices, of home visits from doctors and little social interaction with my peers due to my mother's condition.

So for me, Nanna and my godparents were my constancy: warm, comforting and all enveloping. Nanna shielded me from the realities of life, scrimping and saving to keep us clothed and fed. But there were some things that even Nana couldn't protect me from, and one of those was Mum.

Children can find familial upheaval difficult to handle at the best of times; what happened in my tenth year was more of an eruption than an upheaval.

Suddenly Mum was an 'in-patient' at a psychiatric unit. No warnings, no signs, she was just there. For months I was told she needed to withdraw from the prescription drugs that were damaging her liver. But I knew something else was going on. I had no concept of this 'group therapy' thing Mum kept telling me about, I was just unhappy and confused at having to make conversation once a week with a woman who was now even more of a stranger than she'd been before. It was also blatantly obvious that she was extremely hostile to Nanna. I feared my visits to her in the hospital. I hated to be confronted by the other patients who shuffled along the corridors or darted furtive glances at me whilst I sat in the cafeteria with my mother. They seemed like tortured souls, tight-lipped and tragic, their angst apparent even to a child. Somehow this hospital for people with 'problems', or 'mind sickness' as my mother described it, was to its inmates both a refuge and a prison.

Mum checked into the 'unit' with perfectly coiffured hair and high heels; she left resembling a refugee from Woodstock: barefoot, with her long hair flowing down the back of the obligatory caftan. She'd also decided that it was time to play happy families, but for that a 'daddy' was needed. And she had him in tow.

Roger Barrantes had been in and out of psychiatric hospitals for years. He was in his late 30s, lanky, with a large hooked nose and dirty hair. His eyes had met Mum's across a crowded group-therapy session and that was that. Mum and Roger arrived at our home and promptly announced to Nanna that she was no longer a part of 'our' family and would have to find accommodation of her own within twenty-four hours. Svengali-like, my mother was mesmerised, and acquiesced to his every pronouncement. Then they dropped the other bombshell: I was going with them to their new love nest.

Nanna found a tiny flat in Carnegie, a suburb adjoining Murrumbeena, whilst Mum moved us into a small one-bedroom flat with a kitchenette and miniscule bathroom which overlooked the railway line and provided a cacophony of scheduled trains chugging at fairly regular intervals. I was devastated. Suddenly the only constant in my life had been banished: I was instructed that I was forbidden to see or even speak to my grandmother. Mum explained to me that Nanna was to blame for every single thing which had gone wrong in her life.

Apparently Mum viewed this sudden domestic upheaval as a blow struck for independence. My mother was a fool, even I could see that. She was just swapping one form of dependency for another. I barely knew my mother and I certainly had no desire to know Roger any better than I already did. I blamed him and Mum's psychiatrists for her illogical behaviour. She seemed to constantly glance at him for approval and validation and was incapable of making an independent and resolved decision on anything without Roger's assent.

The first night in the new flat was one of the most bewildering, miserable and frightening of my life. I realised that with Christmas fast approaching it would be impossible to see Nanna – I had never spent Christmas without her and she would be alone. I didn't understand why I was needed to complete this bizarre plan of my mother's, or why Roger was so insistent on taking me with them. Nothing seemed to make sense any more as I lay bunched up in a ball beneath the floral sheet Nanna had sewn a couple of months before. I just sobbed and sobbed and sobbed. I must have been crying so much that I didn't hear Roger open the door and come in.

He sat down on the right side of my bed and placed his hand on my calf. He said that 'they' had agreed that he would be the best one to calm me down and relax me. He said that I was being very 'uncooperative' and making this whole situation more difficult for Mum than it need be. He said that I must do as he told me, that he was here because Mum wanted him here and that I had to 'cooperate' with him. He told me that he was a microbiologist and a physicist – practically a doctor, he said, except he hadn't done the final exam – and that I must do exactly as I was told.

Roger was to repeat this declaration about his education and qualifications to many other people over the passing years. It was all lies. He had never even completed university. The truth, as I know it, is that he once worked as a laboratory cleaner for a large ice-cream company and that that was the only stable job he was ever able to hold down.

As I lay there sobbing, he told me that my nanna was mentally sick and I would be better off without her. He said he knew what was best for me – and that Mum trusted his judgement and wanted him to put me to sleep. Then he ordered me to lie flat on my back so he could relax me properly. When I didn't do as I was told, he said again that I was not 'cooperating' and that this was my home now and I must obey. When I finally did roll onto my back, he ordered me to keep my eyes closed tightly and not allow any part of my body to move whilst he 'massaged' me. And then he began to touch me. He started at my feet and kept talking as his hands continued up my legs, telling me that I was now being 'cooperative'.

I lay there, stiff as a board, with tears coming through under my lashes as he stroked me. My mind raced at a thousand miles a second; my brain spun round and round until I felt dizzy. Inside my head I could hear myself screaming and screaming and screaming at him to stop. Why was he doing this? Why was Mum sitting in the lounge room next door and letting him do this? The spinning in my head got worse and I realised I had to get to the bathroom, had to get away. I flung him from me as hard as I could and lunged for the bathroom door, slamming it shut behind me. I heard his voice through the door as I was vomiting into the toilet bowl. 'Don't worry,' he said, 'you'll get used to my relaxation techniques. Your mother has.'

When I finally came out of the bathroom, the bedroom was empty. Only my bed appeared wrong and out of place. Even with Teddy, Panda and Lambkin sitting on my pillows, I knew that it was no longer the safe haven it had always been. I also understood my new life. I was part of a package deal: my mother had traded me for a mate.

I had been right about my tenth birthday: it was the beginning of the end of my childhood.

This litany of psychological traumas didn't make me that positively disposed to therapy, but even I had to admit that my life after the abduction was spinning out of control. However once I had begun twice-weekly discussions with a psychotherapist, a clarity of thought allowed me to look at the broader picture of my life, and to sketch out what sort of condition I wanted to be in once I reached my final destination and the day when I could hold my children again.

The freedom to express my emotions – unfettered by social constraints – was like water to a parched man in the desert. Liberated at last from the social niceties and sensitivities which had tainted all my conversations since the abduction of the children, it was a relief to be able to dissect the torments sleep presented for me and to rail against the platitudes people felt compelled to mouth in my direction. What could I say when faced with a sympathetic look on a stranger's face, a comforting hand touching my own and the never-to-be-forgotten line delivered in a quavering tone: 'I know how you feel, my cat just died.' (In a deeper part of myself, I realised that grief is relative – only the inner emotional experiences of the person empathising with me could weigh their commiserations – so I had learned to take a deep breath and utter comforting words in return.)

Fortunately, I could laugh and cry about what became known as the 'cat bereavement' episode, and so many others, unconstrained by the fear of causing offence or my deeply ingrained need to be polite. Nothing seemed to throw this compassionate woman at all, so tremendously skilled and sensible was she, a clinical child psychiatrist specialising in grief counselling. Despite all my initial misgivings, she managed to arm me with self-knowledge and new foundations for coping. The next phase of life I was about to enter – travelling overseas to report on the very crime that had so upset my own life – would require all my new-found equilibrium, but with her encouragement I straightened my shoulders and leapt across the breach.

Six

Two Candles

I'll be the first to admit that deciding to embark on a complicated four-and-a-half-week film shoot across twenty-three cities, eight nations and three continents with a budget as tight as an opera singer's corset was probably not one of my most rational decisions, but it did seem logical at the time.

I wanted to create a cohesive documentary on what child abduction is, and how it is dealt with around the world; to show the social, emotional and political ramifications, and to try to educate parents not to use their children like cudgels with which to beat each other around the head. I decided to profile a number of parental child abduction cases across the world – the children and the families left behind, from New York to Israel, France to Algeria, Belgium to Morocco, Sydney to South Africa via Monaco, and England to Egypt, rounding off with a look at the workings of the United Nations Committee on the Rights of the Child in Geneva.

The title came easily. It would be called *Empty Arms – Broken Hearts*. This simple phrase was a succinct summation of my own thoughts and the exhausting futility of all my legal challenges to date, and the personal pleas I made to my former husband's representatives for just one single phone conversation with Shahirah and Iddin.

My inner battle would be to make my mind function and my intellect work during the filming, even as my soul screamed with every breath: 'I love you, I love you, come home safe, my babies.'

So my odyssey began. In order to make *Empty Arms – Broken Hearts* a well-rounded documentary that I hoped wouldn't be overly parochial, I'd devised a filming schedule which, had I known better, I would have taken an extra set of feet, three more weeks, energy supplements and a lock pick.

Fortunately, the three-member film crew consisted of personal friends and Iain (who was also co-producer alongside me), as the four of us would be living in close proximity for over a month with only two rest days. On our tight budget, we were travelling economy class on all flights – a big concession when you consider that two of the crew were over six feet tall – and sharing rooms. When we marshalled at the airport, even with the camera, lights and sound kit pared back to only the barest necessities, our luggage totalled eighteen individually tagged pieces. All the equipment had been registered with international import and export authorities, separately itemised, guaranteed, insured and held under international 'carnet' documents (a pre-paid bond arrangement to ensure that no nefarious on-selling activities were taking place).

By the time we finished filming we had travelled to twenty-six locations and been strapped inside all manner of aircraft. We'd rented seven self-drive cars, hired one dilapidated limousine, escaped with our lives in a battered old Mercedes Benz, journeyed in umpteen taxis, sped along in a French bullet train and hadn't lost one item of luggage.

In many ways the documentary was a confrontation with

my greatest fears and nightmares – one that was necessary, though, if I was to stay true to my children and what they might one day know of me. On my odyssey I would re-enter an Islamic state, with much trepidation, and walk the streets of London on a bright spring day with a young boy who had been abducted by his father four times in a campaign of terror and control. Most often, I would see my own face in those of the other parents – a mirror to which, in my lowest moments, I wished my eyes were blinded.

The huge amount of coverage my family's case had generated led to the public perception that I had some sort of extra power or sterling connections in the palm of my hand and led to other desperate parents contacting me, begging for my assistance or offering information for the documentary. Looking back now, I realise how bizarre it is to research anything without using the Internet. It seems incongruous that in 1994 I didn't even have email. Instead I burned up telephone lines at all hours of the day and night, following leads and fleshing out snippets of individual stories and family tragedy that often reflected my own.

Before we left Australia, I had made contact with scores of parents around the globe who'd lost their children to kidnap, and I had become privy to some of their darkest moments. Now I wanted the documentary to show that none of us was alone in our despair. I'd also discovered the correct terminology to identify myself: I was now officially a 'left-behind' parent.

Shockingly, I had found that far from parental child abduction being confined to a handful of rocky relationships, the international statistics were ominously robust and rapidly increasing.

In 1994, not many nations kept centralised databases on

the numbers of children abducted overseas (today, in 2007, this is changing and laws have tightened); however, according to Reunite, an affiliate of the British Lord Chancellor's Department and the British charitable organisation responsible for assisting victims of child abduction, the United Kingdom was losing an estimated 1,400 children each year. That's the equivalent of forty kindergartens suddenly being removed from the face of Britain. In France, the estimates for 1994 put the number at 1,000 *dossiers*, a term used to identify the individual family names, masking the probability that multiple siblings from those thousand families had been kidnapped in that year. Australia kept no comprehensive records in the early 1990s, but official estimates stood at eighty to one hundred cases per year. From the United States, more than 800 children had been taken overseas in 1993 and categorised under the heading of 'Hague Convention Abductions' – those statistics were even higher if you added the hundreds of children abducted by family members to countries outside the jurisdiction of the Hague Convention.

Thirteen years on, the estimated numbers of kidnapped children involved in unresolved cases, and hailing from Western nations, still stands at the 1994 figure of 30,000. Many of these children are trapped in a legal void – scattered and hidden in different parts of the world, cut off from all they once knew and loved.

The *Hague Convention on the Civil Aspects of Child Abduction* is a multilateral international treaty, which came into being in the mid–1980s, to combat the escalating incidence of international parental child abduction.

Simply put, a child taken from a Hague Convention country to another Hague Convention signatory nation must be returned to his or her normal country of residence.

Working along the lines of an extradition agreement, the Convention isn't meant to be used to determine custody rights or other matters. Its primary function is to ensure the safe return of a child to their habitual domicile and to entrust the appropriate courts in that country to hear all the issues pertaining to welfare and custody. Gradually, over the past fifteen years, the Hague Convention has been adopted and ratified by more and more nations. (In 2007, the number of signatory nations was seventy-six, compared to only forty-one in 1995.) Many Middle Eastern, African, Asian and South American nations are still non-signatories to the treaty, which means that children abducted to or from these places have no legal safety net to protect them and assist in their repatriation to their homelands. Iddin and Shahirah weren't covered by the Hague Convention as Malaysia is not a signatory – there was no safety net for my children.

In any case, even signatory countries sometimes evince confusion or plain pig-headedness when faced with a Hague Convention matter. A significant sector of European Union member states, although Convention signatories, do not readily return children. France and Germany are very difficult countries to deal with in this area of law as there appears to be great internal confusion about the rights of sovereignty versus the precedence of international treaties and self-determination. Tragically this often hampers the proper implementation of the Convention. A strange form of nationalism, sometimes tinged with racism or sexism, can also put a spoke in the wheels of a child's future. Quite a number of former European colonies and protectorates (such as Algeria and Morocco) are known to automatically refuse to return a child if the abducting parent is one of their own nationals – it is a strange form of what I term 'post-colonial backlash'.

* * *

Coming into New York City from the airport, we saw the enormous buildings of Manhattan and the myriad lights reflecting off the Hudson River in the twilight. Then, from our midtown hotel, we took a cab to Brooklyn.

In front of an uninspiring brownstone building, we met a father whose little girl had vanished, aged four, six years earlier in 1988. Quietly mannered, with a neat salt-and-pepper beard and hound-dog eyes, he took us into his spartan living room. He sat and spoke about his daughter as the cameras rolled and the hot television lights reflected off the blinds. As he talked, HIS hands constantly wandered to the dog-eared photographs arrayed on the arm of his chair.

His former wife had scrambled for valid reasons to disallow the father and his grandparents from having contact with the child. Unsubstantiated claims were thrown into the legal arena and proved to be unfounded but by that time the child had been spirited out of America and into Israel, where the mother and daughter simply disappeared and have not been heard of since. How bitter it was to reflect on the grave disservice women inflict on each other and society with such untrue allegations.

My first instance of face-to-face contact with another left-behind parent of longstanding provided me with a concrete example of the effect of a child's long absence. Before me – devoid of window dressing – the emotions and the heartache had been so nakedly revealed in his eyes.

A frustrating misconception that only fathers abduct children has prevailed for a long time. But abduction is not a gender issue – it's so often about power and revenge.

Leaving Brooklyn that night, I turned my head to look out the window of the cab so the others wouldn't see the tears that welled in my eyes and trickled down my cheeks. As we headed back to Manhattan, steam rose wraith-like from the subway manholes that dotted the city's streets and whispered upwards against the chill of the early April night as if to echo my wavering hopes that my own children would return before I, too, had six years of yearning etched deeply on my face.

Although in the middle of the documentary, no filming was scheduled until later in the day, so I had the luxury of time on my own and the privacy of my own thoughts. Turning uptown from 38th Street, I swung onto Fifth Avenue in search of a deli to answer my hankering for a smoked salmon bagel. Instead I came upon the towering Victorian Gothic facade of St Patrick's Cathedral. The enormous circular stained-glass window suspended above the main entrance caught the sunlight and refracted its colours onto the forecourt. Drawn up the front steps by some strange imperative, I noticed a side door standing open and found myself poised within the threshold.

I hadn't been inside a church for a long time. With the exception of Christmas and my beloved nanna's funeral, I'd purposefully stayed away from any building of Christian worship to guard against public conclusions that religion was a huge mainstay in my life. The Christianity versus Islam debate had become such an issue in the media after the kidnap of Iddin and Shah that I had perhaps over-analysed how my attendance at a church would be perceived publicly. Nor had I wanted to further inflame my former husband's religious sensibilities, or those of his supporters. Here though, in a city thousands of miles away from prying eyes, I was anonymous.

I *never* prayed; I simply wasn't what one would call religious. In fact, I certainly wasn't a Catholic by virtue of my own convictions on abortion and divorce; but instinctively I reached out my hand for two tapers. Touching the wicks of both slim candles to one of the small flames, I added mine to the long bank of votive candles flickering in the draughty vestibule of the cathedral. Sinking to my knees in the nearest pew, I murmured under my breath a plea to some higher power I could not even name or identify, but knew existed.

'Please bring them home to me, please keep them safe, please let them know I love them with all my heart and soul – always.'

And so began a pattern for me wherever I was in the world (except Australia). I would seek out the oldest church, regardless of denomination, and light two votive candles, always compelled to murmur the same hopeful words about my children. That simple and private action became as much an imperative of hope to me as it was an act of defiance. The flames flickering in their holders were primitive and ancient, spiritual and timeless, symbolising humankind's ingenuity and resourcefulness and my own burning desire to keep my kidnapped children safe from the coldness of the act perpetrated against them.

I was almost at the end of my epic journey to film the effects of child abduction. Paris would be the second last stop before London. As I stood at the window of my hotel – a strange crooked building on the Rue de Rivoli with minuscule balconies and creaking, crooked floors – I saw the Eiffel Tower for the first time. That most romantic of images. The sky was the deep azure that only a European twilight can provide and all of Paris seemed to glow golden. For a few moments my breath was taken away by the sheer beauty and enchantment of that magical city. But then my chest grew tight, and the absence of my children became a palpable void in my body.

Instinctively, I reached inside my jacket pocket and touched Iddin and Shah's photograph. Their spiritual presence, if not their physical, made my resolve strengthen even though I had begun to feel daunted and drained by the confrontations with officialdom and the mutual tears with parents who'd also been deprived of the joy of watching their children grow and mature.

I made my way to Notre Dame Cathedral for a modicum of respite, pulled again by some illogical reasoning that urged me to seek out the votive tapers in the nave and light two for Iddin and Shahirah. As always, I uttered my mantra of love and protection and stumbled out into the evening, squaring my shoulders for the tasks ahead.

My marriage to Iain had fallen apart a third of the way through the filming – at the end of our shoot in the United States. We were airborne on a United Airlines flight above the Atlantic Ocean, between Washington and Paris, when just in time for the late-night meal service Iain opened his eyes from what had appeared to be a very deep sleep and spewed forth the words 'I divorce you, I divorce you, I divorce you', looking straight into my eyes with unblinking clarity. Oddly, he chose the Islamic method to pronounce this. I sat speechless, trying to find words to counter his startling statement. Continuing, he said that he had decided that he didn't 'want to be married to a famous woman', that he was 'the senior journalist and should have written the first book'. There had been no arguments, no sniping to precipitate these statements. In part, I understood how he felt – I wouldn't have wanted to be married to me at that stage of my existence either.

I tried whispered pleadings and reasoning, but amidst a planeload of strangers it was difficult to come up with the words to save our crushed marriage. Shattered, I retreated to the airline toilets to weep, and remained there until turbulence forced me out to a vacant seat in another part of the plane at the flight attendant's insistence.

Although Iain later asserted he hadn't meant what he said, to me, in my deepest emotional core, I knew that he had been brutally and horrifyingly frank. It spelled the death knell of trust, eroding what had remained of my feelings of security and the certainty of stability I had placed in our marriage. In my mind it was a blow from which our relationship would never recover and a betrayal. The edge of the cliff had simply crumbled beneath my feet and ironically, I hadn't even realised I was standing at the precipice.

Iain and I would continue to work together for some time after his pronouncement. Our intimacy had dissolved even though we ostensibly resided at the same address. On a barely conscious level, because of what had transpired on the flight, I realise that I began to go into self-preservation mode, which was barely perceptible to outsiders because I had so much experience in putting up a facade. I withdrew into survival mode, locked off parts of myself and sought a new existence, purpose and identity away from our disintegrated marriage.

Empty Arms – Broken Hearts went on to screen internationally and was awarded a special commendation for outstanding contribution to the United Nations Year of the Family. Around the world, the documentary has been used as a teaching film for judges and practitioners working in the areas of parental child abduction and family law.

My hope is that the documentary changed the attitudes of people towards this crime of revenge and power. As one thirteen-year-old child, a victim of abduction interviewed for the film, said, 'I hope that any parent who watches this film and is thinking of kidnapping their own children will stop and think about how much it will hurt the children. Don't do it.'

Simple, sage advice from the mouth of a babe.

Seven

The Empty Arms Network

I became more and more despondent on the day of Shahirah's ninth birthday and the second anniversary of the children's kidnap. A heavy bout of depression had settled on my shoulders after completing the documentary filming and I felt unable to shake it off. In hindsight, one of the main contributors was the film itself and the gradual realisation that it might be years before I saw my own children once more. I had written my first book, about the abduction and my early life, and the deep reflection that this required had brought all the demons of my childhood abuse to the surface: issues I'd never dealt with seemed to engulf me and I no longer had my identity as a mother of young children, with which I had defined my self-worth.

For all intents and purposes, Iddin and Shah had been, I believe, in Bahrin's eyes, surgically excised from my life with commendable efficiency. Their absence confronted me daily at all levels of my life and I felt my inactivity as a nurturer keenly. Conforming to Bahrin's dictates that I only communicate with my children via the cold and impersonal offices of his lawyers in Melbourne, I set about choosing a birthday present for Shahirah and also a small gift for Iddin. Two years is a lot of growing time and I felt as if I were inflicting my own disembowelment as I attempted to write a loving birthday card and upbeat notes to my children whose tastes were now unknown to me. Especially as I knew I could probably expect no response or acknowledgement of my tokens of love. It was a horrible pattern of attempted contact which I would continue for over a decade.

I was mentally and physically exhausted, having for months pushed myself to the limit. Sleep continued to elude me, or was filled with nightmarish images and unrequited longings for the children. Tears flowed unbidden at the most inconvenient moments and wouldn't stop; sometimes they were prompted by recognisable issues or triggers, in other instances not. Gradually, the vaguely enticing option of a chemically induced repose began to take on an attraction. Until that time, I had always been adamantly opposed to sedating away the pain. Prescription drugs offered to me by medicos, or from the secret stashes of well-meaning friends, were crutches I had steadfastly rejected, and recreational drugs offered no solution to my insomnia.

'Three hours of relaxed sleep and then the natural body clock will take over. It's a way of resetting your sleep patterns,' was how my doctor described the effect of the mild sleeping tablets I obtained in my capitulation. Tinged somewhat with a fatalistic attitude, and fuelled by a desperation simply to 'switch off' and escape, I downed ten pills in one swallow and snuggled into my duvet and comfortably arranged pillows. The promise of a deep sleep was sensually attractive after two years of broken rest. There was also a feeling of playing Russian roulette with the possibility of not waking up, of simply sleeping for as long as my body decided it needed to.

Exhaustion led me into a delusion of hope, of being able to find Iddin and Shahirah in my undisturbed sleep, of being able to touch their faces and smell the uniqueness of them once more. In some convoluted way I reasoned that by giving up control to a chemical, I was conversely taking control of my ability to find a dream where I might encounter Iddin and Shah without the terrors of separation and overwhelming grief that coloured everyday life as I now knew it.

It's easy to understand why sleep deprivation is such a favoured tool with interrogators and torturers: reality is suspended for the victim, and rational thought is bent and worn down.

Even though I was obviously in a quite deep despair, I was still a control freak: I took the precaution of leaving a note explaining what I had ingested and why, along with a few instructions, such as not to call an ambulance and to just let me rest. Not terribly sensible and, in hindsight, overly dramatic, I admit, but at the time, it seemed organised and responsible. However, when I was discovered sleeping so heavily about three hours into a blissfully dreamless and deep sleep, panic ensued and an ambulance was summoned.

I came to a rude awakening on a hospital trolley surrounded by strangers. A very young and earnest-looking doctor was bent over me, demanding to know why I had attempted suicide and threatening a commitment – not of the romantic kind – should I offer the incorrect answer. Evaluating my situation as hurriedly as my still foggy brain allowed, I ascertained that I was a new arrival in the hospital and hadn't had my stomach pumped, but was in serious jeopardy of ending up in either a straightjacket or, worse, in an open-backed hospital gown. Even more horrendous was the thought of ending up on the front page of the morning newspapers in lurid bold type: KIDNAP MUM'S TRAGIC SUICIDE BID, PICTURES INSIDE! or PRINCESS POPS PILLS! Scrambling for the right words to prove my sanity and liberate myself, I attempted to explain the situation with as much clarity as possible but only managed a pretty good imitation of a fish – my mouth opening and closing accompanied by a groaning 'orruummm'. My tongue seemed to be incredibly attracted to the roof of my mouth and rather too large for its normal space.

So much for the first try. The situation was now serious and my befuddlement was starting to clear, accelerated by the patronising look on the young doctor's face, which was rather blurred as my spectacles, no doubt, were still sitting atop my nightstand. Concentrating on the doctor's next question, I realised that he was speaking with a broad Scottish accent. The foreign brogue explained the absence of a spark of recognition in his eyes which was all too present in the attending nurses' faces I could see hovering behind his shoulder.

'If you commit me overnight, I will sue you,' seemed to have the desired effect of at least holding his attention. I followed up with a slurred, 'I am fully in control of my faculties and do not need to be committed, thank you very much.'

'Tell me why you are so depressed, Jacqueline,' the doctor questioned.

I was rather tempted to point out that as we had not been formally introduced, I'd prefer him to refrain from using my Christian name but thought holding my tongue on that point the wiser option. Instead I answered with the obvious.

'Because my children were kidnapped by their father and—'

'I think you're confused, Jacqueline,' he interjected with saccharine tones and careful enunciation, even adding a vague pat to my hand. 'Your husband hasn't . . . he's . . . er—'

The doctor was cut off by an urgent tugging on his sleeve and a hurried whisper in his ear from one of the nurses. *Comprehension* and curiosity suddenly lit up his face. I was going to have to choose – would I sing for my supper or take the 'high dudgeon' road? I chose 'high dudgeon'.

Ten minutes later I was discharged.

Did I really try to commit suicide that night? In truth I'm not sure. At the point when I took those pills, did I want to die? Let's just say that as I was floating away I didn't want to wake up; I was just too tired. (In any case, the dose I took probably wouldn't have proved lethal.)

Thank goodness my stupid actions remained off the front page and I was able to salvage some shreds of rational thought and determination. I would have to make a choice: either become an eternal victim, in which case I might as well have crawled into a corner and died, or attempt to turn a negative into a positive and try to hang on until I saw Shah and Iddin again.

I knew that I had to keep busy to fill the void left by my absent children; to make some sense of the empty existence I was close to leading.

I decided to harness all the knowledge I'd gathered during the making of the documentary and establish an organisation – called the Empty Arms Network – to offer support to victims of parental child abduction, both on a domestic and an international level.

I was still receiving so many phone calls from parents in similar circumstances to my own. All these parents, male and female, from Australia and overseas, asked me for guidance or assistance with their cases. I felt strongly that no one should have to go through this nightmare alone. Setting up the Empty Arms Network seemed the logical thing to do.

So, I decided to formalise what I was already doing. And to ensure autonomy, I'd fund the network myself using the royalties from my first book and any other income I could garner. I was determined that the Empty Arms Network would be a 'not for profit' organisation able to call on the expertise of a broad cross-section of skilled solicitors, psychologists and like-minded support organisations around the world with whom I had already established viable contacts while filming. By putting in place reciprocal arrangements with my international counterparts for my skill set, much of the ruinous costs for left-behind parents would be circumvented or reduced. There would be no full-time staff except me, as wages were out of the question. It all seemed to make perfect sense. Although my decision to not recoup expenses (such as international phone calls) from the parents I helped was quite a financial drain, I wanted no fingers pointed for profiteering.

From the years 1994 to 2006, I was involved in the safe repatriation of sixty-four abducted children from country to country all around the world. Hong Kong to Columbia, Australia to Lebanon, the United Kingdom to Malaysia, the United States to Australia, France to New Zealand via Australia, Germany to the United States, Argentina to Jordan, Sweden to Australia, Finland to Belgium, Ireland to Indonesia, Singapore to Canada, New Zealand to Libya, Australia to Greece, USA to Thailand, Great Britain to Haiti, Palestine to Paris. The list goes on . . .

Following the success of *Empty Arms – Broken Hearts* and the headway I was making with my work at the abduction coalface, it seemed I'd finally earned my battle stripes, or at least that was the unwritten text of an invitation I received to give a speech on parental child abduction at an international family law conference. Ironically, I had crossed into the ranks of experts and was no longer on the victim side of the river. My gratitude to the then Chief Justice of the Family Court of Australia, Alastair Nicholson, will always be something I feel deeply. Justice Nicholson took a risk in pushing for my inclusion on the programme of speakers, and his trust in me is something I can never repay, for it was to set me on a path that would reshape my life and give me purpose.

With some trepidation I embarked on my first public speaking engagement, so nauseous from nerves that I had refrained from eating for twenty-four hours. Opening my lecture with an audio-visual montage of comments made by children who had been abducted, projected behind me on a screen, was a choice I made to instil maximum impact. Using their words to segue into an overall picture of jurisdictional attitudes proved to be a device that captured their attention. Standing behind the lectern, and quaking in my carefully chosen red suit and black suede shoes, I delivered my paper on the sociological effects of child abduction, not realising that it would be the first of many such seminars and conferences I would find myself attending in far-flung places around the world.

As the third year after the abduction of my children loomed, news came to me in a late-night telephone call that Bryan Walter Wickham, one of Bahrin's paid accomplices (the other two being Singapore nationals), was apprehended by officers of the US Marshals Service in Florida, USA.

Interpol, and ironically the media, had searched for Wickham all over the world, from the Philippines (where it was suspected he had nefarious links) to Scotland, where he had lived until he emigrated to Australia. When this utter stranger had assisted in the abduction of my children, he had left his own kids and his wife, Sheila, behind in Australia. (Hypocritically, at a later time he was to repeatedly espouse the sanctity of family ties and children!) Neither Wickham nor his wife had met Iddin or Shah prior to the abduction, but in every interview Sheila Wickham gave following her husband's arrest, she condoned their illegal removal from the only secure home and family they had ever known. I suppose it was the gleam of all the cash and gold bullion paid to her husband for his part in the crime that eased her moral qualms – although one wonders whether Bryan Wickham has ever possessed any morals.

Wickham had been working in West Palm Beach, Florida, on various building sites since December 1992. From what I could gather, the FBI and US law enforcement agents had successfully pieced together his trail from fingerprints and a random vehicle registration check which some sharp-eyed officer had picked up as being connected to Wickham. Apparently, he had arrived in West Palm Beach five months after the kidnap and settled comfortably into an apartment provided by Mr Orville Rodberg, a local businessman, and his son, whose connection to Wickham was never explained. Complete with swimming pool and salubrious surrounds, Wickham had slipped into a sunny Florida lifestyle with great ease and little apparent complication.

The Assistant US Attorney ensured that the American proceedings went smoothly, so with minimal delay following his arrest, Wickham was successfully extradited from the United States and arrived in Australia for trial, pleading guilty to the abduction of Iddin and Shahirah.

Wickham is a convicted criminal with alleged links to prostitution, tax evasion and money laundering – so it makes my flesh creep to know that he was anywhere near my children.

In court, he told an extraordinary tale of deceit, double-crossing and his own eventual abandonment by Bahrin. He implicated the government of Indonesia and its military in the kidnap, and maintained that he had assisted Bahrin because of his love of children.

He was sentenced on 5 May 1995 to eighteen months' imprisonment, a reduced sentence because he had pleaded guilty. Subsequently he served only half of his sentence, as he was given a probation period of nine months. The usual maximum penalty for the crime of kidnapping is three years per offence. However, Wickham was not through with us yet.

From prison he sent a message, offering to sell me the full details of the kidnap of my children – what they purportedly said, what was done to them, how they behaved and reacted, and so on. Apparently, he felt very clever at having pleaded guilty, and so avoiding cross-examination in court: he had preserved the juicy bits of his story intact so he could cash in on the abduction. It was, the messenger told me, his insurance policy.

Of course, part of me felt compelled to know even the minutest detail of my babies' ordeal. But this was a disgusting ploy to extract money from me. He had already ripped the essence of my life away; I was damned if he'd get one more thing from me.

Another Christmas loomed, taunting me with the children's absence. I placed the children's photograph under the tree and took another snapshot to mark the passing of time. Unbelievably, it had become years since I last saw or spoke to Iddin and Shahirah. I'd missed their birthdays, Shah's teeth falling out and, most of all, their wonderful personalities and laughter. The pain didn't ease but I learned to cope with it for the most part. I've heard that amputees often retain a memory of a lost limb, feel its presence and sensations – maybe that's what I was experiencing.

I had written my first book as a way of allowing Shahirah and Iddin some insight into my personality, and to communicate my reactions, motivations and the choices I had made in my life. I wanted them to have tangible proof of my love for them. It seemed important to put it all down on paper – given how unpredictable life can be. I felt that *Once I Was a Princess* was my insurance policy against an uncertain timeline and left a part of me for them, to delve into one day in the future. Though it was a double-edged blade I had drawn from the scabbard, making me even more exposed to strangers by the nakedness of thought I'd included in the book.

The emotional minefield of the children's absence deployed itself in my daily path, and the grieving continued in a vicious circle of ebbing and flowing tides that washed over me. I wasn't coping as well on certain levels as I did in the first year or two; I just lived in hope.

Eight

Warrior Professors and the Power of Tears

Our convoy of Land Cruisers rattled its way through the Rift Valley, across open savannah country and a dry lake bed stretching twenty kilometres in either direction – one chalky shimmering mass of compacted earth corrugated by thousands of years of tide and wind. Above vultures circled in search of weakened prey and the odd flock of migrating birds cast geometric shadows on the parched plain that was dotted by trees and low spiky shrubs. Across the border in Tanzania, Mount Kilimanjaro, the highest peak in Africa, loomed starkly in the distance, pure white snow caps atop rugged dark contours, revealed only when the low-lying clouds dissipated as if by magic. The sky, a somewhat overcast grey-blue, undisturbed by commercial jets, stretched endlessly to meet the horizon.

We were driving across the cradle of humanity, the hollow of creation, through the middle of the Amboseli Game Reserve, home to the largest population of elephants in East Africa, where animals roam free and humans are as dependent on Mother Nature as the beasts and flora. It was the kind of journey that shakes bones loose and covers everything in a fine red dust that clings to the skin and colours every strand of hair a warm terracotta.

Wildebeest, horned, bearded and broad-backed, pelts a musty grey, slowed the progress of our vehicles as we lessened our pace to allow these strange-looking animals right of way. Scores of gazelle ran beside us, leaping and darting, hooves barely touching the ground. Two hundred kilometres at a snail's pace on rocky roads and dusty tracks, most of which were little more than vague lines etched across clay riverbeds – and not one complaint entered my head. I wanted to inhale the horizon and stretch my arms open to the sun. My nostrils were full of Africa, rich and spicy, clean and uncontaminated; time seemed organic, hanging in the air. Whenever we paused in our journey, I opened the windows of the truck and sniffed deeply to try to imprint the moment in my mind.

Not even the heat could quell my joy at the surroundings. It was all-exhilarating. The zebras grazing in enormous herds and the giraffes loping nonchalantly in graceful rhythm made me wonder why I'd wasted so much precious time before getting to Africa!

In January 1995, my friend Bill Searle, executive producer for *Neighbours*, had been developing an innovative storyline for the show with a charitable theme linked to the humanitarian organisation World Vision. The soap opera would be filmed in Africa. I had flippantly put my hand up when I heard about the shoot but hadn't really expected to end up travelling with the actors and becoming part of the film crew – it just sort of fell into place. I was aware of the popularity of Neighbours around the world and its long run on British television, but as far as I was concerned it was a half-hour of television I never watched.

I'd been vaccinated for nine different tropical and potentially deadly diseases, and spent some time studying rudimentary Swahili!

Occasionally now, a cloud of dust in the distance would begin to take shape, gradually revealing a tall slim figure clad in a bright red and cobalt blue *shuka* – one length of fabric worn as a sarong and the other over the shoulder, like a Scottish plaid. Without exception these men held long six-foot staffs or spears and would nod or wave a greeting as we passed. They were Maasai warriors out for an evenly paced trek across the vast plain. Amboseli was not only host to a plethora of animals, it was also a part of Maasailand, the traditional home of the Maasai tribespeople, some of whom would be taking part in the shoot.

Towards the end of the day we reached vivid green swamplands fed by underground streams from the melting snows of Kilimanjaro. Birds in abundance swooped and dallied around the water's edge, while ripples and several sets of ears and eyes peeking up from the centre of one pool indicated hippos swimming and romancing in the water. All of us found it hard to contain our whoops of delight when we caught sight of our first herd of elephants. A cow and her baby played in the shallows, swimming in circles with trunks raised like periscopes; the rest of the family bathed and snorted water into the air as little white birds hopped casually back and forth on the elephants' backs, feeding off tiny parasites.

I wished my children could've been beside me to revel in this cornucopia of wildlife and nature. I could almost hear Iddin's exclamations of excitement as he drew my attention to a baby elephant swimming awkwardly, or Shahirah's voice, along with a tugging on my sleeve, as a giraffe strolled into view. As always, Iddin and Shah's laminated photograph was in the depths of my pocket. I remembered a quote from some wise soul: 'Being a mother means that your heart is no longer yours; it wanders wherever your children do.'

The heat and often long treks to location made filming exhausting. By the end of the day we'd return to Camp Tortillis and dive into refreshing showers and then fall into bed as early as possible to gear up for the next day. I tried all of these approaches on the first four evenings, doing everything I could think of to ensure a full night's sleep, but to no avail. It was not such a problem falling asleep as it was staying asleep.

Like clockwork I'd find myself awakening at 3 a.m., my ears fully alert and listening to the amazing silence of the bush. It's very stillness like a heavy velvet curtain, Indian ink blue and full of timeless secrets. The odd animal call or rustling in the darkness seemed only to enhance the silence rather than break it. Opening my tent flap I could discern the vague outline of Mount Kilimanjaro, snow peaks glistening in the moonlight, and sometimes I could pick up the faintest scent of a passing animal. No glow of light came from the other tents, no shadows moved against canvas; I alone was awake in the Kenyan night. 'It', the thing that made me wake, had no reason or form, no logic or debatable points.

I could almost hear my own heart beating and feel its slow measured rhythm: no pounding or thumping, no adrenalin rush of fear – just an uncomplicated and dependently steady pulsing. Yet for all my lack of anxiety, for all the calm and stillness surrounding me, it was as if my entire emotional being was a large transparent bowl of marbles. Every marble a different size, weight or colour, and each seemed to encapsulate a facet of my inner, unidentifiable essence. I would watch as the bowl hurled its contents into the air in front of me, and it was as if I were watching my own emotions descend with no sense of order in slow motion to the ground and arrange themselves in patterns on the bare earth, each one different from the last.

With this emotional 'awakeness' came tears. Not anguished or despairing, not angry or bereft. I simply cried big warm dollops of salt water. Each time I wiped them away more would form and spill from my eyes; each time I attempted to curb them, to halt their flow, my body would vehemently object and erupt in spine-shaking sobs. So I let the tears come. Until just before dawn, the rivulets of my inner essence coursed down my cheeks as I 'watched' the African silence outside my tent.

On the fifth night I slept through until Kilimanjaro's snow cap was tinged pink by the dawn. I slept and dreamed endless images of my children with no nightmares or terrors, just happy open memories. 'It' came no more.

Perhaps because I had listened to Africa's silence, or perhaps it was because I'd finally listened to my own, I felt ready for more of life.

Until that time, guilt and longing for Iddin and Shahirah had curtailed even my most fleeting moments of elation and happiness. Each time I wandered off the path of grief, a trip switch was thrown in the very centre of me and I would plunge into self-castigation at my disloyalty to my children. But this place changed things: Africa gave me permission to be happy, yet still grieve. Without for a moment forgetting the loss of my children and the love I felt for them, I simply discovered the capacity to enjoy the present moment without a feeling of betrayal.

One lunchtime, Mongo, a tall and majestic Maasai warrior who was fluent in English, Maasai, Swahili and Italian (he'd won a scholarship to study in Rome), asked me to accompany him to the local school, just outside the location of our film shoot. We walked about a hundred metres outside the main village to a clearing facing Mount Kilimanjaro – elephants to the left of me, and wildebeest and zebra to the right. There, beneath the umbrella-like shade of a thorny tortillis tree, were thirty perfectly aligned white rocks. This, said Mongo proudly, was his school.

There were no textbooks or coloured pencils for the children, no brightly illustrated storybooks or encyclopaedias, just this one determined and dedicated man balancing before me on one leg in the Maasai way.

Covered in red ochre, heavily beautified with beads and tribal scarring on his cheeks, carrying a hunting spear and a fly switch made from a wild boar's tail, and wearing a shuka flung casually over one shoulder, Mongo was a teacher with more tenacity than I had ever before encountered. Mongo's pupils might learn to write the alphabet in the dirt and to read and spell by rote, but they were taught by an amazing and dedicated person who was willing to work with all his heart and soul to give them an education. It didn't take long to realise that what Mongo lacked in equipment was more than made up for by his determination and utter commitment to his people.

Remembering that I had four children's books packed in my bag for emergency gifts (a practice I had begun when still living with the royal family), I delivered them to Mongo at the first opportunity. Seven days later, when filming in the village came to an end and it was time to bid farewell to my new family, Mongo invited me back to his school. This time, thirty small children stood and gleefully recited the entire contents of one of the books I had given Mongo. To say I was astonished would be an understatement; in awe is a more appropriate description. This man, this teacher, who, in Western terms, possessed nothing of material value or wealth, had given thirty children the great gift of imagination, in under a week!

Nine

Operation Book Power

From the day I left Africa, my life evolved with more meaning and focus than I had ever believed possible after losing Iddin and Shah. For what came out of Maasailand with me was the spark of an idea – if four books could stimulate children in the middle of the bush and help them to read, what would a full library do for them? The youngsters I'd met sat on the ground and used the bare earth as both blackboard and notebook, writing lessons in the dirt, yet these conditions did nothing to hamper their voracious desire to learn. The children had held those small books I'd given them, I saw a delight and wonder on their faces that would put to shame the affluent educational institutions of the first world.

So, when I first returned from Kenya, I contacted my Australian publisher and convinced them to give me a selection of children's books valued at A$25,000 to donate to some of the schools and the orphanage I had visited. Organising the shipment of the books to Kenya, and their distribution, took a little bit of wrangling, but it didn't prove too difficult once the customs and export details were sorted through. My royalties and salary from the work I was doing in the media helped pay the shipping costs.

This fledgling project was another small connection with my own children. I had read them their favourite Mem Fox books, along with many others, when they were little. Later, I'd seen delight in their faces as we explored the Chronicles of Narnia together. I hoped that Shahirah and Iddin recalled our bedtime stories and the secret worlds only accessible through reading; I wanted them to hold onto that treasure tenaciously no matter what they were encountering as they grew.

Nourishment comes in so many forms that sometimes it is easy to neglect intellectual needs in favour of purely physical sustenance. Many humanitarian organisations do a magnificent job in setting up feeding stations and health programmes, but I wanted to feed children's intellects as well.

If you give people the ability to read, you give them the ability to be self-determining and independent. A woman can read a contraceptive packet, or a government notice about immunisation for her children. Factual and life-saving knowledge of HIV-AIDS becomes accessible. A farmer can gather information on rotational crops and irrigation. A villager can apply for funding for a well to be dug, thereby securing a safe water supply for an entire community, and individuals can make informed decisions about political reform and democracy.

Widespread literacy is a way of ensuring that a nation is not forever dependent on international aid. This is what Mongo saw for the Maasai and understood to be the practical impact of words and comprehension.

Exactly how to do this on a large scale was what stumped me. It was frustrating to be so enthusiastic, but to lack the key that would make it all happen.

* * *

My very dear and trusted friend John Udorovic had repeatedly told me that God was giving me tasks to tackle and skills to use that were solely meant for me. John was adamant that what I was going through would eventually make sense, and that the pain of my children's abduction was an opportunity to help other people, to offer insight or empathy others probably didn't have. I'd pooh-poohed that notion but now harnessing my experience made sense.

I decided that I would stop procrastinating and take a leap of faith, using my instinct that the notion of taking thousands of books to Africa to build libraries and reading centres would work. I decided to follow my own motto – 'We live in hope'.

So I picked up the phone and began to talk to the powers that be, people in publishing and working for the airlines who could help me realise my mission. I did not ask for money, as being responsible for funds and financial transactions was well beyond my capabilities and would make the project just another charity. I was after goods and services instead.

In this way Operation Book Power was born in 1996 – a non-profit programme to facilitate child literacy in third-world countries. There were no salaries to pay, mostly because there was no staff – there was just me, and whatever help I could pick up along the way.

I was overwhelmed by the positive response from well-known publishing names such as Penguin, Pan Macmillan, Rigby Heinemann, Random House, Reader's Digest and Macmillan Education. They had no hesitation in donating a huge and diverse range of books – from children's fiction and illustrated books through to encyclopaedias and textbooks. In total, twenty-eight tonnes of books were earmarked for shipment, with a retail value topping A$750,000.

What delighted me so much was that the people at the publishing houses instinctively understood what Operation Book Power was all about and threw themselves behind it with a passion.

I bombarded potential donors and supporters with my verbal pictures and enthusiasm and the clincher was pledging that I would personally be at each and every one of the deliveries and would see the whole project through from start to finish. In other words, I would be getting my hands dirty in the field and guarantee that none of the donations would be wasted or diverted.

As a thank you, I organised magazine coverage and television and radio stories that mentioned all the companies supporting Book Power – which we termed a 'Christmas Present for the Children of Africa'.

So many people had been sceptical about my idea, warning that it wouldn't work or that I wouldn't be able to arrange things on my own without years of preparation and a lot of money, so it was enormously satisfying to see Book Power coming to fruition. To avoid problems with the various African nations' customs departments, I approached the Ambassadors and High Commissioners from those countries at their respective embassies and opened a frank and cheeky dialogue with all of them. Each of the diplomats proved to be an enthusiastic supporter of the project and bent over backwards to smooth the way with the various bureaucracies. Having the support of the embassies also short-circuited the prospect of being coerced into paying bribes by lower-ranking officials on the ground in Africa.

By travelling with the shipment I could assure the donors that the books were really reaching the children who needed them, as well as sort out any problems that might crop up.

Distributing such a large number of books by ourselves was problematic, so I began to tap into the already established infrastructure of education projects and humanitarian aid organisations in Africa.

Book Power could distribute thousands of books in Kenya under the auspices of World Vision International's educational programmes and also through CARE International affiliates. Similarly, READ Education Trust, President Nelson Mandela's brainchild, would help with distribution in South Africa. After consultation with these agencies, I was able to work out which areas and schools were most in need. Each school would then receive a consignment of approximately 2,000 publications – a cross-section of all the books donated – as well as teachers' packs and some stationery. If Book Power was going into an area without an established school, then the community had to have a secure, weatherproof structure in which to house the books. This meant that a whole community could benefit, in terms of accessing the materials, as an undertaking had to be given that an evening reading programme would be set up to assist semi-literate adults as well.

Operation Book Power ran until 2000. It had extended to Bosnia in 1997, assisting in the re-establishment of schools throughout the Tuzla and Sarajevo regions, in a bid to restore some normality to the lives of children affected by the long war. Later, we distributed books to Swaziland, Malawi and Zimbabwe, as well as keeping up our work in South Africa and Kenya.

Seeing the children in the Book Power programmes was a balm for my longing for my own two dear ones. I was meeting thousands of children each year, reading stories to them in the middle of war zones, or sitting in a field with giraffes and zebras — but I didn't know if I could still identify Shahirah's giggle or Iddin's voice. Beyond my need, though, I was confident in the belief that literacy is every child's right. Just like clean water, medical care and enough food to eat, literacy is a genuine core need — it is the tool that delivers independence and self-sufficiency.

Ten

The Cavernous Shell

Returning from another overseas trip with Operation Book Power, I tallied up the years and months since I had last been allowed to hold my children. I shook my head in disbelief as I realised that almost five years had passed since Shahirah and Iddin had been kidnapped.

It was late afternoon when my cab drew up to the house, but this was not the home I wanted it to be. I was afraid to go inside and confront my grief. But I was due to begin my three-monthly ritual of making formal requests for access to Iddin and Shahirah, and that could only be done if I remained in Melbourne for a time. I had imposed this debasement on Bahrin's lawyers and anyone else who would listen as a regimen my battered emotions could cope with and still bounce back from the shattering of my composure as I begged and cajoled – without ending up in an asylum. So I stiffened my shoulders and headed up the front steps.

We had moved to this large, two-storey residence just months after the kidnap, when our original rented home was put up for sale. Daisy, my rocking horse, stood sentinel in the upstairs window – a beacon to Iddin and Shahirah that this was their home. Solid and safe, on a big block of land with a private garden, the house was in the same suburb from which the children had been taken, and therefore easier for them to come home to in the future.

In these high, large rooms, I bunkered down now, barely going out except to work or shop for groceries, or occasionally to see a movie or go to the theatre. I developed ploys to minimise my contact with the outside world. For example, I often pretended to be my own secretary so that I could choose whether or not to continue a conversation.

Most people didn't seem to know what to make of me. My reactions weren't victim-like; I didn't want to put on a show of grief for public consumption. Some members of the media seemed to resent my infrequent outings. I accepted some invitations to opening nights extended by the television network I now worked for, but still some journalists were viciously judgemental – apparently they would have been happier had I slashed my wrists and been done with it, or maintained an air of black-clad perpetual mourning. It was far more comfortable for them if I sat in the victim box they had chosen for me. I was resented for making a living and I was resented for not being quiet about the abduction of my children. A woman who shows strength following a personal tragedy is often vilified by the media, whereas a man is allowed to move on, and even acquires kudos for his fortitude and the new life he builds for himself.

With the help of my dear friend Deb, I had transformed the new house into a welcoming place, a home that could at any moment be bursting at the seams with children ... except that the only child living here was my teenage stepdaughter, Skye; the two small kids for whom I pined were still missing. But Iddin and Shahirah's rooms were set up, their treasures carefully stored and the playhouse in the garden stocked with their bicycles and sundry summer amusements. Their early paintings I had framed and hung in pride of place in the family room next to the kitchen, and I displayed their sculptural achievements and swimming certificates on the sideboard. Photographs were everywhere, a huge family pinboard echoed life long past, and reminders of Iddin and Shah's existence adorned every room in the house. I kept Iddin's handwritten recipe for spaghetti on the door of the fridge until it faded and disintegrated, and I cried when it could no longer be salvaged with sticky tape.

This private world was insular and narrow; as long as I held onto the possibility of the children returning I would still be their mother and could kid myself I was in charge somehow.

However, there were some things that I couldn't bear to look at or think about, and the sewing machine was one. Craft and creativity had been such a big part of my life with the children that the machine was now too painful to touch – and besides, I had no creativity of that nature left in me. After the children were kidnapped, I used my sewing machine only twice: once when a girlfriend was getting married and asked me to make a special outfit for her infant son, and again when Skye asked me to make a dress for her school dance. On the dining table I cut out the red crêpe material she had chosen for the formal gown and pinned it together for the first fitting; Skye was ecstatic as only a teenager can be. But I was gutted. At the first opportunity, I locked myself in the bathroom upstairs, to feign taking a shower, so I could sob out my frustration and an enormous dose of grief. I wanted to be sewing for my stepdaughter *and* my biological children. I had made things for Iddin and Shah since before they'd been born; it was a big part of who I was. I'd loved making dress-up clothes, tailoring summer frocks and boardshorts, and fabricating dolls' clothing from scraps and remnants.

In truth, I had turned the house into a prison as much as a refuge. And I was too frightened to leave permanently.

To leave would be to acknowledge that our family of two small children and three big ones, with two parents in love with each other, all living in a house where kids and visitors happily came and went, was over. It would also have thrown up a whole other set of problems under Islamic law – another complication in trying to obtain contact with the children.

If it were known I was single, Bahrin would ensure I was branded an immoral woman, with no rights to her children. Iddin and Shah and I had a far better chance of reuniting if I was ostensibly a married woman. It was not the best of situations, but the needs of my children took priority, and any glimmer of hope that one day I might be allowed a phone call or a letter was what kept me sane, and ruthless about keeping up appearances.

No one except my closest girlfriends knew that my heart and soul were in tatters behind my relatively composed facade. They were my loyal and understanding sounding boards. They kept my secret thoughts safe and were tolerant of my foibles and my hare-brained schemes. They were the truest friends imaginable. With them I was allowed to express myself with no judgements, just unwavering support. But most of all, I could be sad with these great women; they would always allow me that luxury. And when I doubted myself, I would pick up the phone and speak to my beloved friend Patsy Heymans in Belgium; she was always determined and always soothed my fears and tiredness. I had met Patsy whilst making a documentary on child abduction; our connection was instantaneous and her empathy natural and insightful. Patsy had herself experienced what I was going through, having had three of her own children abducted and hidden for seven years by a vengeful former husband.

It truly felt as if I had started to live three, almost separate, lives: an intellectual one, in which I could feel the pull of aid work and the need to help, and couldn't stop my mind planning humanitarian projects; the second, where I went through the daily motions of cooking, working and engaging with others; and the third, in which I lived in the past but hoped and prayed for a future with my children. I had no idea how to integrate my three lives and the effort to do so left me perplexed and exhausted.

The fight to see Iddin and Shahirah went on. I never gave up, although as years went past, it was necessary to scale back my demands and just hope to be allowed a phone call, if not face-to-face contact. I was now allowed to write letters to a formula prescribed by Bahrin. But they shredded my insides. I could include no words of love and was not allowed to tell the children I wanted them to come home. I was required to send the letters via Bahrin's Australian solicitors, who would inspect every item before deciding whether or not to send them on to my own children! This whole grand concession, which was made around 1995, had been a public relations exercise for Bahrin and his lawyers. And I was very sceptical that the children would ever receive anything I sent them, either through sanctioned means or via normal post services. But write to his formula I did, even when sending birthday presents, though I tried to circumvent the censorship in various ways. One year I secretly inserted a videotaped message to Shah and Iddin into a *Star Trek* film, hoping that the children might see the film on their own.

Desperation drove me to reach out in whatever way I could devise. I mailed postcards from wherever I travelled in the world, always careful of the words I used and aware of the double-edged sword I was handing my former husband. The postcards' meaning could so easily be twisted – 'There is your mother, having a wonderful time flitting all over the globe.'

But the three-monthly attempts at contact were terribly draining. I'd be paralysed with apprehension for hours beforehand, procrastinating and finding distractions to keep me away from the task. Finally, I would place a businesslike phone call to Bahrin's legal representatives in Melbourne requesting telephone access to my own children; next, I'd try all the telephone numbers I had for the various residences of the royal family, then I'd move on to their business contact numbers. Finally, I would sit in my bedroom cradling the Malaysian phonebook that a friend had obtained for me on a business sojourn there, and try listings for anyone who might remotely be able to help. Begging strangers for assistance became second nature to me – asking them to help me slip a message to my children, or give me some insight into Shahirah's and Iddin's appearance and activities. I had no shame in making my requests. The humiliation mattered not a jot; the foul language directed at me rolled off my back like drops of oil, though the nasty laughter as I burst into tears incensed me with the probability of what Shahirah and Iddin were going through. I felt beaten down and distressed for my children – they were being raised by these seemingly heartless people, surrounded by human beings prejudiced by a religion and deaf to their humanity. Only one of them in all those years spoke to me kindly, and he was later to ridicule me on the Internet for political gain. How could I help my babies when they were so far away and deliberately alienated from me?

For another six-and-a-half years I would continue this ritual of abasement, this challenge to get through to my children or to garner news of them.

But beating my head against a brick wall might have been more effective in the long run — I could have killed a few brain cells and felt a lot less pain. (In 2006 the children told me that none of my letters or gifts had reached them.)

A journalist from a Sunday newspaper phoned me one Saturday afternoon, just before her publication went to print, to let me know she had interviewed my former husband in Malaysia.

'Your children hate you, the prince told me,' she crowed. 'They are far better off in Malaysia — that's obvious.'

This woman had travelled to Malaysia and been entertained royally for her exclusive story, but had not clapped eyes on the children, let alone spoken to them. Nor had she ever met me. When I asked her for my children's telephone number she admitted having it but refused to give it to me, citing journalistic ethics. It seemed a convenient chestnut that could so abrogate parental rights.

By the end of the conversation I was enraged. Tracking down her editor on a Saturday was no mean feat. But if the journalist had my children's contact numbers — the direct telephone numbers for the house in which they were living — then surely I had a right to have them? After all, under Australian law, I was the legal custodial guardian and parent of the two children.

But the hour-long telephone conversation with the editor proved to be another demoralising exercise in futility: I could 'attempt to obtain a court order for the number', but the editor assured me the newspaper would not otherwise release the children's contact details. Iddin and Shah might still be minors and I might still be the legal custodial parent in Australia, but the editor had to protect her sources. I simply couldn't afford what it would cost me to try to garner a telephone number via court order. It would have taken a least a week in court in any case, and by that time the article would have gone to print and Bahrin would have again changed his telephone number.

So I was a mother stripped of all role in my children's existence; a journalist had more access to them than I did.

I hung up the phone. My chest tightened to suffocation point – then coughing and retching took over, for the first time in two years. I had to get out, I had to go somewhere away from this phone where I knew I would be compelled to dial and redial the editor in my manic state of grief. I didn't want to beg strangers for help any more; I was repelled to think that my family and I would be the hot topic of conversation for that journalist and her editor that night, over casual drinks or a quiet dinner in a restaurant.

The children's absence from the house was too tangible. Night was falling. I threw myself into the car and drove to the last park the children had played in before they were taken. It sprawled next to the river, and a hill overlooked the playing fields below. I chose an old oak tree at the top of the hill; I could see the lights of the city in the distance as I slid down the trunk of the tree to sit on the grass beneath, the fabric of my dress catching on the jagged bark, my knees drawn closely to my chest. I teetered on the brink of simply taking myself out of life's equation, removing the temptation for self-serving members of the media to try to make a name for themselves by climbing on the shoulders of Iddin and Shahirah. If I ceased to exist, the story was over; the children would be left alone, at least.

I sat there most of the night as the rain fell, turning a pack of razor blades over and over in my hands. For a short while I did make horizontal cuts into my skin and watched with detached pain as the blood slowly oozed out. I suddenly understood why self-mutilation in abused girls is so prevalent; for those delicious minutes I could channel all the hurt and grief and all the pain and yearning to one tangible and visible place on my body. It was a release, a glorious and seductive release, to be able to pinpoint my pain and shift it from my soul to somewhere else.

Did I have the guts to slash my wrists more effectively? Apparently not. At 4 a.m. I got back into my car and drove to a friend's house and knocked on the door. When Andrew opened it he hardly blinked at my drenched and bedraggled state; instead, he led me unquestioningly to his guest room as I muttered about newspapers and the children, tears all the while running down my face. Grabbing a towel and a T-shirt from a drying rack, he tossed them to me and left me to get changed, returning with a cup of hot tea. He told me to get into bed and covered me with the duvet, watched me drink the tea, then switched off the light. I slept for five hours, then sheepishly surfaced.

I found Andrew in his kitchen making coffee, a newspaper spread on the counter.

'Thanks for last night, umm, this morning,' I volunteered.

'No sweat, mate,' he answered with a gentle grin. 'You've done the same for me in the past when I was going through a rough patch.'

We said no more; he was a mate in the old Aussie way and

he didn't expect any explanations. Instead we sat in silence at the table, and he began to flick through the pages of the dreaded Sunday paper.

Something had to give: I couldn't go on like this.

Eleven

Finding Oxygen

'Nicolas van Waard,' he offered by way of introduction, inclining his head slightly. I blinked a little; for a split second I wasn't sure if he had also clicked his heels – he was so much of a European caricature that I stifled a titter.

Around us, the 'A-list' were making the rounds of a sumptuous buffet: lobster, prawns, smoked salmon and ice sculptures covered the tables. It was 7 a.m. on Melbourne Cup day, the first Tuesday in November, when the whole of Australia comes to a standstill for a horse race. Attending one of the pre-race early morning breakfasts was de rigueur for socialites and visiting and local celebrities. I had no intentions of going to the racecourse, I was merely fulfilling my commitment to the television network by rousing myself at the crack of dawn and dressing to the nines in an apple green tailored suit, matching high-crowned hat, trimmed with silk roses in a shade of dusky pink my grandmother always described as 'ashes of roses', cream high-heeled shoes and bag. This would be my one appearance of the day. I planned to leave at 10 a.m. and head to my neighbour's barbecue where a comfortable pair of jeans and a sun hat would be my attire of choice once I wriggled out of the suit and heels.

Some of us were here for work, but still champagne flowed freely in the ballroom of the Grand Hyatt Hotel. Gentlemen were dressed in morning or lounge suits, feathers and flowers abounded upon the ladies' hats and press photographers circled their willing prey feverishly. Jewellery twinkled in the early morning light, cutting through the ceiling-height windows at an angle, as a pianist fingered the ivories in the midst of all the chatter.

Turning from scooping up some oysters, my fork slid sideways, clattering to the marble floor, and I met with a solid wall of grey striped morning coat. Glancing up, I had to lean backwards to see the face atop the shoulders – I stand five feet three inches and the owner of the broad-shouldered jacket was at least six foot six. The face that grinned down at me was hovering at nose-bleed height, but we somehow managed to knock heads as each of us bobbed down to retrieve my lost fork.

With a flourish, Nicholas van Waard retrieved my oyster fork from the marble floor and held it for just a fraction too long.

His accent had a cultured Euro-traveller edge to it – his English impeccable and precise as we continued with some small talk. I had to stop myself from staring: Nicolas was tall and stomach-flippingly attractive, with greyish-green eyes, tightly cropped blond hair and a measured assurance, all wrapped up in immaculate tailoring and an elegant ease. Not handsome in a symmetrical or chiselled way, but handsome nonetheless. His eyes crinkled when he smiled, and he smiled almost constantly as we spoke.

At first I thought him to be German, and then realised probably Dutch or Swiss. Wrong on all counts, Nicolas pointed out, as he revealed he was in fact Belgian – Flemish, to be precise. Belgian, thank God, I muttered under my breath. Finally, here was something about which I could converse instead of gawping at him like an awkward schoolgirl. Mentally I blessed Patsy and my visits to the small French and Flemish (Dutch) speaking nation of Belgium – at least I knew my way around there and could namedrop the places I loved and had visited. Nicolas was genuinely surprised that I was so familiar with his country, and even the university he had attended, as I had a friend who was a professor there.

I was shocked at myself; this visceral lust was something I'd never before encountered. Grappling to get my brain into gear, I listened with, I suspect, a slightly glazed look in my eye: Nicolas was saying that he travelled regularly to Australia from Belgium. He handed me his business card with one of those mesmerising smiles I wondered how he could keep producing and I discovered he was *the* chocolate industry! Not just chocolate of a pedestrian nature, not dabbling in sales of the cruder forms of the sweet: he was a director of the most wonderful chocolate company in the world! (I knew this unequivocally, for I am of course a chocolate aficionado; chocolate was the first true love of my life and my constant companion since I had been old enough to save my pocket money and spend it on the stuff.) I felt like a stumbling knight finally catching sight of the Holy Grail. Now Nicolas was asking me very politely for my number! I swear I could see a halo around his head.

What a heady combination: chocolate, Belgium, a good wit and sex appeal to boot. Cue violins and cupids shooting arrows around us, fireworks, and rivers of chocolate praline. We parted then, melting back into the crowd of revellers, but I caught sight of Nicolas again fleetingly, and he inclined his head and smiled goodbye across the room as he was ushered by his hosts towards a waiting limousine.

Four days later, ten kilograms of the finest Belgian chocolate, presented in beautiful tins, arrived at my front door by courier, accompanied by a note from Nicolas. It read simply: 'May I contact you? Respectfully, Nicolas.'

Devouring the first two kilos of pralines in twenty-four hours, I pondered my answer, and chatted with my trusted friends. Point by point we mulled over my position. I had no desire to carry out a romance in the full glare of the media, nor did I want to be anything less than discreet out of respect to Iain, especially if this was only a transient affair by letter. Nicolas was far away, safely removed from everything and everyone in Australia. He probably knew nothing of my story. Why not indulge in a flirtation? Anyway, perhaps it was time for a hobby.

So Nicolas and I began to correspond, and long-distance phone calls were soon arriving from all around the world.

An envelope posted from Tokyo might contain a page torn from an in-flight magazine – the image a set of fluffy clouds with an original poem scrawled in Nicolas's small script across the paper. A phone call from Buenos Aires as Nicolas stood at the window of his hotel might describe his view of an elderly couple dancing the tango in a cobblestoned laneway near the waterfront. A Parisian menu might turn up with 'Thoughts of you and what can be' penned on it.

This was fast turning into a dalliance of thoughts and words flitting in both directions – the articulation stimulating the cerebral nature of romance and seducing me with my own weakness. I was being wooed with charm and sophistication, and I relished every minute of this non-physical, but highly sensual affair.

Nicolas gave very, very, *very* good letter.

* * *

Around this time I was asked to participate in a television pilot being made by one of Rupert Murdoch's family's companies. The idea was to translate the reportage element of *Marie Claire* into the television medium. Ordinary people thrust into extraordinary situations – this was the angle *Marie Claire* wanted for their first TV programme. The pilot *Marie Claire TV* would be shown at the Cannes television 'love fest' called MIPCOM. This, it was hoped, would launch another global idea in 'lifestyle/magazine' television. I would be the subject of the lead feature story for the pilot. My agreement to participate was mostly driven by the fact that this was another opportunity to highlight the international problem of parental child abduction and the impact on the children and families involved.

Jennifer, the producer for part one of the pilot, arrived at my home one February day in 1997 to film an in-depth profile, highlighting my work in the field of child abduction. She and her crew gave off a vague air of disappointment that I picked up on during the two days of filming. In Jennifer's preconceived film treatment, she had pictured me to be 'Spartan' and pared back in my decorating style and had thought she'd capture me against a very minimalist atmosphere – all moody angles and modern furnishings. Confessing all to me in a fit of amused chuckles, she had been quite taken aback to find that I lived amidst a plethora of family photographs on every surface and with paintings and bright artwork adorning the walls. Candles covered every possible surface and were juxtaposed with my not inconsiderable collection of African stone sculptures and personal treasures.

Eventually, we worked out a compromise; I was filmed against a moody lighting arrangement on the tall staircase of my house, clad in a sombre but slinky long, grey dress, my disembodied voice running over the images. Part two of the film package was sprung on me quite suddenly. Could I fly to London and meet with Pamela Green, a left-behind parent I had been involved with, whose three children had finally been returned to her with some assistance from me and my contacts in Washington. It would, I was assured, be a whirlwind trip of just two days. Mr Murdoch's finances would make sure I did it in comfort and with haste. I was glad to hear that, as the journey from Melbourne to London would take twenty-nine hours or more – quite an exhausting slog in a couple of days.

Having been advised in the past by the Australian government that it was unwise for me to travel to Europe over Malaysian airspace (as I faced arrest and a quagmire of political and diplomatic complications), I had become used to taking the long way round – flying over Russia to arrive in western Europe. So, after an uneventful transit of a few hours at Hong Kong airport, the flight took off just after 10.45 p.m.

But shortly into our ascent, a horrendously loud grinding was heard throughout the cabin. Nervous but silent looks were exchanged, and a great deal of shifting in seats went on. One of the flight attendants answered the intercom phone, then pulled her seatbelt a little tighter.

Presently, the captain's voice came across the cabin speakers. It seemed the landing gear would not retract properly, and we would have to return to Hong Kong. First, though, we would need to circle the ocean to dump our excess fuel.

'That'd be right!' was my first thought. 'I decide not to top myself so I can see my kids one day and I end up going down in a fiery plane crash – just my bloody luck!' I automatically reached into my pocket and touched Iddin and Shahirah's photographs for reassurance.

A sudden yelp interrupted these self-pitying musings – the man across the aisle appeared to have a personal grooming aid tangled in his nose hairs; its duty-free packaging lay on the seat beside him. He had no option but to yank the gadget free! I stifled a nervous giggle with my hand. Where were the drinks in first class when you really needed one?

It took two hours to dump the excess fuel over the South China Sea. On the screen at the front of the cabin, a tiny image of our aircraft flew in seemingly aimless circles around an artificial ocean.

Finally, below us, we could see fire engines lined up at the edge of the tarmac, and Hong Kong airport and landing strip lit up like Christmas trees. The screeching from our engines was deafening, made louder by the pounding of my heart as I clasped my hands around my knees and had a meaningful conversation with my kneecaps and toes.

And then we painfully and awkwardly ground to a lopsided halt on the runway. A collective exhalation was audible to all; the passengers cheered and clapped as the cabin crew rose swiftly to pop the hatches.

In the end we all got to launch ourselves down the slippery, yellow rubber emergency slide!

I was relieved to have had a safe landing, but strangely hadn't experienced any real terror, just nervousness, during the ordeal. I didn't want to die, but I had become fatalistic about my life. If I couldn't be with Iddin and Shah, I didn't really care much what happened to me.

After finally clearing customs and immigration at Heathrow airport, I made my way wearily to the hotel. Arriving there in the early evening, I found an invitation in my room from the 'part two' *Marie Claire* producer, Judith Curran, welcoming me, and suggesting that we meet at 8 p.m. in the bar downstairs for a nightcap, and to introduce ourselves and go over the next day's shooting schedule.

Judith admits she already had a vague impression of me formed by news reports; 'severely traumatised is how I remembered you' she has since told me.

'You sat down on that stool next to me, Jack, and smiled as you rejected a glass of wine in favour of a pot of chamomile tea. I, of course, opted for the wine, staying true to my Kiwi blood. I thought you couldn't drink because of that Chinese gene – obviously I was later to discover how wrong I was.'

In point of fact, I was too jet-lagged to sit and sip wine; my head was already hazy enough. Besides, I wanted to take stock of my new companion. Judith was gorgeously blonde with blue eyes and a broad smile emanating from red-coated lips. She was full bosomed (which made me glance down sadly at my own 32B chest), utterly self-possessed and intelligent. I was mind-numbingly exhausted and barely able to string a coherent sentence together; I hoped I made a modicum of sense as I stared at Judith's face in a haze of travel-induced exhaustion as she ran through the shooting schedule for the next day.

We eventually parted to chase our pillows after an hour or more and I remember wondering, as I glanced over at Judith while we waited for the elevator, if this woman might possibly end up becoming a friend.

Next morning I drove with the crew down to Surrey for our scheduled meeting with Pamela Green, grateful that Judith's cameraman and sound recordist seemed to be quietly good natured and not too gung-ho.

When she greeted us at her front door, Pamela was bursting with pride and excitement. She was delighted to be able to introduce me to her complete family at long last, and we filled the half-hour before filming with rapid exchanges of news, and private insights into the difficulties her family faced as they tried to reintegrate their disparate experiences and trauma.

The interview, which at *Marie Claire*'s request focused on the path I had played in this family's reunion, went off without a hitch. But it hammered home to me the terrible contrast now between my reality and hers. Pamela had her children back.

Pamela's finances were modest, almost parlous, and her family large. The abduction and the years her children had been missing had clearly taken a huge toll psychologically on all of them. As we left I wondered how Pamela would deal with the teenage rebellion just discernible beneath the surface of her children's now impeccable demeanour. I had no idea how I would handle my lost children when eventually they returned – but I would more than welcome the opportunity to deal with the challenge. I just needed the chance to have them home.

As we travelled back to London in the car, Judith and I talked about her work and her schedule for the next day. An interview with Paula Yates, the British rock chick icon, was next on Judith's agenda. As my return flight to Australia wasn't until the next evening, I asked Judith if I could tag along. We seemed to have struck up a friendship.

'Jacqueline, good evening,' he called across the lobby as I came in, pronouncing my name in the French manner. 'I was in the neighbourhood, and thought I would say hello.'

In a beige trench coat, light-blue shirt and well-pressed jeans, Nicolas van Waard was beaming across the marble expanse like a naughty schoolboy.

Quite taken aback I shook my head to clear it. 'Since when is London your neighbourhood?' I'd had a big day, following a long and hair-raising flight – I'd almost forgotten emailing him about my trip!

'Well, Belgium's only next door if you take a plane.' He was as full of smiles and laughter as when I'd met him. 'Shall we go for a walk, perhaps have a drink? Come,' – he took my arm – 'let us walk,' and he turned me back into the revolving doors.

I tried to fall into step beside him, but our difference in height made me feel like a trotting Shetland beside a thoroughbred. I asked him to slow down. His hand encompassed mine in the crook of his arm, and I grappled for casual conversation.

I was still bemused by his sudden appearance. Missives and phone calls were one thing; a living, breathing six foot six male was entirely another kettle of fish. At that moment, I hadn't the foggiest if I wanted that fish fried or stuffed back in the cool room.

We chatted over snifters of brandy in the bar of Claridge's Hotel. The spark between us was there again, undeniable and intense. But I felt awkward. If only his eyes would stop twinkling at me in that way, I thought, I might be able to drag my mind into better focus. His body language was relaxed and he spoke of inconsequential things, with a hint of self-consciousness that made him even more charming.

Eventually, we went out into the cool English night and began to walk back to my hotel. Nicolas was gazing at me intently and it was both compelling and disquieting.

We were strolling through a colonnade not far from the British Museum when some delicate bronze sculptures caught my eye in the window of a gallery. Turning back from the glass I felt Nicolas's arms go around me and draw me into an embrace, one large, strong hand in the small of my back and another very gently cradling my head, fingers tangling slightly in my hair as his lips came down to mine. Only the first brush of his mouth was tentative; in me, a dam burst and I found myself standing on my toes to better reach him and pull his mouth firmly to my own as I wrapped my arms around his neck and kissed him back. We drew away from each other and, breathless and electrified from our first kiss, I pushed every other thought from my mind and reached out one finger to trace his lips. Nicolas raised one eyebrow – part query, part statement – and then quickly turned and hailed a passing cab. He stroked my face and repeatedly kissed my hand and the inside of my wrist. In five quiet minutes the taxi brought us to my hotel.

We made love and talked in between times for most of the night. I felt freed for the first time in so long I couldn't recall what this liberation was; my mind was happy and guilt-free.

Nicolas was a passionate and imaginative man, I discovered, not just in his correspondence to me, but also during the most intimate of moments, and for this I was grateful and relieved. I didn't want to have taken the risk of being so exposed, only to find myself counting down the minutes until I could extract myself from an awkward mistake. Up until then, I had felt leaden and quite dead within, and now I was waking up to my more womanly and secret side.

In the early dawn light, I watched Nicolas slide into his clothes after a quick shower, and attempted to frame my thoughts. I asked him if he could understand that I wanted our relationship to remain private from my world – Australia and everything else that made up the complications of my life. That was a place I needed to keep separate from what I had discovered the night before with him.

'Can we just be whatever this is?' I asked him, proud to be trying to keep control where I had failed abysmally in past relationships.

'Only if we can be together again soon,' he replied, not willing to hear my meaning. 'After all, we both travel. I'm decorating my new apartment in Antwerp, maybe you'd have some ideas on that.'

Then, more gently, he told me he'd read my book. 'If you'd been through only half the things you describe, I would still be honoured by your trust.' He bent and kissed my forehead.

I was quite taken aback. I had been researched by my lover! Somehow, I felt doubly exposed.

'Nicolas, I can't offer you a domestic situation if that's what you want, but if you can accept my life and all its erratic commitments, then – let's just be ourselves, warts and all.' I vaguely registered that my language became strangely formal.

Nicolas bent to kiss me deeply. Then he gathered up his trench coat and touched the tips of his fingers to his lips as he reached for the door handle.

'I will see you soon. Either I will come to you, or you to me.' He stated it as a matter of fact, and then he was gone.

Lying back against the pillows, imagining him soon on a plane, I ruminated on what Nicolas and I could be to each other. I wasn't heart-thumpingly in love with him, but this disarming Flemish man was deeply attractive and compelling. Though he spoke French, English, Flemish, Spanish and German, Nicolas was charmingly self-deprecating and was, I suspected, endowed with a very big brain and a formidable will. Profoundly colour blind, he'd said with a chuckle and a shrug that he couldn't even tell what hue my lingerie was the night before!

Rising from the bed and entering the shower, I turned the

taps to as hot as I could bear and immersed myself under the water jets, still thinking of Nicolas. He'd said he was an avid sportsman. Handball was his passion; just a few years earlier, he had won a gold medal in the sport. Catholic, but lapsed, his family was influential in right-wing politics. It seemed Nicolas's father had played a significant role in Belgian life, and his siblings were all highly educated intellectuals.

With our different backgrounds, would Nicolas be willing to work out a relationship on terms agreeable to us both? And at long distance, as well? I didn't want to venture into the realms of proprietorial behaviour again; I was not willing to be someone's trophy any more, nor to give up my newly found determination and independence.

I knew that men always seemed to cling to an image of me that was only a facet of my self, and bore no true resemblance to the many parts of me incorporated as a whole woman. I'd been defined by others as an *objet d'art*, a breeder, a beddable filly. Now I was heading into uncharted territory. I felt that I could do more, be more and achieve more to make my children proud, and I had no desire to be compartmentalised all over again. That was a price too high for passion, comfort and intimacy. Besides, when one is placed on a pedestal, it's an awfully long way to fall.

I would always conform to societal attitudes and expectations in terms of manners and the ebb and flow of social intercourse, but I knew I would now refuse to be limited by my gender or the projections of short-sighted males interested in jumping my bones, or simply shielding me from the big bad ways of the world.

I had paid an inordinately heavy price to arrive at this point in my life and though there weren't many jobs around for fallen princesses who had been to hell and back, I was not going to step backwards into a stifling cocoon. Whatever I became and whatever I did in the future would be as honest and as real as I hoped my children would be in their futures, royal or not.

Twelve

Wayward Women and Wine

Beginning a new day in an utterly happy frame of mind was a forgotten art for me. It was only as I applied lipstick in the mirror and saw that I was smiling that the felicity of my mood registered. Grabbing my oversized handbag, I swung out of the hotel room and hurried to rendezvous with Judith and the crew downstairs. I felt relaxed and pleased to be just tagging along on someone else's shoot, and more than a little curious about the subject of the morning's filming.

Judith and I chatted in the car as four of us wended our way through the backstreets of Chelsea until we pulled up in front of a terrace house in a quiet street.

The front door was opened by a young woman. We were ushered into the front parlour and asked to wait. It was a quirky room, rather small and dimly lit: the bow window overlooking the street was taken up by an enormous empty birdcage resembling the Taj Mahal, wreathed in fairy lights and silk flowers. The room seemed crowded. The fireplace and mantelpiece were filled with flowers, small oil paintings and Russian religious icons; a couch was laden with plump cushions and leopard-skin throws; the bare wooden boards of the floor were strewn with baby toys. And the surfaces of the coffee tables and sideboards were groaning with children's artwork and packets of photographs. Vases of lilies threw out their heady scent.

Judith had the crew set up lighting and position the camera so that cables snaked their way across the floor, and an air of expectation now permeated the room.

Paula Yates tottered in casually. Slim-hipped and buxom, her blonde cropped hair ruffled and funky, ankle-strap shoes encasing her feet and a latte-coloured lace dress clinging to every curve of her body. On anyone else that dress would have looked dowdy, but on Paula Yates it was pure rock chick meets lady-who-lunches.

Paula Yates, it seemed, would give a testimonial to Dinnigan's designs. Following introductions all round, Judith and Paula settled down to the interview.

Paula chatted readily to Judith and seemed both relaxed and eloquent. The interview was over quickly: Paula's former career as a television host and interviewer meant she hit her mark swiftly and controlled the flow of conversation with Judith.

Afterwards, as Pieter and Mark packed up the camera gear, Paula turned her attention to me as Judith explained my presence, and why I was in London for such a brief visit. Paula's eyes sparked up at Judith's precised explanation. 'I've heard about you from a friend,' she said. 'I'd like to get a hold of your book.' She intimated that her divorce from Bob Geldof was becoming quite rocky and sought to find parallels between us, which made me feel a tad uncomfortable.

'Michael [Hutchence, of INXS fame] and Bob swapped houses to make sure the girls were happy,' she said, when I told her how much I liked her funky home. Going on, Paula explained that her ex-husband, Bob, had agreed to move into her partner Michael's house not far away and that she and Michael took up residence in Bob's house with the three girls and their own child, Tigerlily. This logical and generous decision seemed at odds with the other things she was saying about Bob, so I did my best to steer away from the topic all together.

We talked about our children, comparing notes on breastfeeding (of which we were both strong advocates) and the amazing perspective motherhood created in our lives. Casually discussing Michael and talking about her four daughters animated Paula more than anything else we touched upon. Her distress at the effect the tabloid media had on her day-to-day activities with her children was deep and bitter. Paparazzi, she told me, had once pushed one of her young daughters over as Paula and the children walked down the street. The result had been a photograph of Paula hauling her child to her feet with an enraged expression on her face, captioned 'Furious Paula belts teary daughter', or something to that effect. Clearly, Paula was a woman in love with and much loved by her girls. In the background, the baby, Tigerlily, could be heard beginning to demand a feed. Paula hastily snatched a piece of paper and a pen from a teetering stack on a shelf and scribbled down her telephone number and address, urging me to ring her and keep in touch.

'Give me yours too. Quick!' she demanded, as she thrust the pen and a corner of the paper in my direction. 'Genuinely, ring me,' she emphasised, 'I want to talk some more; we'll go out and have dinner or something.' She hugged and kissed me goodbye.

Judith laughed as we emerged onto the footpath. 'Gawd, you two! What a lovely woman. Pity Michael wasn't there too,' Judith said with a twinkle in her eye.

'Yes, on both counts,' I agreed, 'but there's an undercurrent of fragility under all that front.'

Glancing quickly at my watch, I ventured a thought. 'Judith, do you want to go shopping?' I asked with a little grin and knowing that she had no more filming that day. 'We can fit in a bite of lunch, too, before I have to head for the airport.'

'Sure,' she replied casually.

To this day, Judith maintains that her head still spins when she remembers the first time we went shopping together.

Our shopping lust sated at last, we retired to a café where we could gloat over our bargains and feed our growling stomachs. A glass or two of wine soon loosened our tongues, and we talked about all manner of things as I let down my guard. Gently probed by Judith, I felt an enormous weight lift from my shoulders as I let my shell slide to the floor. I took a risk at being myself, and Judith reciprocated.

In that tiny crowded café, Judith sat with tears streaming down her face as she listened to me unburden myself. I knew then that Judith was someone I could trust implicitly.

Even though time was tight, I asked our hotel-bound cab to detour via Trafalgar Square. There was something I simply had to do before leaving London.

St Martin-in-the-Fields is my favourite church, the place where I felt closer to the children than anywhere else. Its tower and blue-faced clock beckoned me inside whenever I was in the city. Reciting my mantra and lighting candles for the children there gave me a sense of peace I never felt anywhere else.

Judith did not bat an eyelid as I went through this most private of rituals. It was truly the start of an amazing friendship.

That evening, we both boarded flights home to different

cities in Australia, but within a week had talked on the telephone, establishing a pattern of raucous laughter and unadulterated truth that still prevails, even though we are usually separated by oceans.

Thirteen

We Are What We Make of Ourselves

In early 1997, the various threads of my life began to intertwine to form some sort of self-determining tapestry. The week I arrived home from London, an invitation plopped into the letterbox asking me to speak at the World Congress on Family Law and the Rights of Children and Youth in June that year. The congress was to take place in San Francisco, and the honorary chairperson being the then First Lady, Hillary Rodham Clinton. The topic of my presentation, the governing committee wrote, would be 'The Impact of Parental Child Abduction: From the Inside Looking Out – A Practical Guide to Casework'. Only a matter of days after that, I received another invitation, this time to brief the US State Department, specifically the division which handles international parental abduction. The State Department would be happy for me to set the date to coincide with the congress.

A foreign government had asked me to speak, but not my own. The irony was not lost on me.

Up until a few months earlier, the Australian government had seemed to view me as a canker on the butt of ministerial dignity. My constant lobbying to try to force them to do something humane and supportive towards my two small children, who were Australian citizens, was met with animosity. But when a federal election rolled around in March 1997, there was a dramatic political change for Australia with the election of a Liberal (conservative) government under John Howard as Prime Minister. Just twenty-four hours later, I received a telephone call from the new Foreign Affairs Minister. He caught me in my car, returning from a speaking engagement in rural Victoria.

How did I think his department and he personally could be of assistance with my abducted children, he asked.

To say I was gobsmacked would be an understatement! Until then, I had been refused any direct contact with the minister and his stance since the kidnapping had been obstinate and resentful, which had only served to raise my ire. Relations between us had degenerated into a sniping match in the media. So to get a call from the new minister left me feeling as if I were having an out-of-body experience. Not only that, he then moved the conversation to the procedures and attitudes of his department in terms of international abduction and consular response, and simple, plain compassion and lateral thinking. The conversation went on for more than two hours and left me feeling bewildered and just a little more hopeful.

The new minister had probably been advised that it was better to woo me with honey than vinegar, so I would prove to be less vitriolic towards the new political incumbents when discussing the plight of Iddin and Shahirah. I wasn't naive, but I was hopeful. And the change in attitude within the all-powerful Department of Foreign Affairs and Trade was noticeable within weeks. For this I was truthfully and humbly grateful.

Small changes, admittedly, but the wheels of change turn very slowly, I knew.

Shortly before the new Prime Minister's first official state visit abroad – to Malaysia – his chief of staff called to say that the Prime Minister was willing to intercede on my behalf, on a personal and private basis, with the then Prime Minister of Malaysia, Mahathir Mohamad. Did I have any objections? Objections! What was there to object to? I'd had my fingers, toes, eyes and all other bodily parts crossed for years, wishing for such a profound change in political attitude!

If I wished, said the chief of staff, I could put together some personal possessions and mementos, which Mr Howard would deliver to the Malaysian Prime Minister with the request they be passed on to Iddin and Shah.

I wept as I hung up the phone. At last, my own government was willing to show some compassion towards my children. It had taken five long years and a change in the political landscape to effect this turnaround.

I decided to send Iddin and Shah a multi-image photo frame – pictures of myself, my nanna and other family members and friends, all labelled with our pet names in case the children's memories were a little hazy. I was sure that neither of the children would have seen a photo of me since the kidnapping. It had been too long since I had held them and they had seen me smile.

Allowing myself a little hope, I worked feverishly on the collage, obsessively rearranging it until I felt it to be just right.

The Prime Minister, I was told, wanted no political gain from his actions, nor did he expect any positive publicity from me waxing lyrical about what he was doing in the press. This was the kindness of one parent to another.

I went to ground for the duration of Mr Howard's state visit. No journalist would be able to elicit a comment from me on the Prime Minister's trip; too much was at stake. In private, I bit my nails and paced the floor – all I could think of was that my children might finally be receiving tangible proof that I was still fighting for them, that I loved them with every fibre of my being.

Confirmation of the safe delivery of the package came through twenty-four hours after the Prime Minister's return to Australia. His aide assured me that Mr Howard had politely but firmly put my case to the Malaysian Prime Minister for compassionate contact with Iddin and Shahirah, and that the Malaysian leader told him he would make a personal request to the Terengganu royal family that the children be allowed to receive my gift on humanitarian grounds. I was tentatively hopeful.

In January the following year, a parcel was delivered to me – it contained the large picture frame.

The back had been defaced with slogans in Malay, and my gift had then been deposited on the reception desk of Australia's High Commission in Kuala Lumpur by one of my former husband's minions. It was obvious it had never reached my children. From there, the gift was returned by diplomatic pouch to Australia, and back to me.

At least I'd had ten months imagining that I had been watching over my children with a loving smile.

Nicolas had managed to make two business trips to Australia in as many months, but now he was urging me to come to Belgium. The thought appealed, and I had work to do in several parts of the world. As well, Antwerp might be a good base for the aid activities I'd been increasingly involved in, and which were becoming focused on the Balkans. As well, it made it simple to meet up with Paula Yates and Michael Hutchence to examine a proposal Paula had come up with during what had become a flood of phone calls from her to me. At all hours of the day and night, Paula had taken to ringing me; sometimes she insisted doggedly that I expand on specific incidents that she had read about in my first book. For her, the telling of my story in black and white did not sate her, she wanted the smaller details, the exact nature of what I felt when I met my father for the first time at the age of thirteen and he was dying from cancer.

Often her train of thought went off on tangents mid-conversation. 'How do you keep going when everyone is out to get you?' she cryptically asked me one night during a tearful phone call that had interrupted a dinner party I was hosting. 'Don't they get it, I just love my children and that should be what counts,' she sobbed, as she audibly dragged in a breath of air. 'I'm fighting for my girls everyday, harder and harder, just like you are for your two.'

I found it hard to decipher if the battle Paula was referring to was against the insatiable media, or against a legal system over custody issues. More and more I got the impression that Paula swung from wanting to defend herself, her love life and her children in the media, to not giving a fig if she was the subject of tabloid gossip and moral outrage in Britain.

Australia, though, was a different kettle of fish. Seemingly, Paula had become anxious to change the perception people in Michael's country had of her; she was determined to dispel the innuendo and mistrust that swirled around her in Australia as well as Britain, garnered mostly from very negative press coverage. Michael also had chipped in during a couple of telephone calls.

'I'm f***ing sick of people heaping shit on Paula. She's an amazing woman and an incredible mum,' he told me heatedly. 'They just don't get it, or us, and it's hurting the kids.' Michael conveyed his frustrations about Paula's divorce proceedings and the scandal which had come to light about their apparent drug use. He came across as a man determined to protect his woman, and was clearly deeply hurt and bewildered by the vitriol spurting forth in the scandal sheets about her. For a man at home strutting the international rock stage, his vulnerability and bewilderment were obviously a new phenomena to him, and probably exacerbated by the emotional upheaval of becoming a father.

INXS, Michael's band, were working in the UK on the release of a new album. 'Come on over to us and we can work out a way for you to write,' she said. Michael and Paula would speak to me about their personal lives and the baby they shared, Tigerlily. 'We'll give you an exclusive to write about us for a magazine; Michael says the *Women's Weekly* is the one to go for in Australia,' Paula pushed. 'I trust you, I like how you wrote your book and we could handle you being around the family as a friend. How about it, will you ask the magazine if they're interested?'

We agreed that I would spend a couple of weeks hanging about with Paula and her family, and that anything that happened during that time would remain off the record unless Paula and Michael gave the green light. Then, the formal interview would take place – if Michael judged me to be OK. The *Women's Weekly* editor jumped at the offer of the exclusive, even with such bizarre conditions attached.

I was perplexed. I had only written a few magazine pieces at that point. This was a story that was much sought after. And I still didn't know Paula very well – snatched phone calls don't really constitute a proper friendship. But she did seem to relate to me as if we were both going through the same sort of experience. I racked my brain, trying to see what parallels she saw between us and what I could do to help steady her unvoiced anxiety. Still, I wanted to have an excuse to be in Europe for a while, and the money would also help.

I decided to stay away from Australia for a few months.

A close friend of Nicholas's kindly collected me from the airport and drove me into Antwerp, as Nicholas was in Hong Kong at the time on business. She gave me the key to the newly renovated flat and left me at the vestibule, to explore my new abode and the picturesque old city.

As soon as I entered the spacious art deco apartment, I noticed that every aspect of the decor was in a derivation of beige. Perhaps, I thought ruefully, I should have had a look at the interior designer's sketches when Nicolas had asked me to. (A year later, during a conversation at a literary dinner, I came to understand the implications of Nicolas's profound colour blindness, and his perceptions of the world around him. My fair skin, which Nicolas kept urging me to suntan, apparently appeared grey to him, similar to the rotting flesh of a corpse!)

'Beige, Jacqueline,' Nicolas himself would explain, 'is the only colour I know I can identify.' Well, the decorator had taken him at his word — unrelentingly. The apartment was like being trapped inside a giant puddle of milky coffee, with no cookie or cake on the side to expand the tastebuds.

Outside, though, a gracious city was waiting. I fell in love with the home of the great artist Rubens and the amazing architecture of the town. Five days on my own gave me time to walk the side streets and wander into the Gros Platz (Town Square) with its aged cobblestones and medieval rooflines. In the ancient cathedral I lit votive candles for my children; this religious focal point of Antwerp had stood solidly for centuries, and I felt my mantra of hope and protection echoing among thousands of whispered supplications already uttered in this holy place.

Having come across the flower and produce market, I staggered back to the apartment laden with long-stemmed roses, pungent cheeses and punnets of fresh, sweet raspberries. It was blissful to have no television in the house and to be able to concentrate on my writing and my forays of exploration. It had been a long time since I'd had the luxury of aloneness. (I'd spent so much time in recent years in the abduction arena or doing media for my book that I relished the thought of being alone and silent.)

Then I contacted Paula and arranged to dash over to London for dinner with her and Michael. I hopped on the Eurostar and then cabbed it to the house in Chelsea. The older girls were out for the evening, so Paula, Michael and I sat and talked for a while before dinner. The attraction they had for each other was palpable and evident in the way all the little intimacies gelled together. I envied their easy body language as they sat draped over one another, Michael's leg across her lap as he half-reclined on the compact couch in front of the window.

It was a bizarre evening that left me feeling like Alice through the looking glass. A whirl of paparazzi jostling us as we made our way into the restaurant, meeting vaguely named people, all of whom seemed to want a piece of the high-profile couple whenever they stepped outside their front door. A day later I was safely back in Antwerp wondering what the next instalment of that scenario would be. Phoning my mentor and literary agent in Sydney, I told him about it.

'Play it through, my dear,' he drawled, 'just play it through.'

Fourteen

A Continental Inspection

If there is one thing I loathe, it's being evaluated for my suitability – for anything. All my old insecurities come to the fore, and I immediately feel on the defensive – as if I'm a horse having its withers and teeth checked.

Over dinner with Nicolas's friends, though, this sensation of being inspected quickly dispelled. I was amidst new bosom buddies! They were a diverse but accepting crowd: one an artist, another a newspaper editor; one woman was a partner in a multinational accounting firm and her husband an architect.

'Watch out for this man,' one teased, 'we're sick of him sabotaging a good thing every time we get used to someone.'

Nicolas looked more uncomfortable than pleased.

'Shush,' chided his wife under her breath. Then, in French: 'She'll run and we'll have to do this all over again with another new one. Besides, this one has a brain and deportment, thank God.'

I maintained a fixed smile and pretended not to understand what she had just said; discretion was an automatic part of my disease to please!

But a few nights later, in a restaurant near Antwerp's waterfront, my feeling of unease was further compounded when Nicolas began to make derogatory comments to his friends about a couple sitting at a nearby table.

'Homophile,' Nicolas muttered to one of his friends with a disapproving grimace. 'Let's move.' Regrettably, I chose not to question this quiet comment as we were in a group. Luckily we stayed put at our original table. But the remark didn't bode well for the future if this was an example of his prejudices or homophobic fears. I had a number of homosexual friends and I wasn't about to have them insulted by anyone with whom I was associated, romantically or otherwise.

For the next couple of weeks I was in a holding pattern with the Paula and Michael story. I met up with them again a couple of times, and Paula phoned strangely often. Her anger at her former husband seemed to be building as Michael and she melded their lives even more closely than before, but also had to contend with the legalities of the British family law system. I still had difficulty understanding why Paula's diatribes about Geldof grew, and had to bite my tongue a couple of times as she kept wanting to make Geldof and my former husband interchangeable. Finally I told Paula that I worried she was not making sense about her worries that Bob would gain the children full time via court order. Perhaps I was naive, but I wanted to add some perspective to her view.

'Paula, if you and Michael aren't shooting up or beating the kids, no one, not the British High Court or anyone, is going to take your kids away. And I don't think that Bob would have gone to all the trouble of making sure his girls were secure in a familiar environment at the house if he just wants to screw you over. No one is going to kidnap your girls.' I finished with ill-concealed exasperation that I immediately regretted.

There was a stunned silence and I waited for her to tell me to go to hell. But she didn't and when she did speak I was surprised that she sounded chastened for a couple of minutes and then exasperated yet again when she ended our call with: 'But you don't know him. The stuff in court and everything else – he's the devil incarnate.'

'Paula,' I growled, 'things get bad when a marriage crumbles and everyone gets angry, but this isn't helping the kids.'

'Hmm . . . OK,' she replied, then said goodbye.

I went to sleep that night pondering the improbability of 'Saint Bob' of Live Aid renown crossing the ring of fire and becoming Hades' new recruit.

Nicolas had commitments during the day, taking business trips to Spain, Germany and France, and occasionally staying away overnight, which allowed me the freedom of doing exactly what I wanted. My beloved friend Patsy drove up to see me a couple of times from her home in the south of Belgium, which was wonderful. We walked to the park opposite the apartment to accommodate her need to be outdoors and talked until our voices were hoarse. But when they met, Nicolas and Patsy took an instant dislike to each other – so vehement was Patsy's hostility that I was left speechless. What passed quickly between them in French and Flemish was a bit of a mystery to me. Patsy refused to speak Flemish and Nicolas refused to speak French: they parried each other's verbal thrusts in two different languages! It's funny to look back on now, but at the time it seemed a weird turn of events which reflected the long rivalry between the different regions of Belgium: the industrial base of the country, Flemish-speaking Flanders, and the farming and agricultural zone in Wallonie, the French speaking part of the tiny nation. It was even weirder given that Patsy was married to a Flemish man, Walter. Now I suspect her bizarre reaction was compounded by Nicolas's family's public profile on the right wing of politics, but Patsy still refuses to go into what she terms 'the insults' of that day.

When Nicolas and I were together, our relationship was electric and volatile. As long as our conversations steered clear of politics, humanitarian causes and ethnicity, we were fine! Nicolas had a tendency to be inscrutable, a trait I found at odds with the openness of his letters and phone calls, and although our private time continued to be passionate, he had difficulty understanding my growing commitment to humanitarian projects.

I was greedy or sensible, I can't decide which, but I did know that my lover had to at least accept my convictions as well-founded and more than just a diversion. On paper or in the bedroom Nicolas was sensational; in reality, at close quarters ... well, I began to mutter 'fascist' under my breath – not an ideal sentiment. Intellectual sparring was one thing, the ugliness of prejudice was another.

Just as I was due to fly to San Francisco, things came to a head between us.

That evening we had returned to the apartment from a black-tie dinner at his club, when he began objecting to a working trip to Bosnia (just emerging from five years of war) that I was planning later that year. It was the final straw. I told him it would be better if he didn't join me in New York the following month, that we simply weren't working, and that to continue romantically would be a mistake.

It was all very civilised. We agreed to part – and we both knew it was for the best.

Patsy was inordinately and most indecorously pleased.

'Bravo, Jacqueline!' she exclaimed on the phone. '*Ffffoof* to him, what a relief to hear this news! Don't worry about him, he *is* a fascist like you said.'

And so I boarded my plane for the US with no regrets about the time Nicolas and I had spent together. We had been refreshingly honest with each other. After so much hurting in recent years, and such deep disappointments in past relationships, my time with Nicolas had restored my self-confidence and self-esteem as a woman. Walking away now on my own terms made me feel in control. I understood that it is possible to retain your identity and not subjugate it to your partner – I had finally learned this secret at the age of thirty-three.

A friendship was the best Nicolas and I could now hope for, but at least the chocolate had been divine.

Fifteen

There but for the . . .

Bosnia was next.

I had hooked up with a couple of large aid organisations and would be looking at their work and filming some of their rehabilitation projects in Bosnia with a view to the footage possibly being used for a documentary or in fundraising.

Only weeks earlier, Diana, Princess of Wales, had been working in the region and now, tragically, she was dead. The world was saddened and concerned for her young sons – I felt so devastated that her boys would never have the opportunity to know her adult to adult. She and I had both had difficult royal marriages and had been thrown in at the deep end at a very young age. But despite her difficulties, her bright personality had struck a chord with so many people around the world and her dedication to anti-landmine campaigning had brought its horrors before the world, and had garnered her true respect.

When Diana and I had met many years before, we had both been young mothers, she a shining star on the world stage – a princess by marriage in Britain, and I a minor princess in Malaysia. Comparing notes, I remember how I had giggled and quipped to her that we had obviously been brought in to our respective families to beef up the apparent lack of chin in the males of the line. Our DNA was a source of amusement to us both over the years – especially in light of the sad fist we both made of toeing the royal lines. It would be safe to say that whilst we both excelled at ribbon cutting and curtseying, our 'common touch' was far too tactile and down to earth for the rarefied air our respective royal families believed they breathed. She'd phoned me not long before her tragic accident, just days ahead of her famed dress auction at Christie's in 1997, when we had both been in New York, and I remember her good-natured laughter. Now I was setting off for Bosnia, a place we'd talked about, and would be spending time with some of the people Diana had been with so recently. On the day of her funeral, I was in transit on my way to Bosnia. In a nondescript hotel room I, like millions of others around the globe, watched her farewell on the television with deep sadness for her children and for the many charities I knew she was committed to on such a personal level. She and I were born two years apart, and our birthdays were separated by only four days. I had married my prince in early 1981 and she in July of the same year. Our children had been born at similar times and we had both struggled to find our way amidst very rigid royal families. Ultimately, we had both lost our children, except I still had hope I would one day see my own. It was an eerie feeling.

My time in Bosnia would affect me more deeply than the work in Africa had done, or at least it affected me in a very different way. The bombed-out buildings and the pockmarked walls of mortar-shelled homes could have belonged to any town in any first-world country. I saw evidence of war in situations I could equate to my own nation and my own life:

to transpose these scenes to Melbourne's suburbs wasn't such a great leap to make. I could finally understand what it had been like in Belgium or London after bombings and war. Any of the villages we drove through or walked around could have been places I loved in my own safe and peaceful country. The terms and conditions of war were such an alien concept for someone of my age from a country that had never witnessed mechanised conflict on its soil.

In Bosnia, this hell on earth had been the result of extremes of jingoism and inverse xenophobia aligning in a feeding frenzy akin to that of sharks scenting blood. And the rest of the world had stood by and remorselessly allowed genocide to occur.

With the signing of the historic Dayton Peace Agreement earlier in the year, a fragile peace had descended on the region, enabling a real evaluation of what these most vulnerable and displaced people needed in terms of humanitarian assistance and I felt passionately that I wanted to find a small way to contribute.

At the point on the map marked as the major crossing of the Savva River and the route into Bosnia from Croatia were massive pontoons upon which a giant raft had been constructed, in lieu of the bombed-out bridge which lurched to the side – two sad halves smashed to smithereens. Vehicles queued here to make the crossing. The wait was tedious, but all seemed resigned to it for a turn on the raft as it ferried passengers, cars and the odd lorry in either direction.

In the inevitable four-wheel drive, the trip to Tuzla, our first stop, took seven hours over mountainous terrain and winding roads damaged by landmines and neglect. Often single-lane and blind-cornered, the road ran through scenery of incongruous beauty in the midst of mindless vandalism.

Abandoned and partially destroyed homes bore racist clichés, the marks of automatic weapons and posters of wanted war criminals.

The Republic of Bosnia Herzegovina is a patchwork of opposing territories and demilitarised exclusion zones. My experiences there were also a patchwork, of tears and laughter, culture and brutality, gentleness and strength.

I had taken pains to attempt some fluency in the local language. My basic phrases, and apparently Croatian pronunciation, would get me by I hoped.

Tuzla itself is a small town, with its business district of eight or nine streets nestled at the bottom of surrounding hills. The architecture has a distinctly Italian flavour, in the way the piazzas with coffee shops and archways worked outwards from the now-notorious civic centre. It was here that, during a supposed ceasefire, a mortar attack had killed scores of young children one summer afternoon.

Shortly after my arrival in Tuzla, I had been contacted by Sandra, a young woman of Bosnian-Croatian extraction who had been told by a mutual friend to expect me. Very tall and slim, with lively blue eyes and blonde hair, Sandra had worked as a translator with the International Red Cross during the war, and later with Norwegian People's Aid. One evening, as she and I walked around her garden, Sandra tried to explain what the siege conditions had been like. Sandra spoke of her father and his death during the war, and how she and her mother had survived through sheer tenacity, refusing to leave their home even when the shelling shattered windows and mortars lobbed into the garden beds. They had hosted Princess Diana on her short overnight visit there as their home had one fully intact bathroom and bedroom. Both women had very fond memories of Diana and her innate ability to simply muck in and be a normal house guest. Sandra laughed as she told me she had found the Princess up to her elbows in soap suds at the kitchen sink as she tackled the dishes. 'Fish and house guests go off after three days,' Diana had apparently joked.

The poverty of those living in the semi-permanent refugee communities was dire. I worked with some of the children for a short while and heard their stories and sat beside them as they drew images of nightmares and bloodied limbs and lost fathers. The largest group among them were the women of Srebrenica, who had been herded at gunpoint from their village, taking only what possessions they could carry in their arms. All males over the age of seven – the entire male populace of 7,000 human beings – were subsequently slaughtered and consigned to secret mass graves in a ham-fisted attempt to cover the massacre.

One day, a pale woman, accompanied by her young son, who could have been no older than seven, came into the office where I was discussing aid distribution with some colleagues.

'Excuse me, I was wondering if you have some soap, as I would like to wash my children?' she asked politely. I replied that we were only an administrative office and the warehouse was some distance away. I offered a biscuit to her little boy and he took it but refrained from eating. This seemed odd in a child of his age and just as I was contemplating his behaviour, his mother swayed on her feet and collapsed to the floor.

When she came to, we prised her story from her. Her dignity and reticence were humbling. Over a cup of tea, the woman explained that she and her three children were living rough beneath a bridge, her husband was dead and the small family had been itinerant for nearly eighteen months. Awkwardly I thrust the remainder of the biscuits at her child, and made plans to find some proper accommodation for her and the children.

Two things will always stay with me about that day. First, for all the difficulties this brave woman was encountering, her dignity and self-respect had not allowed her to lose her sense of pride in cleanliness for her children and herself. Secondly, her little boy did not nibble a single crumb from the packet of biscuits until he shared, with great gravity and restraint, the treats with his younger siblings.

The Organisation for Security and Cooperation in Europe (OSCE) and the United Nations Stabilisation Force (SFOR) had accredited me to observe and report on the first elections since the end of the war. Having been assigned to one of the largest contingents of the US military forces stationed in the Balkans, I was to make my way from Tuzla to Eagle Base, an army camp just outside the town of Brcko.

Street signs and highway postings were few and far between in those days, so it was rather a tense trip as I navigated to instructions scribbled on a scrap of paper, such as: 'Turning for left around white pole exactly 7.8 kilometres south-east of last highway road, then looking for big rock.'

In contrast, the army base was an advertisement for the might of the American military machine. It was as if everything had been done to ensure that a slice of downtown USA had been lifted and deposited in Bosnia. The accommodation for the infantry units was mostly in tents linked by above-ground wooden duckboards to keep the soldiers out of the mud. I was housed in a secure and private tent adjacent to mostly female soldiers. There was a chapel, a library, two huge canteens offering Coke and fried chicken, a pool hall, computer centre and cinema, all constructed from demountable materials. The jewel in the crown for any under-resourced aid worker was the company 'PX', a one-stop shop and home-away-from-home convenience store where you could buy anything from Tampax to T-shirts, shampoo and CDs. (Strictly speaking, it was for the exclusive use of serving US personnel, but with loads of eyelash batting and begging I was allowed to tick off my shopping list – a copious one filled with requests from aid workers around Tuzla who had gotten wind of my foray into US military territory.)

As part of my assignment with OSCE, I travelled with the infantry units out of Eagle Base in tanks and armoured Humvees. Always travelling in a convoy of four vehicles and armed to the teeth, the peacekeepers patrolled the surrounding areas every hour to ensure that the democratic political process was not impeded by harassment or gunfire.

My first 'insertion' into a Humvee was quite disturbing. Wearing the mandatory flak jacket, I was seated hard up against the legs of a soldier who stood for the entire journey facing backwards, his head and arms poking out the top of the vehicle as he manned a machine gun to cover our rear. And anchored to the central column of the Humvee, pointing more or less into my face, were the soldiers' M16s, long-necked and deadly. More disturbing, though, was that after the first frightening day of such casual exposure to firearms, I became quite nonchalant about the guns that were always everywhere.

Every now and again, the patrol would pull over and check on the situation in a village or at a polling booth. Sometimes the soldiers bent their non-fraternisation rule and talked to children and handed out sweets. It was fascinating to watch the young Americans throwing basketball hoops with refugee children in the middle of an aid camp. Despite being dressed in full battle fatigues, helmets and flak jackets, for ten minutes these soldiers would seem little older than the children with whom they played.

It was during one of these stops that a quirk of fate brought me my only first-hand news of Iddin and Shah in many years.

We had halted the convoy to inspect a small town just outside Serb territory. Intermittent rain was falling from a grey sky and the sides of the road were sludgy and uneven. The tracks from our vehicles made deep impressions and my feet slid awkwardly in the mud. No building here was unmarked by the war: the facade of each house had been sprayed with shrapnel and no glass remained in any window. The weather was kept out with old flour sacks and sheets of plastic stamped with the United Nations emblem in blue. Many roofs were missing and walls were riddled with gaping holes. Very few trees remained; most had been cut down for firewood for the rickety camp stoves of the largely refugee population.

Four armed GIs surrounded the captain and me as we made our way towards the partially bombed-out building housing the polling booths, which were staffed by volunteers from all over Europe. Suddenly, a member of the United Nations International Police Taskforce hailed me – in Malay!

The man seemed dumbfounded to see me amidst an official SFOR escort and wearing a flak jacket in the middle of Bosnia. Under the circumstances, I was no less surprised to hear someone address me in Malay.

'Do you want to know about your children?' he asked. 'The prince says you aren't interested and don't care about them.'

In quick order, I felt stunned, mocked, then elated – and then determined to focus, to obtain as much information as I possibly could.

After some gentle pleading, the Malaysian police officer finally relented and looked me full in the eyes.

'So you really want to know?' he sneered intently.

I quashed an impulse to slap his face for his condescending arrogance and focused on remaining calm.

'Yes, of course I do, I want to know how tall they are, I'm desperate to know anything about my children. Have you seen them in the newspapers?' I spoke in Malay, but not daring to hope.

And then he told me.

Before coming to Bosnia, this man had been seconded to the Terengganu police contingent and had spent quite a lot of time at the Badariah Palace, on royal detail. I had to suck my stomach in and lock my knees to stop from falling over when he said, with just a hint of a smug smile, 'I looked after your son, Prince Iddin, a few times.'

Forcing myself to keep calm and quiet, I struggled to avoid grabbing him by the collar and shaking more information from him. I just had to allow his contemptuous power play; I had to allow him to feel his superiority over me. And finally, he did volunteer a little more.

'Prince Iddin is very tall. He's at least six foot, maybe even six foot three.'

The man could tell me no more and knew very little of Shahirah.

In the end I took my leave with as much dignity as I could, and made my way around the corner of a bombed-out building, the bewildered GIs surrounding me closely. They hadn't understood a word we'd said as the entire conversation had been conducted in Malay. Out of sight of the Malaysian policeman, I bent over double and began to dry retch and sob.

Trying to compose myself, I managed to blurt out an abridged explanation of my distress to the American soldiers. Then, removing his helmet and scratching his head, the sergeant, whose name was Larry – a beefy guy of twenty-five from Indiana – drawled out a question that made me laugh and shrug off my gloom.

'Do you want us to go fix him, ma'am?' he asked solicitously.

I wasn't sure if Larry meant the UN police officer or my ex-husband, but for a split second I allowed myself the luxury of imagining what Bahrin would do if a platoon of American soldiers turned up on his doorstep!

I thanked Larry, but declined the offer.

For days following this incident, my thoughts swirled around my head and pulled me in so many directions. I was thankful that I'd had a snippet of vaguely first-hand information on Iddin, but I was also despondent and incensed that these details had to be learned from a stranger with dubious goodwill. But this was what my motherhood had been reduced to – tabloid-like observations.

Filing into Sarajevo's battle-scarred Olympic Stadium on a clear but chilly evening, I made my way past rings of NATO tanks, barbed wire cordons and fully armed UN troops. AWACS (Airborne Warning and Control System) airplanes circled above to exclude a missile attack by zealots. The need for security was very real as a cowboy mentality still prevailed. Searchlights lit up the sky as I underwent two security pat-downs by burly Italian soldiers before gaining admittance to Sarajevo's most eagerly awaited event since the ceasefire: an amazing rock concert by Irish band U2.

There was a mood of intense expectation as the 45,000-strong crowd waited for the group to take to the stage. The concert was a symbol that the formerly besieged city was living in the 'normal' world again. People aged five to fifty-five leapt to their feet as the first guitar riff filled the stadium. Thousands of cigarette lighters flickered and swayed in unison and the crowd began to sing. Bono, U2's vocalist, had tears streaming down his face as he exhorted the audience to fuck the war and celebrate peace. For one night, the people of Bosnia became a force united around one goal – to hear one of the biggest international rock bands from a small island with its own history of internal conflict. Sarajevans were cemented together that night by the one thing that transcends language and hatred: music.

I will always count that as one of the most unforgettable nights of my life. My respect for U2 and Bono's activism turned me into a fan – the band had fulfilled a promise made during the height of the bloody war and never wavered from the commitment.

Yet another evening, I found myself in the grounds of a fort. Built atop one of the hills overlooking Sarajevo, it had served as the perfect vantage point for heavy artillery and snipers. Looking down, I saw a cemetery nestled at the base of the hill. Hundreds of simple white headstones marked the graves. I descended the hill and saw that the majority of the graves were quite new. A fragile gate set into a green picket fence opened into the cemetery. Other people were inside, trimming grass and tending plots, but it took me several minutes to realise that all of them were elderly. The natural order of life and death had been disrupted by the war – parents and grandparents were tending the graves of the young. Lives full of promise had been obliterated by civil conflict and religious demarcation.

I paced slowly up and down the rows of headstones until I noticed that the dates in one portion of the cemetery all related to one particular day. All twenty-six graves were those of children killed in an apparently calculated mortar attack. These children had been the same ages as Shahirah and Iddin.

Looking more closely, I suddenly felt as if the oxygen had been sucked from my lungs and time jolted to a halt. I hurried now from one grave to the next. Two graves carried the same first name as Iddin's: Baharuddin; three others were the graves of little girls – one was called Shahirah and the other two Aishah, Shah's middle name. It was so wrong, so terrifying! Children aren't meant to die before their parents and children are not supposed to be the targeted victims of bloody conflict.

None of us in the world outside that strife-torn territory can escape responsibility for what happened to the children of Bosnia. How many of us watched the coverage of the war on CNN or the BBC over dinner or aperitifs, changing the channel when it became too graphic? Where was our loud united voice demanding strong intervention and peace? Why are we so scared of pacifism, of peaceful and humane political will? Why, even today, as we watch military actions around the world and the carnage of terrorism grips us by the throat, do our political leaders not listen to our calls for peaceful solutions to conflict? This is not just a failing in Westernised societies, it is an obscene crime perpetrated by all those who advocate religious intolerance, violence and cultural supremacy, and hide behind religion or politics.

War can never be the answer to our problems.

Sixteen

Keep on Running and Don't Look Back

The often-talked-about interview I was meant to write never happened, though both Paula and Michael talked with me about it intermittently. Only a couple of weeks earlier, before Michael's death, I received a garbled phone call from him from New York – upset, but very protective of Paula. He wondered if she and all four of her daughters could use my house in Melbourne as a bolt hole if they followed him to Australia in the coming weeks. 'You've got a pretty normal big old house, haven't you?' he queried. 'It might be a solution to our problems.' He ended the call by saying Paula would be in touch soon.

Paula never called and I didn't speak to her until after Michael's funeral, where she'd sat in the front row of the church, cradling their daughter, Tigerlily, and weeping silently. Around her were Michael's glamorous ex-lovers, including singer Kylie Minogue and model Helena Christensen. The atmosphere was simultaneously maudlin and fashionable, an incongruous mix, but understandable given the circumstances. The who's who of show business and the fact that the funeral was being televised live ensured a confusion of media and mourning. I sat next to an old acquaintance as members of Michael Hutchence's family reflected on their loss.

Paparazzi and tabloid media hounded Paula after the funeral, sliding notes underneath her hotel room door trying to provoke a comment on Michael's death. She was forced to go into hiding in a hotel-cum-serviced appartment in Sydney – inconsolable, and adamant that Michael had not deliberately taken his own life. I managed to reach her on the phone and we spoke twice in the days after the funeral.

'He didn't fucking kill himself,' Paula sobbed and sobbed. 'He wouldn't do that to us. Why won't anyone listen? It was a fucking accident.'

'I don't understand how it happened either, darling,' I offered inadequately.

'You saw how he loved us, he did, he did, aren't I right?' She pleaded over and over for my agreement, which I readily gave, bewildered by what had transpired on the night that Michael had been found dead in the Ritz Carlton hotel. Michael was talking about the future when he had called me that night, weeks earlier. I didn't know what I could do for Paula and Tiger; I knew she had a friend travelling with her but offered to help with the baby. I had no choice but to leave it at that.

After the trip to Bosnia, I often found myself thinking of the women I had met there who were living in such difficult conditions. My mind's eye kept returning to the woman who had asked for a piece of soap with which to wash her children, and to the other women who'd approached me – not asking for food, but seeking feminine hygiene products, wondering if I had any left over from my personal stock. I couldn't think of anything worse for a woman already beaten down by volatile and degrading circumstances than being without sanitary pads or tampons to deal with their menstrual flow, and it wasn't as if there were alternatives available. Toilet paper was an expensive commodity and often missing from the shelves in stores, so it wasn't even possible to stuff wadded tissue in one's knickers. And money, if the women of Bosnia had any, was for food and fuel to cook with, not commodities that most women in first-world countries take for granted.

So in 1998 I developed a project called Operation Angel, which aimed to assist women and children caught in the middle of conflict. Donations were not a focus of the project: I was after goods and help in kind that were practical and appropriate.

The main project that year was to collect hygiene and sanitary products from Australian businesses and the public to give to women and children in the volatile Balkans. A funky television commercial promoting the idea was made with the help of members of the film industry, many of whom donated their services. Airlifting a huge shipment of sanitary pads, soap, deodorant and shampoo seemed a feasible and practical way of restoring a little bit of dignity. The campaign collected more than A$600,000 worth of goods.

In hindsight, I was pushing myself too hard. I'd been to Vienna to meet with executives of (the now defunct) Lauda Air to get a Boeing 777 aircraft for an Operation Angel airlift to the Balkans. Then, in quick succession, I lectured in Scandinavia, Belgium, Hong Kong, South Africa, Paris and Washington.

I could be accused of running away, I suppose, when I travelled outside Australia, even though the attempt would be futile and escape itself unachievable. But travelling made the hollowness in me moderately bearable for a short time.

Occasionally, when attending conferences on human rights issues or international law, I was asked by other delegates about my own children. Many meant well, but some were dispassionate academics out to make a name for themselves in a newish field – it irritated me that they treated left-behind parents as a species to be studied and regurgitated for intellectual merit, ignoring the humanity of their terrible situation.

I always felt a churning of nausea in these situations, and I would excuse myself at the earliest opportunity to escape to the nearest loo, to gather my breathing and quell the tears that always threatened. It was imperative that I kept my self-control. My children were constantly and continuously on my mind, they weren't shoved into a safe space in my head and summoned forth as and when I wished to be a grieving performance act. I had not been allowed even a single phone call with my children after so many years. But I was ineffective if I showed too much hurt; at all costs I wanted to maintain a distinction between myself and the often tightly wound left-behind parents who sometimes turned up at these conferences with only personal barrows to push. To behave in anything but a professional manner would have been a huge disservice to the cause as a whole. My view was the bigger picture, for every contact and scintilla of intellectual respect I garnered I had the potential to help other children and their parents. And maybe, just maybe, my own children would benefit in the long run.

In Washington for a week-long conference organised by the National Center for Missing and Exploited Children, I met a new player on the international parental child abduction scene, the dynamo Catherine Laylle, newly married to Sir Christopher Meyer, Britain's Ambassador to the United States.

Lady Meyer was an elegant and sophisticated blonde woman of French and Russian heritage who had previously worked in London as a commodities broker. Foremost though, Catherine was a mother, who, like me, was a left-behind parent. Her struggle to secure the return of her two boys, Alexander and Constantin, who had been kidnapped in 1994 by their father, a German national, had proved as futile as my own.

Until the time of their removal from Catherine's custody, the boys had been living with her in London, where she had rebuilt her life following the marital split. The children were nine and seven when they were retained in Germany following an access visit. When Catherine and I met, neither boy had been allowed more than a cursory form of contact with his mother. Ten years older than me, Catherine had exhausted every legal avenue open to her to gain her boys' return, and nearly beggared herself in the process. But still she had lobbied and doorknocked.

One day this odyssey had brought her to Christopher Meyer's office, in his capacity as British Ambassador to Germany. Several months later they married and she found herself on a plane and in a new role — as first lady of the British Embassy in the US.

Thrust upon the diplomatic circuit by her marriage to Christopher, Catherine quickly made her mark on the Washington scene with her style and erudite conversation. Soon active with the National Center for Missing and Exploited Children, the Meyers had offered to host a black-tie dinner at the Embassy for the conference delegates, as well as an afternoon tea.

During pre-dinner small talk, Catherine and I had gravitated to each other, for we both seemed to view our predicaments and the pain of being separated from our children as part of a bigger global picture. Comparing notes and discussing our cases in private was a natural progression. When it was time to go into dinner, I remember the tall figure of Christopher approaching us; he placed a solicitous hand on his wife's shoulder and murmured a very gentle and heartfelt 'Darling' into her ear. She answered with a dazzling smile and a slight bending of her head towards her husband's hand. It was the one time I remember feeling a pang of loneliness that had nothing to do with my children and everything to do with being a woman alone. For as much as I appeared to be independent, the solidarity and obvious romance shown by one of Washington's most glittering couples made my solo struggle seem, for a split second, pitifully solitary and desolate.

Catherine and I farewelled each other at the end of the week with a warm embrace, and a comic exchange of our books on the abduction of our children – there were some things that were just too raw to voice in person. Neither of us were quitters and both of us were determined to work within the system to obtain the best outcome for the most beloved beings in our lives, our children. We were more than capable of looking after ourselves; it was the emotional and psychological impact on our little ones that most concerned us.

Seventeen

Just a Little Bump in the Road

It was almost 1998 already; time seemed to pass at breakneck speed. Inwardly I raged at the ageing of my children and cursed the hours, days and weeks that took me further from them.

I'd come back to New York, after a trip to Kenya, to write some articles – anything to keep me out of Australia on the triple-whammy month I loathed: my birthday was on 5 July, Shahirah's was on the 7th, and the 9th was the anniversary of the kidnapping. Reporters diarised the abduction every year and would approach me for comment, attempting to persuade me to cooperate with articles or television stories they could use to make a name for themselves. Everyone hoped for an exclusive that would serve no purpose in getting the children returned home. The annual black cloud of this period was overwhelming and I would do anything or go anywhere to avoid it.

But then my agent rang and asked me to meet him in Los Angeles, issuing instructions to make sure I had suitable attire for California.

Discussions had begun again about optioning my first

book, but I was singularly unenthused, knowing as I did that Hollywood likes a happy ending, I thought it would be another futile discussion.

The whirlwind of social activity arranged by Tony swooped me up the afternoon I flew in from New York.

I'd not spent much time in La La Land before, and was curious to press my nose up against the window. Some of the glass for this exercise had been organised by an icon of mine, Miss Jackie Collins, whom I had admired for many years. Jackie and I had been introduced during one of her book tours to Australia, when we'd lunched together and generally hit it off. She'd been very kind to me during our encounters, and had done a lot to encourage my writing.

Jackie said she thought her friends would enjoy meeting me – I only hoped I would live up to their expectations. Lunch was scheduled at the famed Le Dôme restaurant on Sunset Boulevard. I shamefacedly changed my dress three times before going.

As I was shown to a huge round table at the rear of the restaurant, I mentally straightened my shoulders and told myself to go with the flow. Immaculately coiffed and wearing a stylish but casual suit and eye-catching jewellery, Jackie now rose to kiss me on both cheeks, and made the introductions. The guests included the exceedingly beautiful Shakira Caine, David Niven Jnr and Joanna Poitier.

Jackie had always struck me as highly intelligent and incredibly droll, a savvy woman who had found her niche as a novelist and knew exactly how to deliver entertainment to her audience. And her friends today were kind and chatty, interested in my aid work and the issues of child abduction. They, too, had ideas about whom I should be introduced to as part of the Hollywood dating game, but I politely and firmly declined. What my nanna would have thought of all this was beyond my imaginings, I just felt a little bit of a fraud, holding my breath before being caught out.

The rest of my sparkling LA sojourn passed in a blur of dinners and lunches, but I couldn't help feeling completely out of my depth.

On my last day in LA, the film producer David Giler had kindly offered to take me to the airport for my evening flight to Australia. We spent the afternoon by his pool, barbecuing steaks, sunning and swimming – a relaxed and make-up-free day.

As I was showering after the swim, I suddenly felt a shiver, as if someone had just walked over my grave.

'That can't be right,' I muttered as I ran my fingers over my right breast close to the armpit. A small lump the size of a pea was there. 'Bugger,' I swore.

I had felt a lump weeks earlier, then it had disappeared. But my breasts had been so unpredictable in recent times – I had even at one stage begun spontaneously lactating due to an excess of oestrogen, a by-product of grieving for the children. Lumps and bumps had become the norm.

Well, there was nothing I could do about this one here and now in Los Angeles, not when I was due to hop on a flight in a few hours. So I swallowed my panic and carried on dressing.

Later, at the airport, I was so distracted as I said goodbye to David that I didn't notice he'd arranged an upgrade for me, to first class, and I hardly acknowledged the man, Wes, to whom he introduced me and who was also travelling to Melbourne. Although we would chat later during the long flight, all I wanted was to sleep and wake up with no stupid little lump making a nuisance of itself.

During transit in New Zealand, Wes lay down on the floor of the VIP lounge and went through the most limber-stretching routine I've ever seen a man achieve. People began to point and a couple of flight attendants asked for an autograph, managing to slip past his bodyguards. Through my haze, I realised that this Wes was Wesley Snipes, the action-movie star.

'Drink this,' said Mandy, my neighbour, as she held out a bowl of miso soup. For days, this was all I could keep down. It turned out that the little lump was more insidious than I had first imagined. A speedy lumpectomy had been performed, and to my immense relief the surgeon believed I would be one of the lucky ones. But as a follow-up, I was having radiotherapy at a nearby hospital, in the very early hours of the morning to avoid any media attention.

Getting over the illness as quickly and as efficiently as I could was the goal that I doggedly fixed my mind upon. I was determined to see Iddin and Shahirah again – dying was simply not an option. For the most part, I closed down emotionally and only had contact with close friends, who kept me going during this time; my focus was on making my body provide the best long-term outcome.

My great regret was that my commitment to Operation Angel had to be wound back. It was tremendously hard to admit that I wasn't able to bring the project the energy it needed, but I simply had no other choice. Fortunately, *New Idea* magazine, the major sponsors and promoters of the programme, stepped into the void and kept the project on track, and not a single whisper leaked out about my condition. The three women at the magazine with whom I liaised kept my health an absolute secret and made no attempt to turn it into a story or abrogate my privacy in any way. Their help and friendship was an amazing watershed in the cut-throat business of women's magazines.

Twelve months later, following some discussions, the magazine became an active fundraiser for breast cancer awareness and research, and I agreed to discuss my (by then) positive outcome publicly in *New Idea*. Someone up there was obviously looking out for me.

Eighteen

A Whole Lot of CARING

Though seven years had gone by, my longing for Shahirah and Iddin had never lessened. I missed their scent, the tantalising mixture of odours unique to one's own children. I even pined for the little irritations, the tangible childhood grime of living in close proximity with your own flesh and blood. Intellectually, I understood that Iddin and Shah were no longer little children, but the memory of their grubby little hands wrapping around my face as their lips came in for a kiss still had the capacity to stop my heart beating and shred my carefully constructed composure. My yearning for them was intransigent and constant, but so too was my anger on their behalf. The fact that Shahirah and Iddin had been possessed and carried off like trophies, to be stripped of independent will and reasoning, made me furious. Unilaterally depriving them of their right to know both of their parents was such an abrogation of the most basic tenet of self-awareness and development and I was fearful of how this deficit would manifest itself in their adult lives.

As for me, I knew I was more than the sum total of the abduction of my children. I never wanted to be mired in the tragedy of their kidnap. Since the earlier days following the loss of the children, my mind had matured and stretched; I'd learned to embrace life's vagaries and become more comfortable in my own skin, less worried about others' perceptions of me and more at home with my reflection in the mirror and with my inner strengths.

I recognise though, particularly since my brush with breast cancer, that much of my strength has come from my friends, my loved ones, and from all that I've had the good fortune to experience and witness around the globe. This element of life has enabled me to contextualise my response to the bombardment of media images that affect society's common conscience.

It is this insight, combined with my irritating and innate stubbornness, that I learned to channel into projects and causes about which I felt passionately – it kept me from going mad and also reinforced to me, at my darkest moments, that getting on with life is what we are all meant to do. That, and creating change if we believe there is a wrong to be righted. I believe that an openly voiced opinion is a way to change the world – the complicity of silence can be as obscene as the injustice itself.

I *know* that one person is able to change the world – it may not be a seismic shift, but simply a shift of heart or a contribution to humankind that can make the existence of another human being more tolerable.

When the situation in Kosovo began to flare up, around the time I became a Special Ambassador for CARE International – one of the world's largest independent emergency relief and development agencies – I hoped I could create a tiny niche from which to make a difference in a complex and diverse forum. The deal breaker when I was discussing my appointment as Special Ambassador with Charles Tapp, then the CEO of CARE Australia, was that I be allowed to work in the field, in conflict and emergency zones. (Fortunately, we'd known each other for years and Charles was used to my 'out of left field' aid ideas, so he didn't view me as entirely demented.) I didn't want to be some token 'rent a celebrity' wheeled out for photo opportunities. I needed assurances that I could continue to get my hands dirty and stomp around in the mud with the people CARE was trying to help. That way, when I participated in public lectures or discussions involving CARE's work, I would not be regurgitating a press officer's briefing: I would be speaking with first-hand experience.

CARE is completely non-sectarian and non-political, an important factor to me as I wanted no religious affiliations which would dilute the purity of the aid work in which I was involved, and no distracting agendas based on gender, race or politics.

During times of emergency, like earthquake, war or famine, the deployment of a CARE International Emergency Response Team (ERT) is rapid, usually within forty-eight hours. They partner with CARE staff already working in that region, and are specially trained and experienced people drawn from around the world, with backgrounds as diverse as engineering, logistics, nursing, infant welfare, media, accounting and military. This was the team I would be joining, the one I had chosen, as I felt I would be most effective in the emergency response role.

I had an enormous feeling of hope inside my chest as I agreed to take on my new role. More than anything, I wanted my children to be proud of me and to one day share in my convictions. I felt as if I was somehow starting a job that could build a bridge over which Shahirah and Iddin might walk one day. Deep down in my heart, I believed passionately that every opportunity I had to assist another human through CARE, I would be furthering the promise of a better and safer world for my own children. If some sort of cosmic balance existed, then perhaps Iddin and Shahirah's lives would be being nurtured by some other woman far away in Malaysia simply because she had the gift of empathy and compassion. It was the single strand of conviction to which I clung when my faith in human beings teetered on an abyss of disdain and disillusionment.

To prepare for my new job in emergency response, I took an advanced first-aid course, so that I wouldn't be at a loss in a difficult situation and could handle resuscitation and bleeding. I also studied the treatment of psycho-trauma, which in some ways was a natural extension of my work in the field of child abduction and its aftermath.

I also had to fulfil further commitments first, on the Hague Convention and child-abduction front, flying to France for meetings with representatives of the European Union, before attending a conference in London on EU policy changes on international parental child abduction that coincided with the release of my book in Britain.

I travelled to London during what was becoming a tumultuous time for CARE. The war in Kosovo was spiralling out of control and scores of refugees were flooding across borders into Albania and Macedonia, seeking sanctuary. NATO had waded into the conflict in an attempt to bring order and was running bombing raids over Belgrade. Compounding the humanitarian emergency, three of CARE's aid workers had been arrested in Serbia as alleged spies and were being detained by President Slobodan Milosevic on espionage charges. I arranged with Charles Tapp to speak about CARE's work in Kosovo and also fundraise during my publicity tour, dovetailing my old life with my new.

The next fourteen days passed in a blur: the EU conference, interviews and myriad book signings. I also became a spokesperson for the Kosovo Crisis Appeal in the United Kingdom and used every opportunity during live-to-air broadcasts to exhort people to donate to the very sensibly centralised fund, which covered the Red Cross, Oxfam, Save the Children, CARE and other agencies, and cut out competitive fundraising in a time of international emergency.

It was a whirlwind of mismatches. Train trips up to Edinburgh to do press; a quick flight to Dublin to appear on a talk show; 5 a.m. starts, and a car picking me up and depositing me at the headquarters of BBC Radio for twenty back-to-back interviews in a windowless bunker for regional radio. Emerging like a mole into the light, I remember feeling confident that I had talked about the crisis in Kosovo and deflected a few questions about myself onto a more important topic.

And there was a gruelling interview with Tim Sebastian for the BBC World programme, *HARDTALK*. Nausea churned my stomach about this interview, for, as Mr Sebastian reminded me just before the camera began to roll, I knew there was a possibility that Iddin and Shahirah might see, or hear of, this particular television piece. *HARDTALK* was broadcast around the globe, with the same episode aired numerous times in the one day, so as I tried to answer Mr Sebastian's probing questions, I imagined the children seeing me for the first time in years. My heart was ready to jump out of my chest with hope and trepidation.

A luncheon meeting with the British managing director of Polaroid was a late addition to an already hectic schedule, but I'd had an idea for a relief initiative for the Kosovo crisis and wished to discuss my proposal with him and he'd readily agreed to meet me.

I outlined the conditions in the refugee camps. Small, lost children, I explained, were often incapable of recounting their proper names or those of their parents, so getting little kids back into the arms of those who loved them was fraught with problems. Photographs would speed up the process enormously, but there was no electricity in the refugee camps, so no way to process film quickly. Polaroid agreed to donate one hundred cameras and thousands of packs of film stock to assist the Red Cross and other agencies in the reunification process for families who had become separated in the flight to safety. It was a lunch that I would bless in the weeks to come.

Nineteen

Bond, Boots and Bastards

Feeling the pressure of a hand grasping the back of my airline seat, I half turned to see who it was. 'Roger Moore,' the throaty deep voice said, in tones familiar the world over. I blinked as he extended his hand to shake mine. A frivolous voice in my head quipped, 'Moore; Roger Moore,' in a bad imitation of the classic James Bond line, and I swallowed hard to focus my attention on the dapper, bespectacled gentleman towering above me. He explained that he had seen me on the BBC recently and was familiar with my background.

The flight from Zurich was taking us to Skopje, the capital of Macedonia and the central command post for much of the humanitarian relief effort during the ongoing war. Roger and his Swedish wife, Kristina (Kiki) Tholstrup, were travelling to Skopje as part of his role as a long-time UNICEF Goodwill Ambassador.

Roger asked if he could introduce me to someone. I was aware that I couldn't have looked less like a 'Bond girl'. I'd tucked my oversized CARE T-Shirt into black cargo pants and cinched them in tight at the waist to keep them up, and my enormous Belgian paratrooper boots took up most of the aisle. But now was not the time to be worrying about elegance — a couple of minutes passed and Roger returned with a smiling black-haired man, who he introduced as Toni Popovski, Minister for the Environment and Urban Planning for the Republic of Macedonia.

'Your Excellency, may I present Special Ambassador for CARE International, the former Princess Yasmin,' said Roger with a resonance so familiar from his films. 'She prefers to be known as Jacqueline Pascarl,' he added, almost as an aside. Cringing inwardly, I smiled and raised an eyebrow at Roger over the minister's shoulder. An almost imperceptible shake of his head was all Roger gave in return. Obviously, Roger knew the non-government organisation (NGO) ropes better than I did. Excusing himself with a smile, 007 turned and took his seat beside his wife, leaving the minister to clamber over my feet and into the vacant seat beside me.

Talk about being thrown in at the deep end! Although I knew the value of being acquainted with a Cabinet member in a host country, I wasn't well prepared and understood none of the political dynamics of Macedonia, but I winged it.

Popovski was in his mid-30s, I gauged, and determined to be charming. He questioned me closely on my role with CARE and the organisation's work with the Kosovar refugees flooding into his country. The Minister said he recognised me from the cover of my book, which he had seen in an airport bookshop. Did I have a copy with me, he asked, as if I was on a promotional tour!

We talked for the rest of the flight and Popovski was insistent that I attend a few of the government and diplomatic functions scheduled over the next few days, as his personal guest. Well, you never know when a private telephone number will come in handy, I thought, as he pressed his business card into my hand. Under his protection I cleared Customs and Immigration.

Walking into an established clique of people is always a hard ask, triple that if it's a group of aid workers with a determination to make the interloper sweat a bit of blood. My first couple of days at the official 'country office' of CARE International were pretty isolating. Many of the Kosovar staff were traumatised by the arrest of three of their colleagues, particularly as a number of them had worked closely with two of them before the war broke out. They felt that they might also be at risk, and their family members left behind in Kosovo during the evacuation. They were refugees themselves, who were trying to function as relief workers in a foreign country. As well, the office director had been called away for operational meetings, and morale was very low.

There is a distinct division between the administration staff at Headquarters and the Emergency Relief Team working in the field. One is about dotting the Is and crossing the Ts, and the other is more worried about food rations for their charges and the supply of potable water at the location at which they are working.

I straddled the two in a weird grey area that confused everyone not privy to the parameters of my role with CARE International. Sometimes *I* was even a little perplexed, as I always felt more akin to the relief workers. I was there to represent CARE with the media, work in general camp management, attend any UN or host-nation gatherings, film enough material of CARE's work to utilise for publicity purposes and generally find a niche for myself. Add to the mix further instructions from CARE's Secretary General, Guy Toussignant. He'd repeatedly impressed upon me the importance of my role as Special Ambassador and the focus he wanted me to put on diplomacy and public image, drawing on any lessons in deportment or conversation I had used in my old life as a royal.

The two sides of aid work needed their counterpart; one without the other is a recipe for chaos. The logistics of such an enormous aid operation were complex and many. Everything has to operate like a domino effect. Money, transport with a reliable fuel supply, national staff (as local employees are called), power, paper, computers (or at least pens), accounting, *in situ* accommodation – they all have to bubble away before you even start helping rebuild shattered lives.

Cynicism is what I expected to encounter – I would have been naive to expect otherwise. I knew that I would have to earn my stripes, and I wanted the opportunity to do so.

A population of 450,000 normally resided in Skopje. Now the city was reeling from the influx of NATO troops, hundreds of United Nations and other NGO aid workers, a gaggle of international media and a huge number of Kosovar refugees, who were sheltering with distant relatives in basements or on living-room floors around the city. Along with all the people confined to the refugee camps that had sprung up in outlying areas, this was a city bursting at the seams.

There was a CARE house in Skopje, but it was already full. So my billet was the Roza Diplomatik, a small hotel in a very quiet location near a Catholic church and within walking distance of the CARE office. Roza Diplomatik was a quirky little place – four storeys high with only twelve rooms, a twisting staircase and an open-air courtyard at the rear, it was more of a family-run pensione than a hotel. With my own bathroom and a working air-conditioner, I could retreat to my room on the top floor when I wasn't on duty or sleeping at one of the refugee camps.

Breakfast was available at the Roza, and drinks and coffee, but otherwise food had to be found at one of the little cafés or restaurants that dotted Skopje. I seldom saw my fellow guests as I had to leave the Roza by 6 a.m. to be on time for the 6.30 a.m. shuttle, and the thirty-minute drive out to Stenkovec II, one of two camps CARE was running and that currently sheltered over 27,000 refugees.

The standard joke around town was that the US government foreign-aid agency (USAID) people staying in my hotel were really CIA operatives. Needless to say, I always checked my cornflakes box for hidden cameras!

Shading my eyes from the sun, I looked up at the UNHCR flag flapping from the flagpole overhead. Danish Fred, one of the UN staffers working at the camp, would finally be satisfied, I mused ruefully; all he had done for the past few days was badger CARE people to have that flagpole erected. Frankly, there were other more pressing matters to deal with but, in the end, a minute's peace was worth it.

I had driven up to the vantage point of Skenkovec II's highest hill for a fifteen-minute break from the fetid air in the alleyways between the tents in G sector. I chugged water from the bottle I kept in my pants' pocket, next to my Leatherman multi-tool, and pulled off my neck scarf and hat. Twenty minutes earlier, I'd been staring down a bulky and aggressive man with a knife and I do admit that it takes a bit out of a girl mentally. It was a bugger too that my walkie-talkie battery had gone flat so I hadn't been able to call for assistance even if I had wanted to. This particular man had taken exception to my asking him and his family to share their tent with another influx of refugees, and he had drawn his knife, saying he was going to slit my throat before he would be forced to share the accommodation. It wasn't the first time — and it wouldn't be the last — that this happened. It seemed standard procedure that men would 'try it on' with me and not one of the blokes with whom I worked. I suppose some of the more macho and traumatised refugees thought they could scare a woman into agreement, but I knew that their bluff had to be called. I calculated that they wouldn't risk committing a crime in which the Macedonian police would inevitably become involved. More importantly though, I knew that if I didn't stand my ground, word would get around and it would be open season on the other aid workers in the camp. The knives would then truly come out to settle disputes and the result would be unrestrained aggression and chaos.

The small hill on which I now sat allowed me to survey the barren camp below. Devoid of trees, it was a swirling dustbowl when any wind was about. Inside each gully of the former quarry, hundreds of tents clung to the rough terrain. The broad high walls created by the old excavations served as makeshift roads that we drove along at very slow speed to avoid accidents. We were without sewerage, running water or electricity — nothing was simple or easy about providing the creature comforts to our refugee inhabitants. Each sector of the camp had been assigned a letter of the alphabet as its designation, and stencilled in red on the side of each tent was this letter with numbers. The system allowed us to allocate resources and count heads in each enclave. Every sector had a representative chosen by the inhabitants to liaise with CARE staff on all matters pertaining to the running of the camp, from bread deliveries to petty grievances. This was important to ensure that the people we were there to help were active participants in decisions affecting their day-to-day existence — there is no room for a patronising attitude in such situations.

The water supply to each sector was sketchy at best but critical to maintain, especially for the thousands of children and elderly for whom we were responsible in the forty-degree summer heat. Every sector had a hosepipe supplying a water source for the scores of families dependent on the corrugated water tanks from which gravity fed the taps. These massive tanks had been an amazing feat of engineering which our designated water and sanitation experts, the charity Oxfam, had constructed on the hill behind me. The tanks were replenished by trucks which ran into the camp twelve hours a day. If the trucks didn't run, the taps wouldn't either, so I had a special dislike of visits from perceived VIPs as water deliveries would be halted for these.

On a smaller hill adjacent to the one on which I sat, a huge yellow form sprawled like some alien spaceship. This was the French Emergency Hospital, an amazing structure that had been inflated like a gigantic children's jumping castle. Powered by diesel-operated generators, it was without a doubt a feat of modern ingenuity and the best design for a field hospital I had ever seen. Fully air-conditioned, it came with sleeping quarters for medical staff, an operating theatre, X-ray department, three wards and a pathology laboratory. As the nights could be very cold in the old quarry and the days blisteringly hot, the hospital was truly a godsend for newborn babies and surgical patients. Staffed by a mix of military doctors and nurses, and paramedic-trained fire-fighters, or *pompières*, the hospital would be with us for just thirty days, the maximum deployment allowed by the French government.

Supplementing their specialist medical care was a small outpatient clinic down on lower ground. Run by International Medical Corps (IMC) and staffed by a handful of volunteer doctors and nurses from around the world, this was the front line in most medical treatments and evaluations. Dentists Without Borders and Pharmacists Without Borders also operated between the three main camps in Macedonia – the other two were Stenkovec I and Cegrane, where I worked occasionally.

Although the UNHCR banner flew over the camp, the United Nations' presence was minimal. CARE International had been officially tasked and contracted by the UN to handle the day-to-day running of Stenkovec II, with an allocated budget for the provision of food, water, shelter and national staff drawn from the population of the camp. (This is the normal procedure in many disaster and war zones to ensure that the expertise of the different aid organisations are fully utilised.) CARE's staff slept in the camp and were responsible for all aspects of its management, and security as well. We were also in charge of the Mother and Baby Units, an expression of CARE's belief that little ones need to be protected and nurtured through tough times by a dedicated nurse educator and staff. These units, dotted around the refugee camp in specially provided tents, ensured that mothers could bathe their children and had access to baby food, formula, potable water and disposable nappies – all essential in maintaining a disease-free environment under very harsh conditions. Women giving birth in the camp were encouraged to breastfeed for their own health and that of their babies. A special nutrition-monitoring programme was also operating to keep up the health of the many children living in this less than ideal situation.

The other agencies working within Stenkovec II and Cegrane camps were the International Committee of the Red Cross (ICRC), who undertook the mammoth task of tracing lost children and adults and reuniting families, and UNICEF, who set up shop in the relatively fresh air on this unimpressive hill. Here they ran a kindergarten, playgroup and school for the children of the camp but still in very dusty conditions – most of the land was denuded of grass.

During daylight hours, in a caravan set up opposite the converted shipping containers that served as our camp management office, IOM (International Organisation for Migration) operated its service. Here displaced people queued for hours to apply for temporary humanitarian relocation to places all over the globe. Every agency present in the camp interfaced and worked together without rivalry – this scenario bore no resemblance to the outside worlds of Australia and the USA, where humanitarian organisations routinely compete for positive publicity and the donor dollar. Emergency relief was an entirely different kettle of fish; that we all pulled together was one of the things I most enjoyed. That and the camaraderie.

The tents provided for the refugees were a hodgepodge of ex-military surplus and donor-provided shelters. It always amused me that the tents in Stenk II seemed to have been erected anywhere in odd clusters and at strange angles to each other – the wonderful and constantly good-humoured pompières and French soldiers had done most of the grunt work – while at Cegrane, German military engineers had laid out the camp with Teutonic efficiency and precision. Global Positioning Satellite beacons in hand, the Germans had striven for exactitude, and as a result their perfectly aligned canvases stretched unswervingly as far as the eye could see, housing 57,000 displaced souls on what had been a rubbish dump.

Overflowing with people from different walks of Kosovar life, time at Stenk II proved challenging. Gypsies, teachers, factory workers, farmers, musicians, college professors, housewives, shopkeepers and plumbers were forced to exist cheek by jowl in stifling conditions devoid of privacy and autonomy.

Fire was a huge and dangerous problem. Candles were prohibited inside the pitch-black tents at night, but this rule was frequently flouted. Cooking fires were another hazard. There was no central kitchen to dole out food in 'wet feedings' (the term used to describe pre-cooked meals) to the inhabitants; instead, a two-day food ration of canned fish or meat, onions, a loaf of bread and some fruit was distributed from a designated point in each sector and recorded on a ration card. There were so many fires in or near tents as a result of cooking fires getting out of control, I still can't believe no one died.

When I flip back through my diary from that time, I realise just how diverse my duties were. The team worked each day with little complaint. The one thing I detested was distributing mattresses, for they were as valuable as gold and as sought after. This job often fell to me because I spoke Bosnian and had picked up a smattering of Albanian, the Kosovar tongue. Slabs of foam the size of a single bed, they were released according to very strict criteria. Essentially, they were reserved for pregnant women, the elderly and the very sick, although if a family had numerous children we could sometimes justify the allocation of one mattress to the entire family group. All the other refugees slept directly on the tent floor, only a groundsheet separating them from the granite beneath. Blankets were given out upon arrival – one each. No pillows were available.

I hated the power I had over the refugees' comfort; I hated that I couldn't offer them more. Most of all, I hated the clamouring and the pleading when the appointed hour for applications rolled around – the desperation shown by

young men on behalf of their womenfolk overwhelmed me.
They seemed to link their self-esteem as males to their ability
to provide a comfortable bed for Grandma or their younger
siblings. In a refugee camp, I learned, men are the ones stalked
by depression and disenfranchisement.

Day after day, I would enter tent dwellings and find
dozens of men lying with their faces turned to the canvas;
their hopelessness was almost palpable. They had lost all they
possessed materially, but worse, many of them had been unable
to protect their female relatives from sexual abuse, rape or
torture at the border crossings controlled by the Serbian forces.
This humiliation sometimes manifested itself in the form of
aggression, knife-wielding and threats. It was the one thing
they could do for their abused women – stake a claim on a
tent and refuse to allow interlopers a foot in the flap. Women,
by the circumstances in which they found themselves, didn't
have the luxury of mourning or solitude; their extended
family depended on them to collect rations and water, wash
clothes and care for the children and the elderly. The gender
division was enormous and the responses to the trauma of
displacement, violence and war were markedly different.

One of my duties was to inspect every tent in my
designated sector for that day and ascertain numbers of people
and available space. Stenkovec II and Cegrane were officially
transit camps, which meant many of the refugees were awaiting
immigration processing and evacuation to temporary safe
havens being offered by nations around the world.

The inhabitants of Stenk II could spend as little as five days
with us or as long as several weeks. Our population ebbed
and flowed to such an extent that it was imperative to take a
headcount regularly and keep track of the spaces becoming
available in tents throughout the camp.

In any given twenty-four-hour period, six buses of fifty people each could be processed to other countries and depart the camp. At night, when the Macedonian government opened its borders — the prime hour being 1 a.m. — an enormous convoy of incoming buses would arrive at our guarded gates, escorted by NATO military or Macedonian police. A snapshot of human trauma and misery was crammed into these convoys with buses meant to carry fifty-five people practically bursting with 120 passengers. On the other side of the border crossing, in the full summer heat, the buses were loaded by the Serb paramilitary when the sun was at its highest. Then the doors were closed. If the refugees were not carrying water, then there was no way to slake their thirst.

I hadn't been prepared at all for the night of my first large arrival. Faces were squashed up hard against glass, people standing and reaching hands through the small sliding windows near the roof of the bus. Tiny children were held up to the slits for some fresh air. Condensation dripping down the glass made it obvious how stiflingly hot the buses were. The Macedonian authorities would not let us open the doors to the buses en masse — we could only process the buses one by one. I wanted to smash windows and pull everyone out, but we couldn't antagonise our hosts.

Our radios had crackled to life just before twilight, warning us that buses would be coming across the border tonight. We had heard rumours all day and I'd had the tents in A sector prepared and the people who had been in them relocated to G sector and throughout C. I was warned to get some rest, but to sleep with my clothes on. At midnight the wail of the police sirens started in the distance, and grew nearer as I pulled on my boots and reached for my headtorch.

As the first bus approached with its interior lights on, we could see the shocked and weary faces of the people crowded into it. We watched as one, two, three, four, five, six buses followed in the wake of the police vehicles, straight past Stenk II's gates and on to Cegrane, three more long, hot hours' drive away. Seven or eight minutes later, a police car swung through our gates followed by eight buses lumbering under the weight of too many passengers. The most immediate need was for water, and we ran up and down the length of the parked vehicles like people possessed, tripping over rocks and tufts of grass, pushing bottles of water through small window openings as the desperate cries for *vodu* – water – sounded from the souls locked inside. The outside temperature was still at least thirty degrees. My frustration was rapidly turning to tear-suppressed anger that we were forbidden to simply fling open the doors to the buses and process everyone in the cooler outdoor air.

Finally, a half-hour or more after the buses had trundled in, we were allowed to direct them around the rabbit warren of our camp to A sector, where we would release the new arrivals. I plunged cross-country, dodging guy ropes and potholes to get to the offloading area fast. The pompières were frantically resetting the arc light that ran off a car battery, and repositioning trucks to illuminate our working area by the headlights as we had no generators to provide electric light. Residents of the camp gathered to help us or in the hope of finding a lost relative or friend.

It was organised chaos, a tragedy of human suffering and shock. Finally opened, the first bus disgorged its cargo – in an explosion of dehydrated, exhausted, weeping and soiled humanity, clasping whatever was most precious in a tight grip. Moments went by before I realised that some of the stiff bundles were tiny babies swaddled in the traditional way with layers of wrapping and string. Overheated, the fragile mites were pale and glassy-eyed. Traumatised toddlers clung to their parents' legs and wailed.

Immediately, paramedics and aid workers made their way rapidly along the lines of squatting and collapsing people, trying first to assess medical requirements.

A woman in her mid-20s holding a baby began to scream. I ran to her, trying to decipher the cause of her distress. Checking the child, who appeared to be no more than a couple of months old, I realised it was barely breathing and had poor skin tone.

'Too hot,' I said to the mother as I pulled the knife from my belt and began frantically to slice away the string and the swaddling around the child.

Sinking to the ground, I placed the baby across my legs and stripped away the last layers, including a putrid plastic shopping bag which had been serving as a nappy. It was a girl and she lay limp in my lap. Pulling off her bonnet, I saw a tuft of blonde hair.

'Come on, sweetie, take a big breath,' I urged her, as the mother wept and pulled at one of my arms.

The baby was terribly thin and covered in a heat rash. I began rubbing her limbs and body, as I yelled to a pompière-paramedic, Jean Paul, for help. Then, taking a chance, I gently blew into her mouth and nose – her pulse was barely registering. After a fraught few seconds, she took a big gasp of air that seemed to inflate her flaccid wee body and, letting out a feeble whimper, she nuzzled for food. At that moment, Jean Paul arrived by my side. Looking at my face, he put a hand on my shoulder and pronounced, '*Aucun probleme, Jacqueline, c'est OK, n'est-ce pas?*' (Is there still a problem, Jacqueline, seems it's

OK now, isn't it?) and quickly moved on to a gunshot wound that had just been identified.

The mother gratefully took the tiny girl from me, and I ld her in sign language and rudimentary Bosnian that it was too hot to wrap her baby. She nodded, beginning to free a breast for her daughter.

Obscenely, human dignity was reduced here to whether I could find a nappy for a baby and a shelter for them both. How could the perpetrators of this ethnic cleansing allow tiny children to lie in excreta, fight for oxygen, and be denied the right to grow up in safety, surrounded by family?

The team were flat out. So many of the new arrivals had been sleeping rough in caves throughout the mountains, or under bushes, as they tried to get to the safety of our camp. Parents were dazed and kids exhausted; all had a haunted look in their eye, an insecurity that transcended the underlying grief, and a bone-weariness shaded with suspicion about their new surroundings.

Making my way up and down the lines of families, I continued to slit open swaddled bundles to cool down overheated and distressed infants. One baby was convulsing, and the pompières transferred it to their truck for the trip to the hospital on the hill. Then a man with a gunshot wound that was still oozing blood and pus was loaded into the truck with the baby and mother.

Group by group, the new arrivals were ushered into the enormous tents that would be their home for the next few days. Tentatively, they followed us into the darkness, where they would have to sleep like sardines against the torsos of strangers, in the most rudimentary conditions. We distributed ration packs, explained the no-candle rule and asked that people use the latrines and not relieve themselves inside the tents.

We left the refugees blinking in the dark. I could hear whimpering and moaning as we walked away. Misery, fear, grief and desperation sound the same in any language and are somehow worse in the dark.

The next night it began all over again.

An intense groan of pain, guttural and exhausted, escaped from the woman's lips. Pushing the damp fringe back off her face, I glanced at my companions. Three concerned sets of eyes caught in the light from my headtorch. A single arc light was set up six metres away, illuminating the night and the line of buses stretched out in front of us.

'*Oui*,' Jean Paul nodded to me, '*le temps pour pousser*' – it was time for the woman, just unloaded from a bus, to push.

'OK,' I said turning back to the woman, who was gripping the edge of my T-shirt in a twisted bunch. Her back was propped against the tyre of the bus, and her pelvis was on a sterile pad that the pompières had placed over my waterproof jacket to keep her from the bare ground. Looking her in the eyes, I urged her in throttled Albanian to push. Switching to Bosnian, I encouraged her, '*guranje*', adding sound effects for good measure. Slipping my right arm around her, I mimed a huge breath in and pushing down. Thank goodness her primal instincts took over. The pompières were taking care of the birthing end, but I took a quick look after she gave two enormous pushes and saw that the baby's head was beginning to crown.

'*Attendez une seconde*,' came the sharp command from Jean Paul; he wanted to avoid any tearing as the head was delivered and had to slow things down.

'*Poor marlo*,' I told her in bad Bosnian, 'slowly, wait', and breathed shallowly for her to copy.

Getting the nod once more from Jean Paul, we all urged her, in a multinational cheer squad, to push. With a guttural wail, the woman concentrated all her strength, and in one gargantuan push the baby slithered out into the waiting hands of Jean Paul.

'*C'est un garçon!*' – a boy – beamed Jean Paul with tears in his eyes. He showed the newest member of the human race to his mother, and the tiny creature let out his first protesting cry of indignation.

There was no beautifully warmed bunny rug for the babe, no delicate clothing, no downy soft towels, just a sterile pad on which the tiny boy was laid while the pompières tied his umbilical cord and cleared his airways. As soon as Jean Paul and the others had finished, I whipped off my CARE T-shirt, turned it inside out for cleanliness, and gave it to them to swaddle the baby, blessing my luck that I had a utilitarian tank-top bra underneath. Once the boy was safely placed in his mother's waiting arms, I helped her unfasten the front of her dress and got the baby to latch a slightly lazy mouth onto her breast. Tears had welled in my eyes and were now beginning to run down my face. By this time, a stretcher had been fetched, and mother and son were transferred to the pompières' truck, to go to the French hospital where the pair would be properly checked and the placenta could be delivered. I climbed up on a tyre, hoisting myself over the edge of the truck, and kissed the woman's cheek gently.

Stepping back, I watched the tail-lights bob unevenly over the rise and then they were gone. I wiped my jacket on the grass as best I could and pulled it on over my tank-top. A few hundred refugees still had to be processed, and my job was to help get them under shelter for the night.

A couple of hours before dawn, I sank onto my sleeping

bag laid out on the floor of the shipping container with as much relish for its embrace as I would have evinced for a feather bed at the Plaza Hotel. Mashing my knapsack into an acceptable repository for my head, and still fully dressed, I reached out a hand to make sure my boots were close by and shut my eyes. Around me, I knew my colleagues were equally as horizontal, and mostly snoring. Three of us lay shoulder to shoulder and another fellow was propped up on a row of boxes under the window. With a stifled groan, I prayed that my bladder would hold out for a couple of hours and promptly plunged into a deep and exhausted sleep – it had been a long seventy-two-hour stint.

When I awoke, it was to the dual reveille of a rooster crowing in the distance and the loud explosion a human fart can make in a confined space. Pulling my arm over my mouth and nose, I half-opened one eye and hazarded a guess at which one of my male colleagues had serenaded the rest of us.

As a rule, aid workers have to be genderless in terms of interaction within the framework of their own organisation. That was the thing about often being the only woman present on an emergency relief mission: it was imperative to be one of the 'boys' and not be viewed as a woman at all. Judging from the fart, I had apparently been successful, although I drew the line at competing on that playing field.

I grinned to myself as the others awoke around me – to think, just ten days ago I was dining in posh London restaurants. It's amazing how quickly you can get used to the whiz of overhead air-to-surface missiles, helicopters and pit latrines!

'*Bonjour, Jacqueline*,' came the exuberant greeting, as I raised my wet head from above the bucket of water where I had been doing my early morning ablutions behind the shipping container. 'You must come to the hospital,' Jean Paul said when he arrived from the adjoining French compound. 'It is the Abanian custom: the new *maman* wants you to give the baby his name.' With a broad grin and a salute, he was gone.

And that is how it came to pass that a small Kosovar baby was named Baharuddin, in honour of my missing son, Iddin. Fortuitously, it was an appropriate name for a Muslim child and not too unusual within his culture.

Holding the precious mite, I whispered his new name into his ear and blessed him with all the love could muster. His mother lay back on her stretcher bed and beamed, while visions of my Iddin as a tiny baby flooded into my mind.

'Stay safe, little one, and grow up safe and strong with your mum; be a good and gentle man,' I cooed to junior Baharuddin, his hours-old eyes blinking at me wisely and his face a solemn study of concentration.

Excusing myself then with a hug and a last kiss, I withdrew quickly, afraid that these tears of joy might change to grief.

Twenty

The Truth about Emergency Sex

id workers are a funny bunch, most of us deeply flawed or carrying some sort of chip on our shoulders that makes us want to do better. We feel compelled to work hands-on in areas rife with death, disease and distress.

Certainly aid workers are deeply committed to a better world and the resolution of human suffering – but are they holier, more noble than the average person on the street? Absolutely not.

Aid work strips away all the defence mechanisms of a person's character and leaves them naked and exposed. Human frailties are unmasked but, more importantly, tremendous human strength and depth of character come to the fore. It's possible to know exactly where you stand with another emergency relief worker within seventy-two hours. That's the time it takes for the real person to appear. Without a doubt, I know that the handful of really close friends I have made during aid assignments are the most reliable, trustworthy and dependable people I have ever met. The best of them can look at a problem and see a lateral solution in no time. Hesitation is not in their lexicon, though caution should be.

In the best of them, intelligent caution combines with dogged determination. I would not hesitate to trust these people with my life, as indeed I have on several occasions.

The difficulty for most aid workers is reintegration into normal life post-deployment. For weeks after getting back to Belgium or Australia, I would feel physically ill at the sight of all the food overflowing on supermarket shelves and have to quash down my contempt when witnessing the stupidity of road rage or unconscious greediness. I felt my detachment and isolation intensely after I returned, my experience more intense because it also added to my unquelled desire for Iddin and Shahirah.

Comparing notes with other aid workers on 'civilian' dinner parties they'd been invited to, I realised that we all come up with similar tales. 'Tell us what it was really like,' is the stock request. Urged at the dinner table by friends and acquaintances to describe Sudan, Bosnia, East Timor, Iraq, Afghanistan or New Orleans, a newly returned aid worker can go one of three ways.

The first, usually preferred by seasoned veterans of emergency deployments, is to provide a heavily censored vignette with a good outcome involving child/mother and clean water or medicine. One nods sagely and shrugs when someone says, 'Well, I think you are wonderful for doing that work, I don't think I could,' and changes the topic swiftly.

The second option is to tell the uncensored truth, describing tortures and rapes, the suppurating wounds and starvation. Then for good measure, relate how it felt to have a child die of measles in one's arms, or what it was like to see the eyes of a child roll back in its head as the infant passes away from starvation. You can attempt to describe how inadequate words are to a woman who has lost everything. People begin to shift in their seats, a glazed look in their eyes takes hold and silence falls over the dinner table. Someone will then make a light-hearted attempt at praise and then offer to open a new bottle of wine to cover the awkwardness. And all the while the aid worker sits with a fixed smile and seethes at the glazed eyes. He or she realises that no one really wants to hear what it's like.

The human mind and soul have their limits, and sometimes a short circuit is needed to avoid a meltdown precipitated by severe trauma and the continual witnessing of man's inhumanity to man, or the indecipherable cruelty of Mother Nature.

In emergency zones, quiet and unremarkable pairings sometimes occur. Each week, staff from different aid organisations might get together to let off steam. These are no dress-up-and-preen-to-disco-music affairs; instead, a precious bottle of Baileys might be shared from tin cups outside a tent, a local café might see fifteen aid workers gather for a meal and a drink, or a small low-key party might be organised, with a few military personnel who have provided direct logistical support as guests. These get-togethers are not a prelude to an orgy or anything of that nature, and any pairings that result are distinct from the drunken snoggings seen in corners of rowdy parties the world over. The interactions I silently observed at these functions often began with a quiet and intense conversation away from the main group, usually about work problems, frustrations with head office responses, and exhaustion.

Somewhere in the midst of shop talk, the dynamics would change just a little – suddenly the pair would both feel safe and utterly devoid of bullshit. Two oddly genderless creatures needing respite devoid of ego and games.

Who better to comprehend the human suffering and barbarity you have witnessed and waded into that day than a fellow aid worker? Where else could you find another person who could see the black-humoured side of unwittingly squelching through human remains? How else to obliterate those images and the memory of the sounds another human being makes as they plunge into the bloody abyss of their tragedy?

Rob and I had met at a United Nations cocktail party to honour a visiting celebrity to Macedonia. We'd been given the dubious honour of attending as the representatives of our respective aid agencies and were each mindful of the politics involved. It was also a fascinating chance to see how the flashy side of international aid carried on in a conflict zone when a VIP comes to town: the incongruity of the celebrity 'meet and greet'. An enormous part of me detested these kind of events; I understood them to be a necessary part of my job, but I inwardly railed because I knew the people inhabiting our camps wouldn't recognise me gussied up and sipping chilled wine only a few kilometres down the road from their shattered subsistence.

For me, this evening had been the third soirée in as many days for the same VIP. After my 5 a.m. start and a day working amidst the sweltering heat of a refugee camp, traipsing up and down the dusty tracks in temperatures topping 103 degrees, I had been dirt-caked twenty minutes before the scheduled start of the reception. I'd just managed to snatch time to peel off my filthy combat boots and grubby CARE T-shirt and cargo pants, hurl myself under the shower at the Roza Diplomatik, and wriggle into the one dress I'd had the foresight to cram into my backpack along with a pair of stiletto-heel sandals. Adding a dab of lip gloss, a slash of eyeliner and mascara in the back of the cab on the way to downtown Skopje, I shook my hair from its plait and walked into the cool of the air-conditioned building. The last thing I felt like doing was making small talk – I'd had a shit of an afternoon trying to find a way of moving an elderly woman around the camp to the latrines without a proper wheelchair. Topping that off, apparently I needed to speak to some guy at the other camp, Stenkovec I, about her predicament, but no one had his mobile number or radio call sign.

Realising I was the last to arrive, and having the bad luck to walk in smack in the middle of what would prove to be a tedious and long-winded speech, I scouted the room for a familiar face. Not a single one, bar the UN country director and the celebrity. Resigning myself to a dismal and dutiful evening, I caught sight of a very tall and lean bald man on the other side of the room who seemed to be finding all the wordy sentiments being expressed as amusing as I was. Dressed in a pale-blue polo shirt and jeans and aged somewhere in his mid-30s, he leaned against a pillar and glanced around the space at regular intervals. Eventually we made eye contact and exchanged wry smiles.

Later, mercifully released from our listening posts, we found ourselves in a group who were discussing the latest sanitation problems at our respective refugee camps. I began relating my difficulties meeting the needs of the elderly lady and adding a few expletives about the elusive 'fixer' at the neighbouring camp being un-contactable. I trailed into silence when I noticed that Rob had broken into a wide grin.

'Do you think all this is funny?' I challenged him.

'No,' he replied, 'it's just that I'm the arsehole you're cursing.'

Sheepishly I apologised, feeling about two feet tall, but he seemed to think it was hilarious.

Looking round the room, I realised that the crowd was thinning and my feet were aching – my stomach was also growling furiously and very audibly. One rumble obviously reached Rob's ears, and he guffawed and asked me if I wanted to grab a bite to eat. Accepting thankfully, we exited the building and I climbed aboard his vehicle, the ubiquitous aid worker transport, a white four-wheel drive.

Minutes later we arrived at a local café, apparently known for its fresh Greek salads and local roast meat dishes. Over dinner, which thankfully arrived swiftly, we chatted about conditions in the camps and the state of our charges in our respective domains. The meal and the conversation went down easily, we used the shorthand peculiar to relief workers around the traps and kept away from the gritty, less palatable topics of the job stresses, our emotional states and the inevitable anger and despair that so many of our ilk carry around just beneath the surface.

Twilight was still to fall as we arrived back at my hotel. Opting for a drink in the open-air courtyard downstairs, we talked some more and when they closed the kitchen we eventually found ourselves upstairs in my room as night fell. It was not love at first sight, or even lust. There was no huge frisson of attraction, it was what it was – comfort and escape in a tumultuous world of crappy war and tragic human consequences – a night off – no thoughts of riding off into the sunset together, no complications, or romance, or expectations. And when it was over, when we'd sweated and laughed together, we made the first move towards a friendship and a mild curiosity about each other. This, as far as I was concerned, was the minefield to navigate, and the item of conversation I was so overly prepared for as to seem too pat and glib. I dreaded trying to explain my background.

'So, what number war is this for you?' I ventured with a pre-emptive strike.

'Err, let's see,' he began, as he reeled off some locales. 'Bosnia, Somalia, Northern Ireland and a couple of places I can't discuss, and here. How about you?'

Pulling myself up on one elbow and tugging the sheet higher, I countered with my list. 'Bosnia just post-war, dabbled in Rwanda and here, Macedonia. Before that, East and South Africa in straight development aid.'

Out of the corner of my eye I noticed Rob shoot a quick look at my CARE International identity card and security name badge which lay on the nightstand.

'So Jack, what's with the alternative name on the official ID?' he quizzed me. 'I know that you're CARE's ambassador, but all the talk tonight was about your work in the field. The title ambassador and now this,' he said jerking his head at the IDs, 'don't exactly scream dirty hands, luv,' he ventured in his southern English accent.

Inwardly I cringed, feeling defensive and exposed as I always did when I had to talk about my past and the reality of my life and its complications. How to pot a history for a lover one hardly knows, and who doesn't have the foggiest about one's background? Should one rise from the bed, wrap oneself in a sheet and grandly declare, 'Once I was a princess, and there aren't a lot of jobs around for us fallen ones.' Or should I spill my soul by ripping open my carefully constructed facade and explain that I had once married into an Islamic royal family as a teenage bride and many years after the marriage was dissolved, my former husband, the prince, abducted both my children in a fit of revenge and cultivated religious fervour. Either way, each of these solutions would leave my emotional composure the worse for wear and my coping mechanisms in tatters.

Leaning over the edge of the bed, I mentally steeled myself as I fished an oversized T-shirt off a pile near my backpack and pulled it over my head. Turning to Rob who was leaning back against the headboard with his hands behind his head, I began to speak. 'Better you hear this from me rather than from the gossip that'll eventually start floating around the aid workers' network.'

I folded myself into a cross-legged position facing him on the bed and continued, my arms crossed over my chest defensively.

'On the 9th of July 1992, my two children, Iddin and Shah, were kidnapped and I haven't seen or spoken to them since – that's six years, ten months and a couple of days.' Before Rob could form a question I was off, outlining all that had passed and all I had lost. I could hear myself talking rapidly and realised that I was like a battleship by this point, steaming ahead at full speed and too raw to draw a breath or pause for comment for fear I ran aground.

'Since the day they were kidnapped by my ex-husband, Bahrin – that's the abbreviated version of his name – I haven't been allowed to see or speak to Shah and Iddin at all – zilch, nada. It all made international headlines at the time, and since. The whole battle was pretty ugly and I was gutted – still am actually, life just fell apart, and if I'm honest, that's a bit of why I'm here. Anyway, I've also written a book about what happened, which has just come out in London, so I schizophrenically arrived here fresh from a huge publicity tour and an international conference.'

Taking a deep breath, I shot my companion a quick look and added, 'CARE appointed me as their Special Ambassador, but only on the criteria I insisted upon. So there you have it, a precised life story.'

Expelling a huge breath of air, Rob opened his mouth, 'Well, bugger me – that makes some of the things I've heard in my travels sound like a walk in the park. My turn then. I'm ex-SAS, did a long deployment in Bosnia before I left the regiment – stuffed up a bit and just got tired of being on the armed side of the fence, so here I am, heading up an NGO mission in a war zone. My mob are here with minimal funding to try and help the refugees who fall through the cracks . . . the disabled, intellectually and physically, as well as the elderly.'

With a flip of his eyebrow he added, 'S'pose that's why I came up in the conversation when you needed a wheelchair for the old lady at your camp. I've got funding for that, and over at Stenk I we've set up a corner of the camp to deal with "special needs" people – you know, the ones at risk and with no families to look after them.'

Scratching his pate, he queried gingerly, 'So just how well known are you in the UK?'

'Enough to have *Times* journo Danny McGrory, who's posted here, want to speak to me while I'm about, and NBC from the US, etc.,' I answered as I saw him wince.

'Hhmmm, great, look, I'm not married or anything, I'm single so there's no worry there, but I loath the tabloid press. I can just see the headline now . . . "The Princess and the Paratrooper".'

I laughed tightly and shrugged. What else could I do? He was right – on a slow news day, a story like that could possibly get up. It would also take the focus off the work CARE was doing in Macedonia and the rest of the Balkans. To risk a headline for something that wasn't even yet defined as a full friendship, let alone a proper love affair, was just unnecessary, and frankly would use up too much energy.

'Hey, I make a bloody good friend and colleague,' I said as I switched off the light.

'Yeah, me too, Jack.'

We saw each other through work as he moved between my camp and his, Stenkovec I, a couple of miles down the road. Sometimes I would hitch a lift to town, or work with him, and we occasionally ate together. Sleeping and sex were just extensions of deep conversations. In the desolation of this place, tenderness was a huge factor in our friendship. Both of us had to be so hard and so focused in our duties that physical and emotional letting go when we were in each other's company often brought us to tears at the strangest times.

We guarded our friendship fiercely, keeping it private and casual when around others. We were watchful against media interest, too.

As the weeks went on, I came to love Rob as a friend with whom I occasionally had sex — or more often than not, someone with whom I wept and slept minus any sexual contact. It was about trust and respite, being emotionally naked and frank together in a very lonely situation. Even now, from a distance and over thousands of miles, we speak by email every so often and we have shared the happiness of our subsequent marriages, and joy in our respective children with goodwill. As the song goes, 'but most of all when snowflakes fall I wish you well'.

The time had come again. I must use the latrine in the CARE compound. I had learned to value my bathroom at my billet extravagantly, and this was a moment I always dreaded. So putrid was the facility that I would hold on for hours longer than was physically good for my bladder!

Approaching the building, I undid my belt and drew a

small bottle of Diorissimo from my pocket and sprayed myself liberally. Taking a huge intake of air before lifting the latch and stepping into the cubicle, I tried not to look down, and was able to hold my breath for the entire procedure.

Emerging with comically bursting lungs, I heard my name called. A CARE worker was approaching with a delivery man proffering a huge beribboned bouquet of carnations. Another utterly surreal moment! I'd already had enough of these off-kilter episodes that day, as a distraught and barely coherent Paula Yates had managed to track me down on my mobile phone.

Handing the bouquet to me with a slight bow, he departed in a government car. This was the second bouquet of flowers I had received that week – in the middle of a refugee camp!

Attached to the flowers was an admiring note from Toni Popovski, the Macedonian Environment and Urban Planning Minister. It was all getting too much. He had already turned up unannounced for a tour around the camp – but at least that had given me the opportunity to ask for more water trucks and an extension of Cegrane camp into the nearby forest.

Good relations with a host government were one thing, having a Cabinet minister as a suitor was quite another! Of course Minister Popovski had been immensely helpful, and as Special Ambassador I had been taken by him to meet both the Prime Minister and the Macedonian President, but this was a delicate situation I wanted to exit from gracefully.

Now, heaving a sigh of bewilderment, I resolved to make the best of the situation. Gathering all the empty plastic water bottles I could find, I drove up to the hospital on the hill. Dividing the carnations, I made up small arrangements for all the female patients in the hospital. The French medicos looked at me as though I was slightly demented, but I reasoned that women the world over deserve flowers for having a baby or surviving surgery, and especially in the middle of a refugee camp, far from home.

Twenty-One

Bread, not Circuses

An uglier form of unwanted male attention can be found anywhere. But this time it was provided by a new member of my own organisation.

He was one of those utterly dysfunctional, weird aid workers that I had sometimes encountered, a war-zone junkie, and he seemed to have decided that his mission was to take a former princess down a peg or two.

His first stunt was to make sure there was no vehicle available late one night to take me from a café where all the CARE staff had been eating in a nearby town to the house CARE had rented for staff in Cegrane township, forcing me to walk two miles alone on the back roads of rural Macedonia with only a headtorch to light my way. 'Bastard,' I muttered under my breath as I walked along the rutted track with my knife open in my hand. But worse was to come.

After a couple of weeks, during which he made it very difficult for me to function in the camp, I found myself alone with this man in the back room of the Cegrane site office, where I had been sorting through boxes. As I straightened up, my back against the wall, he placed his hands either side of my shoulders and began to speak.

'So, if I had a castle, would you shag me?' he leered, his breath hot against my face.

'Not bloody likely!' I retorted.

'You jumped-up bitch,' he hissed as he tried to grope my breast and bring his mouth down onto mine.

Fortunately, Rob had taught me a few self-defence tactics earlier in the week, and I can confidently say that I caused my unpleasant co-worker a significant degree of discomfort. I doubted he would attempt to bother any woman over the following few days or want any sort of 'emergency sex'. Not all aid workers are saints, and occasionally you can come across an utter bastard.

The celebrity visit to an emergency relief zone is a double-edged sword. On one hand, it has the potential to throw a spotlight on tragic circumstances, bringing attention to desperate situations and fuelling the public's financial response. On the other hand, relief workers stationed in conflict and disaster zones often view the intrusion of a celebrity and trailing media pack as a necessary evil they have been directed by head office to facilitate, and they may quietly resent the disruption to the finely calibrated daily routine of the camp.

And disruptive these visits are. During my time in Macedonia, a circus of celebrities came to town: Richard Gere, Bianca Jagger, Hillary Rodham Clinton, Vanessa Redgrave, Roger Moore, the German Foreign Minister, and the Dutch Prime Minister and his wife, to name but a few, all on fact-finding trips, and all, I am sure, genuinely concerned by the human suffering they observed.

But whenever a celebrity pays a lightning-fast visit to a

refugee camp, at least three aid workers attached to the charity with which the celebrity is affiliated must swing off normal duties to act as ushers, answer queries and generally help wrangle the celebrity's entourage, photographers and other hangers-on. With most camps chronically short-staffed, the disruption to normal schedules is huge, and many daily duties in the camp go out the window.

When Hillary Rodham Clinton visited Stenkovec I camp, for example, water and bread deliveries were suspended for the day, for security reasons, and some residents simply didn't get fed. Many of the vital services in the camp ground to a halt as secret service agents swarmed through the old quarry and cleared an area, specially sanitised for Hillary's viewing. I don't believe she got a realistic view of the camp at all. It was hardly her fault that the security and media requirements were so disruptive, and, of course, the political influence Hillary could wield was important. But I often wondered whether VIPs knew what being deprived of bread for a day did to a refugee family with an already tenuous quality of life and, if so, would they still be as determined to observe the woes of humanity at close quarters?

Certainly the movers and shakers of the world, the decision-makers who hold the purse strings, should see at first hand the suffering of others and carry those images and the pungent smells of misery with them as they make determinations on life-and-death issues. But surely it's unnecessary for actors and models to have the same level of access for what is often a glorified photo opportunity.

If the celebrity arrived without fanfare three days before the media phalanx – and without a publicist, bodyguard or entourage – to unpack aid shipments, distribute food rations and live alongside the relief workers . . . if they were exposed to seventy-two hours of reality before fronting a media conference – I wonder how many would opt to send money instead?

Cegrane camp held 57,000 displaced and emotionally shattered people; a rubbish dump converted to a refugee camp; its white granite tiers cut into a steep hillside now bore row after row after row as far as the eye could see of barely weatherproof tents.

Before the Dutch Prime Minister, Mr Wim Kok, came to Cegrane, workers of various aid organisations ran around trying to clean up the camp and briefing all and sundry on proper behaviour. Watching everyone buzzing around like big blowflies, worrying about their T-shirts being stained, made me incredibly pissed off. Medical treatments slowed to a snail's pace, while the putrid pit latrines were cordoned off from the areas designated fit for viewing by the Prime Minister. They were deemed too filthy for his sensibilities.

On the day, the official welcoming party stood in an orderly line to greet the PM, who had just inspected the medical clinic and some tidied-up tents. Standing there as CARE's Special Ambassador, I felt rather grubby: a sudden downpour earlier in the morning had quickly begun to flood a row of tents and I'd had to dig out an overflowing drainage ditch with my hands and the lid of a tin can. Now, dried mud stained my clothing, although I had done the best I could to wash my hands.

When he reached me in the line, the Prime Minister checked that I was actually the CARE Ambassador, then called to his wife, Rita, to join us. By coincidence, she had just finished reading my book in Dutch. We made chit-chat about the work in the camps and the conditions – until the devil in me took hold.

Catching Mr Kok's eye, I boldly asked whether he and his wife would like to see the real refugee camp.

'Absolutely,' he replied emphatically, and to the horror of their entourage, Mr and Mrs Kok followed me as I cut through the cordoned-off area and steered them in the direction of the communal latrines, a few hundred metres away.

As we got closer, the stench was almost overpowering and I explained that each block of five latrines accommodated the needs of almost 2,000 people. With no flushing mechanisms, the latrines were large holes in the ground surrounded by wooden duckboards. There were no showers in the entire camp, I told the stunned couple.

Walking away, we moved to a row of tents that through their open flaps revealed humans at their lowest ebb – their faces defensive or blank, distressed and humiliated by the state to which they had been reduced. The tents were designed to hold six people but each accommodated twenty desperate souls.

Mrs Kok stopped in her tracks and turned to me.

'You know, after the war, when I was a child, I was a refugee,' she confided with tears in her eyes. 'What do you need from us, how can we help?'

'Well, we desperately need the mattresses and funds the government of the Netherlands has pledged to us,' I told her. 'Not in a month, but now. The granite is too hard for the sick and young to sleep on.'

'Wim,' she said, turning to her husband, 'it has to be done.'

The Prime Minister looked me in the eye and took my hand. 'I promise you that I will see what can be done quickly,' he said, and with that his entourage was upon us.

A lot of glares were directed at me from some UNHCR people, but they didn't dare utter a word of rebuke. It was one of those out-of-kilter moments when being a fallen princess really paid off and boundaries of etiquette were blurred for a good cause.

Twenty-four hours later the Dutch money was in the bank, and the foam mattresses arrived forty-eight hours after that.

Driving around Stenk II in the battered old blue utility truck we used to carry refugees and supplies around the camp, I would pull over if I had a few minutes up my sleeve. Time for some fun.

Over the past few weeks the children and their parents had become used to me jumping from the truck and starting up a game in the handiest dusty clearing. Often as I was driving around in the middle of a task, children would run beside the truck and beg me to stop and play. They knew the drill by now.

'Kangaroo, kangaroo,' they shouted excitedly as they hooked into a long conga line behind me and I sang 'Skippy the Bush Kangaroo' at the top of my lungs. 'Hokey Pokey' came next, then 'Kookaburra Sits in the Old Gum Tree' – which ended with my ear-splitting rendition of the mad Aussie bird's call, much to the delight of the adults looking on. I didn't give two hoots if I looked foolish; the children loved a game and I loved watching their faces split with laughter.

Smiles and laughter were such rare commodities in the terrain in which these children were marooned. They needed to have fun; I didn't need my dignity. And every time I made a solemn little face crack into a grin, I blessed my own children and hoped that someone was making them laugh in their captivity. I saw Iddin and Shahirah reflected in every small face that looked up at mine, and longed for them more than ever. For now, the children of the camps were the closest I could come to being with my own children.

One morning, the renowned British photographer Tom Stoddart arrived in our camp and asked if he could photograph the doings of the day. Even though it was part of my job to shepherd the media around Stenk II, I was heartily sick of unscheduled film crews traipsing through the camps and getting in our way, often with little respect for the human tragedy going on around them. On guard, I watched him carefully as he followed aid workers around on their regular tasks. I was surprised to see him first obtain the permission of a chosen subject before he took any photographs. It was a refreshing change, as so many members of the fourth estate came in, shot their footage and departed as if they'd been to observe animals in a zoo. Tom, though, talked to everyone, squatting on his haunches in the dirt, and giving some dignity to people living in very undignified circumstances. This was a man to trust, and admire too.

Kushtrim, a slim young boy aged twelve, was our youngest Kosovar volunteer. A pensive and gentle boy, he had brought his elderly grandmother into Stenkovec II in a wheelbarrow, hauling her over mountainous terrain to reach us. They were the only ones of their entire family to have survived the brutal slaughter and had been forced to hide beneath the bodies of the dead for two days before escaping into Macedonia. If ever an adolescent had a justifiable reason to become taciturn and sullen with an enormous chip on his shoulder, it was Kushtrim. Instead, he had decided he was my protector and had taken to following me around the camp as I worked.

Someone had reported a 'mad' couple and some 'feral' kids in F sector, and I was sent to investigate. With Kushtrim in tow, I found a man in a catatonic state lying in a pool of urine and his wife, who was probably schizophrenic, defecating in the tent they shared with other people. Their three-year-old daughter was filthy and hungry and was scavenging food from other refugees. The woman seemed oblivious to the barely breathing baby lying on the bedding beside its father. Other refugees said the mother hadn't fed the baby for three days at least. According to passers-by, the couple usually ran a newspaper kiosk in Pristina. Upon arrival, they had slipped through the net at assessment time and were now without the medications they normally took to keep their mental illness in abeyance.

I had to make a rapid decision. Snatching up the non-responsive baby and running to the truck, I handed the flaccid baby to Kushtrim and drove towards the French hospital, but it was too late – it had already been deflated and packed up ready for departure. I diverted our vehicle to the clinic on the lower level and was halfway there when looking up at me with petrified eyes, Kushtrim told me the baby wasn't breathing. I pulled over and began to give the baby CPR on the front seat as Kushtrim tried to help. Blessedly the little one took a small breath and we drove on to the clinic. Once there, the International Medical Corps doctor from California set up a drip for the baby boy and I fed him a bottle of paediatric rehydration as Kushtrim hovered close by. Under the circumstances, the doctor said he could only keep the baby overnight as a favour to me. The small child must return to his parents in the morning. There was nothing more I could do other than arrange a medical visit for the baby's parents and extract a promise from the International Committee of the Red Cross (ICRC) to find medications for them. I knew that without help for the sick parents, the baby would probably die.

Just another day in the camps.

A couple had stumbled off a bus into our camp, the husband barely supporting his wife's weight in his own distress and grief. Their two little girls had been separated from them at the border crossing in the mêlée caused by aggressive paramilitary guards. The parents had protested violently, to no avail. The mother was so severely dehydrated it was nearly impossible to find a vein in which to insert an IV drip. She was almost speechless with worry and shock. I had to bite down on the inside of my cheek so as not to cry with her as I could so easily understand her physical and mental anguish.

Four days passed with no word about the children. I knew the parents' pain: I was looking into my own reflection 10,000 miles from home and seven years on from Shah and Iddin's disappearance.

With one of the Polaroid cameras, I headed to the medical tent where the mother was still being treated. I took three shots of the parents, and organised for Tom to drop them off at the ICRC tracing centres at Cegrane and Stenk I.

Two days later, two little girls at Cegrane, just three and four years old, pointed to their mum and dad's picture – success!

The next day, with tears all around, the family was reunited. I felt relief so sharp my sternum seemed split. I only wished I could conjure up more happy endings.

Twenty-Two

The Fine Line Between
Pleasure and Pain

I left Macedonia in June 1999, just as an official ceasefire took place in Kosovo. I felt ambivalent about returning to Paris and London – the *real* world was where I had been working. I had commitments on behalf of CARE to attend to, but it didn't make my departure any easier, or the goodbyes any less distressing. I had wanted to remain and work on the repatriation of refugees; I wanted so much to see Pristina, the Kosovar capital, and help put the homes of some of my new friends back together. But I was needed for fundraising and publicity duties, and knew that if I stayed in the camps, I would be dangerously close to burning out. I was sick to my stomach with worry about some of the kids in the camps whose parents had been killed and who now found themselves in charge of siblings and elderly relatives at the tender age of twelve or thirteen. Kushtrim was of particular concern, but I made arrangements with another family for him and his grandmother to travel on their tractor when the time came to go home.

Arriving back in Melbourne in July, it took only three days before the nightmares about Iddin and Shah kicked in. It seemed that the familiar surroundings precipitated their return to my subconscious. Nights were no longer a time of rest – I came to believe I slept better in a war zone than at home.

Awakened at night by what sounded like the children's voices calling for me, I would have to get out of bed and look around the house. I knew that it was just some kind of trick that my nightmares played on me, but the longing for Iddin and Shahirah that surged through my body, the ache I felt in my womb, told me that the bond between them and me wasn't broken.

Like Pavlov's dog, I jumped when an email pinged into my box. Could it be true or another hoax? It was from Iddin, the heading told me. But it was an Iddin who didn't seem familiar with any private family history. I could explain that away to myself though, in my desperation to believe my children might be trying to contact me – after so many years, perhaps the children had only hazy memories of what life had been like at home in Melbourne. I held with all my stubbornness to the kernel of hope that pushed its way to the surface even though my rational side told me not to wish for the impossible. I felt physically sick as my head and heart slugged it out for ascendancy.

Every time I did some media in Australia – as I did when I came back from Macedonia – fresh interest would be sparked in my family's case. Either a junior reporter would decide to do something new on the abduction of my children, approaching the 'tragic mother' like a loyal friend; or a twisted stranger would pretend to be one of my children contacting me via the Internet.

Back home, going through the motions, I replied to the

latest 'Iddin' as guardedly as always, asking a few questions – and then spending days compulsively wondering and waiting for a reply.

Four days passed before I heard anything, and then 'Iddin' implored me to 'get us out of here. Hire some guns and muscle and rescue us.' The hoaxer then gave themselves away: 'You asked me if I remembered Granddad – yeah, of course, really worried to hear that he isn't the best. Get me and Shariah home so we can hug him. Just get us home. Love from your son Iddin.'

The children's grandfather had died before they were born – I was only fourteen when my father died in Singapore from throat and nose cancer. And Shahirah's name was misspelt.

There was no way for me to tell if this was a journalist or a kid hoping for money. A story about me contemplating an armed retrieval of my children would make a good headline. But I had neither the time nor the inclination to allow this sicko any more of my attention. Move on and regroup had to be my attitude or I'd never survive.

One thing never changed, though: the concept of what, and who my children were – precious rare gifts, individual spirits whom I loved with all my heart and soul. I hoped and prayed that one day they would find their way home to me.

Twenty-Three

Wanting to Move Heaven and Earth

With an eerie green glow the television screen showed a baby being tossed by a frantic mother over high barbed wire and, by sheer luck, falling into the arms of a UN official. Eyes, terrified and pleading, shone in the night-vision lens of network video cameras – the sheer terror of the East Timorese people. All the while, gunshots and frantic screams came from off-camera.

My own stomach began to churn in agitation as I was drawn unwillingly into the mayhem being broadcast on the monitor before me. This was too close to the bone for me, an echo of the violence and damage I had witnessed in the northern hemisphere summer during the Kosovo war. It was hard to believe that this obscene picture was coming from only a few hundred miles off Australia's own northern shores and far, far too close to my own children and the lives they were leading in the same South-East Asian region.

The catalyst for the unfettered violence the world was witnessing was the Timorese people's declaration of their right to be self-determining and free of Indonesian rule. East Timor's gun-toting, machete-wielding thuggery was in a state of vengeful aggression and violent dissent; armed vigilante militia roamed the streets and pro–independence supporters were being abducted and probably murdered, and the towns torched.

Australian-based aid organisations, including CARE, began to plan for a relief effort, if and when the opportunity arose.

Automatically, I pulled my aid kit from its storage place under the stairs, cramming my knapsack with the bits and pieces I suspected would come in handy when the call came for my deployment to a ravaged war zone. Timor, I reckoned, wouldn't be that different from Malaysia – uncomfortably humid and steamy with plenty of opportunistic mosquitos looking for a taste of imported buffet. Heavy-duty insect repellent, water-purifying tablets, a precious roll of toilet paper in a zip-lock plastic bag and sachets of dehydrated soup were crammed in alongside my med kit, miniature flashlight, sharpened multi-tool and sturdy lace-up boots.

Disembarking in Dili, the tropical heat washed over me, taking my breath away. Sweat and humidity drenched me in seconds. It was day eight of INTERFET, the UN–sanctioned peacekeeping 'International Force in East Timor'. A couple of goats and a horse wandered across the tarmac. For a moment I had a flashback to my time living in Malaysia, and I wondered how Shah and Iddin were coping in the intense and constant heat.

Fluent in Indonesian, I'd joined the emergency response team as interpreter, assistant shelter coordinator and Special Ambassador. My other primary duty was to liaise between CARE International and CMOC (Civilian Military Office of Coordination) at daily briefings to ensure we were aware of safe travel zones and military and militia activity.

The work in Dili seemed never-ending as we were very shorthanded, so it was all hands to the wheel, but it was uplifting and the rewards came with seeing people getting fed, their lives improving bit by bit. There were times when I watched the faces of displaced people light up as we successfully reunited their families and I had to quash the temptation to transpose my own family into that situation. Personal thoughts were almost too distracting, although I was constantly aware that geographically I was so close to Iddin and Shahirah. I had hoped that news of my presence in East Timor might filter through to them in Malaysia, as the conflagration was obviously big news in the region, but I may as well have been on the moon. There was still no breakthrough in my quest for contact.

Everyday was a hard slog in East Timor, the humidity made moving around exhausting, and the sheer scale of what needed to be done to restore society to a functioning community was immense. Our national staff were living in the same conditions as our refugees and it was inspiring and poignant to be surrounded by colleagues who were so committed to moving forward and building a new nation from ruins. I wondered if Iddin or Shahirah were aware of the extent of the upheaval in East Timor and once, in a moment of self-indulgence, I ventured a hope that maybe one of the children had spotted me in the background of a news broadcast. This small thought made me feel guilty when so much suffering was going on around me, but I having to speak and function on a day to day basis speaking Indonesian, a dialect of Malay, brought me strangely close to the children.

As assistant shelter coordinator, I was supervising the setting up of a camp for thousands of demoralised refugees, many of whom were very ill from spending weeks in the jungle with little food and no sanitation. Our main shelter was to be the ruins of a Catholic boys school, Dom Bosco, that had seen a lot of militia activity.

Preparing the burnt-out buildings was a mucky job: the somewhat unstable walls had to be checked and the floors of the buildings had to be cleared of rubble. Weatherproofing with UNHCR tarpaulins was imperative, as the rainy season was fast approaching. I designed a series of lashings with old water bottles filled with dirt to weigh down our temporary roofs. The Canadian sailors from the ship HMCS *Protecteur* and US Marines detailed to assist me proved to be invaluable, climbing precarious roof ridges to secure roof joists. Although I would have preferred if they had been unarmed as I narrowly escaped a bullet that accidentally discharged from a sailor's rifle during one of our rest periods and went whizzing past my head into a spot on the wall where my head had just been! That aside, together we wielded hammers to get the job done as quickly as possible accompanied by a lot of laughter.

Pushing and shoving with all my strength simply wouldn't budge one charred door, to the side of the main hall we were clearing out, so I called over a couple of burly US Special Forces soldiers, otherwise known as Green Berets, to help. A mighty thump from them sent the door flying off its hinges.

Entering the small side room with a shovel and broom, I calculated how long it would take to clear the collapsed roof and began to move debris, assisted by one of the sergeants. We worked for five minutes or more before my shovel struck something that rolled. It was the blackened remains of a person. Reeling back, I half squatted at the doorway and peered at the charred pile that was partly covered by ashes and muck. I unclipped my radio and made a call to INTERFET headquarters, trying to keep my language as innocuous as possible as this was an open frequency. The last thing we wanted was to have a huge crowd of local people descending, trying to identify the morbid discovery. And it would be too distressing for the people whose loved ones had disappeared.

What divides us from those who can snuff out another human being's life without compunction? What provides the impetus to propel a person forward to strike the first blow when anarchy breaks out? I believe that a mob mentality buoys up a deranged absolution of collective guilt, allowing people to act in ways in which they would never usually have enough moral fortitude to do so. It is cowardice of the greatest magnitude.

When the crime investigation unit arrived, we withdrew sombrely to another part of the complex and allowed them to work undisturbed. A number of local priests and nuns were still unaccounted for and this was a place some of them had taken refuge. In my mind, there was no doubt that this was the site of an execution. Two body bags would later leave that small room. I was never to find out whose resting place I had disturbed, but I made my way that afternoon to the large white church near central Dili and lit four candles. One for each of my children, and two for the poor souls who had died amidst so much violence and terror. This time I prayed that my children would never know war first hand.

Sometimes the sheer magnitude of a relief effort can prove almost overwhelming and the individuals you are trying to help become one big blur. Other times, though, you become passionately and personally concerned for a particular person or family. It could be you've made a connection somehow with a single glance, or recognise that this woman or man could so easily, under different circumstances, be a friend you would catch up with over coffee back home. Perhaps one single human being becomes for you the encapsulation of all the sorrow, misery, violence and injustice you have been witnessing on a grander scale. Somehow, you become determined to help this one person and you'll move heaven and earth to do it.

This happened for me twice in East Timor – both times with women called Maria. The first Maria I met as I walked beside the breakwater taking photos of the temporary shelters refugees had erected on Dili's harbour foreshore for CARE fundraising. Maria had two small daughters and a son with her. Bright-eyed and smiling, their vivacity reminded me of Shahirah and Iddin. We began talking and Maria told me she had just returned from West Timor. Her husband had been killed by the militia and all she now owned was packed into a striped carry-all bag with a broken zip. Beside her was the standard issue UNHCR repatriation pack of a yellow HDR (Humanitarian Daily Ration), a bucket, a water storage container and a pan for boiling water.

Maria and her children needed a lift for the last stage of their journey home. So in the CARE truck I drove them to the backstreets of a suburb not far from the cemetery. There, Maria's face crumpled, as she surveyed the ruins of her home for the first time. But she remained dignified, determined not to let her children see the tears in her eyes.

The family prospects were indeed grim: Maria couldn't leave her still-nursing baby and young kids to forage for the basics of life, and she had no man or other relative to help.

I hugged her and said I'd be back soon. At the UNHCR warehouse the supervisor knew me, and pretended not to notice as I pulled a tarp from a pile, along with a reel of rope and bits of plastic for windows. I tucked a couple of blankets into my pile of loot too. Tossing everything into the back of the vehicle, I headed next to the CMOC, where I pleaded for two mosquito nets. Back in the cabin of the truck, I heard a thump — two folding army cots had landed in the tray as well. Not much was said; just a nod and a wink from a friendly Major was all I caught in my rear-vision mirror. It was enough that I came to CMOC in need, as I was not in the habit of asking for favours. Next, at the French INTERFET contingent, I scored some extra ration packs, two kilos of rice, a loaf of bread and some fresh fruit, including oranges just off the supply barge from Darwin. A broom and extra cooking pot and a sharpish knife came from the Thai contingent, and soap, a torch and a new toothbrush from the US Marines.

Four US Special Forces guys with a ladder and a tool kit lashed to their Humvee came back with me to Maria's. Only ninety minutes had passed. Gobsmacked, Maria watched while the Green Berets clambered onto what was left of her roof and repaired it with the tarpaulins. Then they busied themselves with the windows, and suspended the mosquito nets from the charred ceiling beams. After the floor had been swept the army cots came in. Not content with all that, the burly men squatted against the wheels of their vehicle as the delighted children watched them fashion a windchime from razor wire and steel — which we hung very high above the front door, out of the way of little fingers. It wasn't much, but when we were finished, Maria and the children were weather-tight and had a bit of a head start.

What I'd done was against the rules. But I didn't take anything out of the mouths of other refugees, and there are times when rules just have to be broken.

The second Maria was holding a tiny bundle in her arms

in a back room of the Dom Bosco complex, where a priest had given her refuge upon her return from West Timor. A small towel was draped over her baby's head. First asking Maria's permission, I drew back the covering to find a little boy of six months, frail and non-responsive, but suckling at his mother's breast. The child's head was grossly deformed and the size of a basketball. It was obvious the pair needed help, so I contacted INTERFET doctors, who diagnosed the baby as having severe hydrocephaly, or water on the brain — a condition treatable in any first-world nation with surgery and the insertion of shunts to drain away the fluid. The dilemma was that INTERFET couldn't simply airlift a small child out of Timor without a pre-arranged destination and an appropriate paediatric surgical team lined up. All this needed money that simply wasn't available, so after discussing the options with Maria, I set off for the Hotel Turismo in search of a journalist from News Limited to whom I could offer an exclusive in return for a public campaign in Australia to cover the medical and travelling expenses of Maria and her baby. This plan worked out terrifically, and within three days of the story being published in Australia a paediatric surgeon and his team had volunteered to assist, after consultations with the INTERFET medicos. Major Mark McKay from CMOC helped gather all the documents to process temporary travel papers. By the end of the week Maria and her baby were on their way to Melbourne. It was one of those great moments when all concerned felt elated that we had contributed to something truly worthwhile.

But Maria's child had been misdiagnosed. In East Timor proper diagnostic tools simply weren't available, and it was discovered in Australia that the baby's condition was in fact anencephaly — he had been born without a brain. His brain stem controlled his basic bodily functions, but there was absolutely no chance of his developing any higher brain activity. Anencephaly is a birth defect which can often be averted by the simple ingestion of folic acid prior to conception and during the first trimester of pregnancy.

It was a testament to Maria's utter devotion as a mother that she had kept her child alive by simply holding him in her arms virtually without a break and breastfeeding him on demand. Anencephalic infants usually die within a couple of days of birth. There was nothing for the doctors in Melbourne to do, and so, sadly, Maria and her tiny son were sent home to East Timor to be with family and await the inevitable.

After the transit camp was up and running as smoothly as could be expected, it was time to swing onto the distribution of aid to outlying districts. It was imperative that seed for crops was delivered to the rural areas before the rainy season set in and the roads became impassable. I drove with many loads across the steep mountains of the island, though food supplies were unreliable and aid workers, as well as the Timorese, often went short. Most of us lost a lot of weight rapidly, from illness and poor diet. I had arrived in Dili weighing fifty-three kilograms and would go back to Australia eleven weeks later at forty-seven kilograms and looking decidedly gaunt.

The tropics took their toll on each of us to much the same degree: one by one we were struck down with all manner of ailments, from pneumonia (I had it twice and was left with a weakened heart muscle), to dysentery, dengue fever and malaria – typical tropical diseases borne by mosquitoes and flourishing in the tough conditions.

Eventually, I was sent back to Australia on a deafeningly loud 'Herculces' C130 transport plane to recuperate from my second bout of pneumonia. The break forced me to take stock of the past few years and look towards the new with a mixture of trepidation and the desire to make changes.

The year 2000 was just opening and the absence of my children now straddled two centuries.

Twenty-Four

Freedom to Love

Friday, 16 March 2001, 3.41 p.m.

Intense blue eyes fixed on my face in grave concentration and, with just a hint of the quizzical, minute rosebud lips opened from a gentle pucker. As I looked into her captivating eyes I finally knew that everything would be all right. The world had righted itself and nothing seemed so daunting any more. We would be OK, this little person and I.

Verity Isabelle, my daughter, was born with a full head of wavy golden hair and a pianist's long fingers. After months of worry and concern, she was rudely healthy and weighed in at 3.71 kilograms (8 pounds 3 ounces); at 55 centimetres (22 inches) long, she promised to be tall. Her lashes mesmerised me; they lay long and lustrous, sweeping her cheeks and fluttering in her baby dreams.

Turning to my breast just moments after her first examination of me, she began to suckle confidently and with gusto.

'There,' said the obstetrician, 'I told you that you could do it. You know, I've never before delivered a babe down on the floor, so you're an honoured party.'

I assured him that his reputation as the feared head of the Royal Hospital for Women hadn't been tarnished in the least! In an amusing cliché, he had truly ended up being the man who stood by me through a pretty horrendous time. It had been a very difficult pregnancy – I had been hospitalised several times with complications, premature labour, and spent the last three months of Verity's gestation lying down, medicated for a heart problem I'd developed in East Timor.

During the early months of my pregnancy, Paula Yates had begun to telephone me again; sometimes slurred, her words were full of pain. Shortly after this our contact was only sporadic and so sad, although always full of her love for the girls. Tragically Paula would spiral further downwards and be found dead in September 2000, apparently from an accidental overdose. Her former husband, Bob Geldof, turned out to have real depths of compassion and love, becoming legal guardian to Tigerlily and raising her along with her three sisters in a secure and safe family unit.

A parcel arrived for me a week after Paula's death – inside was a gift-wrapped present containing a miniature leopard-print jumpsuit and matching bootees – a gift from Paula for the baby I was carrying.

All my fears about not being capable of unreservedly loving another child disappeared like evaporating fog on a sunny day. My self-doubt and the emotional trauma of the pregnancy receded into nothingness. I could feel in my deepest core that I wasn't as damaged by the kidnap of my older children as I had feared, and that I still had the capacity for the deep and visceral love one feels for one's own child. It came as a relief and a revelation, for intellectually I knew that the nuts and bolts of mothering would be a breeze, it was in the emotional bonding department that I had been worried I would be wonky.

But Verity was not born to heal my wounded heart. Nor have I ever thought of her as a replacement for her older brother and sister. Children are not interchangeable, they are unique individuals in their own right, not mindless extensions of their parents' egos.

Unthinking people often ventured, after Verity's arrival, that she would make up for the loss of her siblings. How little they understood, and how little they knew of the small and determined 'old soul' that Verity is.

'Verity's herself,' I would find myself retorting forcefully, softening my words with a smile. One child doesn't make up for another, and though I delighted in my new baby, her brother and sister were always in my thoughts – and my heart.

I had loved my Peanut (Verity's nickname until late in the pregnancy) from the moment I had held my breath as her strong heartbeat showed up on the ultrasound machine, only weeks after her conception, as my then partner held my hand in the doctor's office. While I'm definitely pro-choice, abortion had never been an option, even though the pregnancy was a surprise considering my medical history and the risks involved. At first, the medicos were dubious that I could carry Verity to full term.

Even now I tell Verity that she was my miracle from God and one of life's greatest gifts. I've always, since she was tiny, whispered in her ear as I've tucked her in at night: 'Mummy chose to grow you in her tummy. I love you as much as all the leaves and all the trees in the whole wide world. I love you with all my heart and all my soul and I always will, no matter what.' And later, when she met the man who would become her real daddy, we added him to her bedtime blessing. 'And Daddy chose to be your daddy – which makes you even more precious, and he loves you up to the moon and back again ten million billion times.'

For the truth is that Verity is not the biological child of my husband, Bill, but he is her father and she is utterly and completely his daughter. He changed her nappies from the time she was a few months old, and rocked her when she had her vaccinations and was hot and whingey with the pain. He carried her around in a baby sling and proudly puffed out his chest when complimented on the beauty of his daughter. Sometimes I suspect that he fell in love with Verity well before his friendship with me turned into love.

When Verity was eleven months and two weeks old, and we were told that she might have leukaemia, just eight days before our wedding, Bill cradled her struggling little body as the doctors searched for a vein from which to collect more blood. Tears were streaming down his face. He's been there for the good times and the bad, for the midnight vomit sessions and the triumph of first steps and milestones achieved. So in every way that it matters to a child's peace and security and self-esteem, Bill is Verity's father.

When Verity was conceived, I was in what I believed to be a long-term and permanent relationship with her biological father. We had plans to resettle in Washington after her birth. I had rearranged my life to be with him, at his request. Then, when I was eight-and-a-half months pregnant, he decided to redraw the boundaries of our relationship. He had re-evaluted his future, he declared. The choice was mine to make, not his, he said earnestly: adopt our baby out at birth, or break up.

As devastating as it was to do, I chose the latter and have never regretted my decision. I loved Verity's father keenly and trustingly, without reservation, and with utter confidence in what I thought was his goodness and his understanding of my personal history. I loved him with the encouragement of some very protective friends and people whom I respected – all were shocked by the outcome, and his feet of clay.

When I asked him why he had begun our relationship in the first place, he explained, in front of friends, that he had viewed me as 'a challenge' and had thought me 'intriguing'. He then walked out of my life forever. I have not seen him since, nor has he ever made a request to meet Verity.

It is one of the most painful and deeply humiliating episodes in my life and one I have tried very hard to rise above and move on from.

But on that warm evening in March as I settled down for an exhausted sleep with newly born Verity nestled in the crook of my arm, I wished for nothing more than a wonderful and fulfilling life for her, and that one day she might meet her big brother and sister.

Twenty-Five

Serendipity and Salsa

A quick rest on the comfortable hotel bed, after a shower and a Danish pastry, meant that Bill was behind in his schedule. Therefore he missed being in the restaurant on the top floor of the World Trade Center.

He phoned me in the middle of the antipodean night.

'It must be one of those tourist joy flights I've seen buzzing over the city.' The words had barely left his mouth when a television cameraman captured vision of another plane, a jetliner, ploughing into the second tower. The images went out live across the two time zones.

The Twin Towers collapsed and the Pentagon burned.

We remained on the line to each other. I asked Bill what he was wearing. I had started to function like an aid worker before war.

'Head down to the Australian Consulate to register; they'll help evacuate you if the need arises. On the way, withdraw as much cash as you can from ATMs – they'll probably go off-line soon – and buy some bottles of fresh water,' I urged him. What would happen next?

Dazed and concerned, Bill followed my instructions,

walking downtown as a tide of humanity surged past him in the opposite direction. New Yorkers covered in ash, dust and debris, starkly white and in shock, moved like a migrating herd as the skyline darkened behind them and an acrid smell choked the city.

Later, returning to the hotel, he managed to get a line to Australia and this time I answered, holding Verity in my arms.

'When and if I get back, we're getting married,' he insisted and I didn't demur.

On 9 March 2002, in front of a gathering of friends from around the world, I married Bill on a late summer afternoon in a beautiful park in front of a chiffon-wrapped rotunda to the music of a string quartet. Verity, Bill and I had our first dance as a married family to the strains of Van Morrison's 'Someone Like You'. Given the lyrics of the song, I couldn't help but grin at the irony of marrying the boy next door.

We had decided to have exactly the type of wedding we wanted. As a special favour, the priest who had conducted Nanna's memorial service and Verity's baptism agreed to marry us in Alexandra Gardens rather than a church. The ceremony was highly personal, and funny as well; one of Bill's most endearing traits is his warm, generous sense of humour.

I wore a very pale pink, strapless A-line dress of Duchess satin with fresh gardenias in my hair and carried a bouquet of David Austin pale pink roses. Verity, our flower girl, was gorgeous in a pale pink frock and satin slippers. Only four days earlier, she had been cleared of suspected leukaemia – we had reason to celebrate indeed. The reception, also in the park, was a casual and relaxed affair, with endless food circulating on trays. Our terrific friends had spent all morning in the park making sure the rotunda was decorated with metres of white chiffon and bowls of roses. As night fell, hundreds of candles illuminated the paths, courtesy of more hardworking friends. I breastfed Verity under a tree as I watched our family and friends sway and twirl to the beats of the salsa band. For Bill's beloved parents, we interspersed the Latin beats with Greek music that made guests erupt in unfettered versions of the Zorba dance – skirts, ties and feet flying in a joyous frenzy. Grannies gripped gorgeous young men, and whoops of enjoyment were punctuated by choruses of 'oopa' as the circle of dancers whirled in the moonlight. It was *My Big Fat Greek Wedding* meets *Barefoot in the Park*. I wondered what Iddin and Shahirah would have made of the day and the eclectic mix of people and music. I would have loved to share such happiness with them; it would have made the day simply perfect.

This was a private occasion that was only to be shared with invited guests. But journalists were determined to gatecrash, jostling a number of our elderly guests out of the way as we were making our vows. As a result, several of our own wedding pictures show us scowling at some presence out of the shot. Eventually, the media were firmly ejected, and the happy day continued in a much more relaxed manner.

Days later, we discovered that hell hath no fury like a reporter scorned. Mean-spiritedly, I was ridiculed in print for remarrying, and wrongly described as wearing a bright yellow dress. In another newspaper, a columnist who had not even been present made up a story about the ceremony, for which his newspaper was forced to print a retraction and apology. Bill is an intensely private person and found the press interest in my life abhorrent.

By some odd quirk of fate, Bill and I had attended the same high school in Melbourne, where I was a couple of years his senior. For years we had lived only a block away from each other and had often seen one another on the street and at various events, from concerts to open-air markets. We knew the same places and shared a lot of tastes and experiences, but most of all we laughed together – a lot.

As I have mentioned, Bill and I had met after Verity was born. I'd realised I wanted to settle back permanently in Australia. Melbourne seemed the best place to raise a child, and some of my closest friends were there – Verity would only benefit from growing up around a great mix of 'aunties' and 'uncles'.

From Sydney, where I was living, I had chosen a house, sight unseen, from an ad in the newspaper. On paper, it had met all my criteria and so, trusting to friends to inspect the house and give it the thumbs-up, I took a twelve-month lease via email and a series of phone calls with the landlord, who had sounded pleasant and professional. He had been born in the house I was renting from him and had purchased the derelict house next door and renovated it himself. He lived there now.

The sun was trying desperately to emerge from behind the clouds on the day two moving trucks and my car converged outside the house. A new life was unfolding for the two of us. Taking Verity from her car restraint, I lifted her into my arms and walked across the street to be greeted by the landlord, Bill, who was standing outside the front gate.

'Welcome!' he said. 'I've taken the day off work in case you need a cup of tea or a quiet place to change the baby.'

And so, over the following months, Bill became my friend, taking an afternoon walk with Verity and me, pushing the pram as we strolled the familiar streets of Hawthorn.

Still, I'd decided not to expose Verity to any transient relationships. Single, I resolved, was the best stance for all concerned. But sometimes I found Bill looking at me in a way that unnerved me. Finally, one day I told him that I simply wasn't a good bet and that I didn't want to lose his friendship by gaining a lover. I urged him to go on the overseas trip he'd been talking about.

'Go find a gorgeous Swedish blonde, or a bombshell in the Greek islands,' I told him. 'You need a girl without baggage.'

A week later, Bill headed off for a two-month trip, hugging Verity and me warmly, and a little wistfully. Almost immediately we knew it was a mistake!

'I shouldn't be here by myself; you and Verity should be with me,' he said on the phone.

And the rest, as they say, is history.

Twenty-Six

Knock, Knock, Who's Really There?

I had never predicated my aid work on religious precepts; rather I had gone out of my way to avoid integrating the projects I set up with religious organisations, as I believe that the most evil of human actions is to define a person's worth by their religious affiliation. In Africa, the Balkans and East Timor, I had refused to label people according to their religious belief and felt appalled at the prospect of a globe divided by creed.

Were we moving towards a world divided along the lines of them and us, Muslim and Christian, and if so, what would be the bridge?

And was a reunion with Iddin and Shahirah now further off than ever?

Then came 9/11. I could only hope that zealotry did not play any part in the Islamic instruction Shah and Iddin would be receiving in their Muslim household.

Christmas came and went. I had relished decorating the Christmas tree, and watching Verity's eyes dance in merriment and excitement as each bauble and ornament was carefully unwrapped and hung in its place. I crowned the tree, as always, with the fairy I had made with Iddin and Shahirah so many years ago.

'Shasha,' said Verity, handing me a little picture frame with Shahirah's photograph inside.

Looping it over a branch, I turned again when Verity tugged at my skirt.

'Iddin,' she insisted imperiously, handing me her brother's picture confidently.

Verity was aware of who they were: pictures of Iddin and Shah filled the house and I had told her since birth stories of their childhood. Now, a deep stab of sadness hit me; it was at this time of year I missed the older kids the most.

Bending over to reach for another ornament, I yelped as the baby in my belly gave a swift kick. I rubbed the little foot pushing against my side. At six months, this was an easier pregnancy than with Verity, but I still had to be careful of my heart. The new baby was due in late April and was a dream come true for Bill and me. We had decided early on that we didn't want Verity to be an 'only child': although she had siblings in Malaysia, they were years older, and even if they were to return tomorrow, they logically wouldn't be playmates for her.

Motherhood this time around was wonderful and amazing – although I admit to being exhausted all the time.

I eased myself into the seat in front of the computer and logged on. I went into the email account for the Empty Arms Network, a mail box I kept for child abduction advocacy. This account did not have my name attached to it as the recipient.

Reposing in the inbox was an email from a sender with the tag 'loveisanillusion' and the title 'Can you help me find my mother'. Mildly interested, I clicked the Open button, expecting it to be from a victim of kidnapping, perhaps in another country.

I almost tipped my chair over backwards!

The email purported to be from my daughter, Shahirah. Something about it – nothing specific, just a feeling – made it different from the others: the tone was so respectful and there didn't seem to be a hidden agenda.

Was this just another hoax? I read the email again, more slowly this time:

> *My name is Shahirah and I am trying to contact my mother, Jacqueline. I would like to speak to her and hope that you are able to help me contact her. My brother and I were taken from Australia a long time ago and I was given this email address by ********.*
> *Sincerely,*
> *Shahirah.*

No matter how hard I remonstrated with myself, I was almost hyperventilating at the prospect that this time it might truly be Shahirah. I struggled to get hold of my emotions, and the baby somersaulted in my tummy, reacting to my surge of adrenalin.

I called to Bill to come and read the email. Much more sceptical than me, Bill wasn't convinced. But he thought I should investigate further, if I felt there might be a possibility of it being true.

Shaking, I immediately telephoned Judith Curran and told her what was unfolding. For simple self-preservation, I had to remain sceptical, and think carefully about replying to whoever this was.

Judith offered to be the intermediary between this new 'Shahirah' and me. We worked out that she could email an explanation to this person, and also a list of questions to which only the real Shahirah would know the answers.

I set to work on the list straightaway, careful not to include any questions to which I had revealed the answers during the thousands of interviews I had done since Iddin and Shahirah's abduction. None of the correct answers would be found in my first book either.

When I had drafted my list, I checked and rechecked it for foolproofness. These were the questions I settled on:

- What was the colour of Shahirah's mosquito netting?

- What was the name of her reversible doll? (Or please describe it.)

- Can you remember what language Shahirah learned at school in Australia?

- Did Shahirah enjoy sleeping in her bed, and please describe it?

- Can Shahirah remember her last birthday party?

With my heart in my mouth, I called Judith back and had her set up a new account in the name 'chocolateslab' – I am a chocoholic after all and it seemed like a lucky name – so that she could forward my questions to 'loveisanillusion'.

Goodness, I mused to myself, if it is Shahirah, what has happened to her to make her adopt such a cynical email tag at the age of only seventeen?

I held my breath and crossed my fingers and toes – I couldn't cross my legs, I was too pregnant. Three days went by. I pretended not to fret, but secretly I did, checking my inbox again and again each day.

We were at the end of January, and Iddin's birthday was fast approaching. I wondered if my birthday card and gift would arrive, or perhaps whether the anniversary might prompt him to contact me. I realised I had held off checking my emails for three hours. Once more, with trepidation, I sat at the computer. Judith had emailed me.

> *Darling Jack,*
> *I received this email this afternoon via the chocolateslab account. Fingers crossed it's positive. Let me know.*
> *Love Juju xxxx*

Opening the attachment with trembling fingers and a lot of secret hope, I scanned its contents.

> *To Chocolateslab,*
> *My favourite doll was a cup-cake doll that smelled like strawberries.*

As I read the opening line I began to shake and an enormous sob escaped from my spinning heart: I could hardly read the rest of the email because of the tears. No outsider could possibly know that five-year-old Shah had gone everywhere with what I always called her 'muffin doll' in her pocket. A miniature freckled figure with a wide skirt made from rubber and resembling a crinoline dress – when Shahirah inverted it, the doll looked like a small cake. It was fruit-scented.

Sloshing tears onto the keyboard, I moved down to the next answer.

> *My mosquito netting was really bright, a really hot pink and my mum sewed it for me.*

The netting had been a source of resigned amusement to me, for at the age of four, Shahirah had stood in the fabric shop and adamantly argued against the delicate shade of pink I was proposing. 'No, Mummy, I want the fluoro one,' insisted my pink-mad daughter. It had been so garish, the family joked that sunglasses were needed to look at it and that the colour would wake Shahirah in the middle of the night!

I think I learned Italian, but I'm not sure.

Italian it was! This whole moment was so surreal: was this truly happening eleven and a half years since she had been snatched from me?

My bed was up really high, not a bunk bed but one with high legs taller than Mum, I climbed a ladder.

No one except someone who had seen this bed would have known how to describe it. Iddin had one the same, but always opted to sleep on a mattress down below so our dog could snuggle up with him at night. No photographs had ever appeared showing its strange configuration, and even if they had, it would have been taken for a bunk bed.

By the time I got to the question about her last birthday party, I was convinced it was Shahirah!

We went to the Plaster Fun House and painted, I think it was raining.

I read the email over and over again, the sobs of joy and relief catching in my throat. Finally convinced I wasn't hallucinating, I searched out Bill and told him. He questioned me closely as I wept. Was I sure no one else could have the answers? No, I assured him, only Shahirah and Iddin.

'That's wonderful, darling, what do you want to do now, and where will we put them?'

Shaking my head, I truly didn't know; Shahirah had made no mention of wanting to return to Australia. She didn't even know it was me. I was a little frightened now; I wanted to make the right impression – it was like a blind date with a child I hardly knew any more.

I decided to email her in the morning. Right then I had to organise Verity's dinner and put her to sleep. Most importantly, I had to collect my thoughts and think everything over.

That night I slept deeply and happily, although when I dreamed of Shahirah I saw a blank spot where her face should be, and a fairly neutral body. But I knew it was her – she held her muffin doll and was wrapped in hot pink.

Twenty-Seven

Out Came the Sunshine

The opening theme to the ABC children's show *Play School* drifted through the study door. Verity was occupied for at least half an hour; the electronic babysitter (commonly known as the television) was a godsend the morning after the night before.

My first step was to open a new blind email address in the name of 'yummy chocolate' which could not be traced back to me – I was aware that perhaps Shah's emails might be monitored and did not want to compromise her security. Then I sat back and felt utterly daunted, staring at the computer screen.

Half an hour to write one of the most important letters of my life, to a child born of my body, whom I knew almost nothing about and who had probably been indoctrinated against me on every level imaginable. Eleven years of pining and hoping and loving to be encapsulated in one electronic transmission.

Mindful that this might be the one and only time I could communicate with my teenage daughter, I took a cleansing breath, and then another. Procrastinating paralysed me. This was the one letter I knew definitely that Shahirah *would* receive after so many long years of being held incommunicado. But rattling around in my mind was the possibility that, even though this letter wouldn't be intercepted, it might still not be entirely private, for I had no idea whether or not Shah confided in her father. In some way, this was a test, but whether I would pass, I simply hadn't the foggiest.

No problem, should be a breeze, no pressure; just make this the best letter you have ever written and get on with it. But still I dithered. 'Out came the sunshine and dried up all the rain, and the incy-wincy spider climbed up the spout again,' came the words of the children's song. I could hear Verity clapping delightedly in the living room. It shook me from my stupor of self-doubt. I had sung this same rhyme to all three of my children, climbing the spider up the drainpipe of my forearm. This was my child I was about to communicate with; she may choose not to answer, I knew, but somewhere inside her must be the toddler who had watched in wonder as her mummy made the rain fall and sun shine just to make her laugh.

Mentally squaring my shoulders I began to type, carefully telling of my love and the joy I had found when her answers to Judith's email test had come through. I felt deeply compelled to tell Shah that I had never given up trying to contact her and her brother, and that I wanted so much to hear her now grown-up voice and to know what she and Iddin looked like.

This was not the time for recriminations against their father, so I remained circumspect on that front.

What did she like to do, what were her hobbies, what sort of music did she listen to, was her favourite colour still pink? Did Iddin still have his blond spot on the back of his head? On and on my questions went.

And then I poured out my emotions.

> *No matter what, I can't, and won't, pretend to be anyone or anything other than me, your mother — warts and all. I have loved you and missed you with every fibre of my heart and all my soul for so many years … I love you millions, billions, trillions and infinities and I always will.*

I also wrote that I had no desire for media attention and that I was very worried that our private communication would become a catalyst for a new press circus. Explaining how I had declined to give any interviews on personal issues for some time as I preferred a quiet life, I hoped that she felt the same.

Then I went on to describe the terrace house in which we lived and the garden.

I decided not to include my telephone number, as I didn't want to pressure Shahirah into any situation that might prove to be too emotionally overwhelming for her. I just prayed with every cell of my body that I would receive a reply. Hitting the send button I forced myself to rise from the desk and leave the room with only a quick backward glance at the computer.

For the next twenty-four hours I did my best to concentrate on the here and now and keep my recalcitrant mind off the electronic ether. Poor Verity sensed my preoccupation and demanded extra cuddles.

To top it off, I had an episode of premature contractions and a trip to the maternity ward in the middle of the night for a check-up on the condition of the baby. Exhausted and with instructions to rest in bed — always such a ridiculous proposition for the mother of an active toddler — I didn't get to check my emails until late the next afternoon — again, thank you *Play School*.

Closing my eyes, I stilled my expectations, but in my heart I was wishing for a miracle. I told myself to remember that

Shah and Iddin lived within a religion and culture so very different to my own. Shahirah might be rebelling on a mild level and the initial contact would be all I got. To even take this leap would be a major initiative for a girl brought up in the royal family that I had known and rejected. Perhaps the first email was just adolescent curiosity that would crumble when faced with the reality of direct contact.

With complex and contradictory emotions swirling through me, I reached out my hand, moving the cursor across the screen and opening my inbox.

My hands began to tremble. There was a reply to my email to Shahirah:

> *Darling Mummy, yes it really is me, your Shah, and I love you too. I miss you SOOO much . . .*

I was gone, I was a weeping mess as I tried to read the rest of this precious communiqué. The stony control I had so often called upon over the preceding decade deserted me and all I could do was hang onto the string as the balloon of hope began to soar skywards. My face began to ache from the broad grin I had, like some sort of idiot, under the tears. She had called me Mummy and she said she loved and missed me – no greeting card could ever top those lines for me. As I sit here writing this chapter I realise that this mental image of the day I had my first reply from Shahirah still makes me break into a happy grin – I can't help it, all the years fall away and I am back in the moment.

I found Bill in the garden; I dared not even whisper the news to him for fear of being overheard. I dragged him indoors and wept in his arms then pulled him to the computer and asked him to read, but illogically wouldn't let him go, so intense was my need to be held at this moment.

It took me several readings of Shah's email to twig that she had attached photographs of herself and Iddin. Overwhelmed again, a fresh wave of tears erupted as I saw my children for the first time in eleven years. Shocking and amazing – here were my little ones inhabiting adult bodies – and to me they were amazingly beautiful. Shahirah explained about each hazy image. Here was one of her without her veil so I could see her hair colour and the way it grew.

Somewhere in the middle of all the text I remember reading that her favourite colour was now green. The knowledge of such a simple preference made my eyes overflow with tears again. I felt a twinge of irritation at my own responses, but then pushed it to one side and just revelled in the moment of happiness.

> *People have secretly told me I look like you and that our hair is the same colour. Do I look like you, I really hope so!!*

A doe-eyed willowy teenager with the luminous beauty of youth stared out of the screen at me. I could see some part of my own face reflected in the photograph, but Shah was very much her own person, and needed no comparison to her ecstatic mother.

Included was a photograph she had made Iddin pose for: it was taken from behind, and yes, he still sported a natural blond spot, the one with which he had been born.

Here was another shock, because at twenty he had been transformed into the image of my father. Gone were the long gangly legs and the stick-thin arms and body; in the gauche boy's place was a stocky young man – handsome, somewhat serious, and fully grown. And he had a beard!

This was better than I had hoped, for even if it all turned pear-shaped and contact was again cut off, I now had photographs – I finally knew what my beloved children looked like, and it appeared that they were both taller than me!

Iddin sent his love, Shahirah wrote, but he was a bit shy and said he would write soon. Could she have my telephone number so she could give me a call when she was able?

'Of course,' I wrote in my reply, full of love and amazement. As sensitively as I could I filled Shahirah in on the existence of Verity and my marriage to Bill. I included news of people I hoped she still remembered and volunteered bits and pieces I prayed would jog her memory and make her feel less awkward about our relationship.

One little niggle had to be dealt with.

'Does your father know you have contacted me?' I typed.

In the back of my mind I doubted very much if he did, and instinctively I feared what his reaction might be if he found out.

But for that moment and that day, I allowed myself unreservedly to feel like the mother of two grown-up children and one little one. I hugged Verity with joy until he squirmed and wriggled away.

What an amazing day! A few minutes had changed my life. After all these years, I had tangible details of the real people my lost children had become.

Twenty-Eight

A Luddite, a Baby and a Healing

'Mummy!' a woman's voice said to me over a crackly line. 'Hello, Mummy, it's me, your Shah.' She spoke in a musical sing-song tone, slightly tentative and enquiring.

'Shah? Oh my God, Shah! Is that really you? You sound so grown up, sweetie,' was all I managed before a dam burst and all I could do was sob.

'Oh, don't cry, Mummy, it's all right,' Shah soothed me. I was instantly flooded with myriad complex and illogical thoughts: distress that I couldn't recognise my own daughter's voice; relief that one of my heart's desires was coming to fruition; panic as I didn't know what to say to this stranger.

I needn't have worried. After I pulled myself together, we just began to talk — awkwardly, yes, but it was wonderful. I realised that this first phone call needed to be approached with honesty, but also as much nonchalance as I could muster eleven years, six months and fifteen days since I last saw my daughter. No sweat, a little voice inside me urged. Bloody hell!

Shah sounded wonderful, simultaneously intelligent and naive, insightful and giggly and hurt — that was in the undercurrent of her voice. Eleven years of being cut off from me, of having her decisions made for her had taken their toll – there was a fragility to our discussion, as though she and I had still to come to grips with the new reality.

Rationally, I knew that I had lived a whole new life since the kidnapping, and so had Shah. I no longer held a position of authority with her; gone were the days when she was six and I was her all-important mother – and this I had to keep in the forefront of my mind as we talked and cried and talked again.

I tried to keep a level tone and failed abysmally. But I must have done something right, because our tentative relationship somehow blossomed. We both took a leap of faith that day and began to occupy a place, however small, in each other's day-to-day lives. For me, Shahirah's presence was a constant – it had been since the day she was born – but for Shahirah, I had to keep telling myself, I probably would be no more than a secret smidgeon in a private part of her thoughts.

For years, I had privately held the conviction that my children would return to see me when they were adults, but I hadn't expected anything before they each reached the age of about twenty-seven. I'd had to think in those terms: I had calmly calculated the years of education then added the time it would take for them to establish themselves either in a career or in marriage, find their own adult voices and break free of their father's all-pervading presence and control. Yes, I had thought, twenty-seven would be a feasible age to come into one's own in the royal family of Terengganu.

Now I saw I had underestimated the vistas the Internet could provide, and I had doubly underestimated my daughter's gutsiness. She was apparently very much my daughter after all – a source of headaches to her father and the stepmothers he had provided my children with. I will admit I got a little pinprick of satisfaction from this knowledge.

What an amazing new dimension technology has brought to the world! The children and I had been censored from each other's lives – but a little bit of 'googling' and Shah had been able to track me down herself. She had learned of my aid work and other activities. And now, with the privacy of her own pre-paid personal mobile phone that couldn't be traced or tracked by other parties, a whole spectrum of possibilities opened up for us.

Privacy and secrecy were the biggest worries I had. Such a development of wonderful happiness! Yet I was forced to maintain silence as far as the outside world was concerned. Shah was still a long way off being considered an adult in Malaysia. Twenty-one was the age of majority there, and even then, a member of an Islamic royal house had severely limited options. Iddin, too, was still not legally an adult. Lord only knew what their father would do if he found out about this contact, for during my conversation with Shah, I was able to gather that the proverbial would really hit the fan if he was to find out. My biggest fear was that Shah would be married off without a choice and would be swallowed up in the great royal abyss.

Following my first phone call with Shah, I wrote a list of people I felt I could safely tell our news. It wasn't so much that I couldn't trust a really broad circle of my friends; rather, everyone I told could perhaps let slip in their excitement this wonderful development for my family . . . and in the end it could be leaked to the press out of joy and excitement, not malice.

Speaking to each in turn, I related my good news. These friends had supported me through my darkest hours and days following the abduction and they all loved Shah very much. Their responses were mainly to burst into sobs of joy, then caution me about the dangers of the situation.

Exhausted by the end of a very emotional day, I lay down with Verity's sleeping form cradled in my arms and fell into a deep sleep of warm and unreserved happiness. Towards dawn though, a cold breath of fear stole into my room. I sat bolt upright beside Bill and extricated my arms from around Verity.

I would have to dissemble from now on. I would have to bend the truth whenever the inevitable question was trotted out: 'Have you spoken to your children?'

How could I get around this innocuous but fraught line of questioning?

And then I came up with my strategy, the manoeuvre that would squeeze me out of the tightest of corners, a stock response that would satisfy the curious. Whenever the question was posed, I would subtly change the subject, just like politicians and diplomats the world over.

'I wish I could hug them, that's all really. It's been so many years now and all I can imagine is how amazing a hug would be. I can't talk about it at the moment because I will burst into tears. I know you understand.' I would finish with an extended hand on the questioner's arm as a thank you – drawing a line under the enquiry and effectively changing the subject.

It wasn't strictly lying, I assured myself shakily; I was telling the truth while avoiding answering the question. Most importantly, and this had to be my paramount concern, I was protecting my children. They had to come first, before any of my prickling sensibilities and the press and public's interest.

But it was enormously hard, I was to find, and so Bill and I began to confine our social activities to either large affairs, like christenings or weddings, or small gatherings with the people who knew what was going on. It was an enormous strain, keeping this huge secret, but it would prove to be worth it for my children's sakes and the tentative steps they were both taking.

My contact with Iddin was initially much more confusing than with his sister. Somehow, with Shah, it had been easy to fall into girltalk.

Luckily, I knew many young men and teenage boys had difficulty verbalising their emotions. I could only imagine this was compounded in my son's case: though he was at the age when most young men in Western society strive to free themselves of the shackles that tie them to their parents, Iddin was firmly in my former husband's sphere of influence.

Quite shy as a child, Iddin had also been a cautious kid, seldom leaping into any activity without first calculating his ability to undertake the task with some success. He had always been the thoughtful one, ruminating long and hard on issues and solutions, so I could only imagine what a can of worms my presence would bring to his now fairly stable existence. I wanted to know and understand the young man he had become, and I realised that any contact I had with him would have to make my appreciation of his adulthood very clear.

I, of all people, had to give him respect, for I strongly suspected that his father, a consummate ringmaster and puppeteer, would still be trying to control every aspect of our eldest child's existence. Intelligent young men need the security of respect and an acknowledgement of equality from their parents as they mature. Without parental trust in his good character and common sense, a son's self-esteem and confidence cannot grow.

Taking the bull by the horns, I rang Iddin at Shah's urging – she gave me his number. I knew that Iddin had not been that comfortable with the written word when he was a child, having been diagnosed with a mild form of dyslexia. So a very quick phone call might be the best way to start. Besides, he was about to turn twenty, and I couldn't possibly miss one more of his birthdays.

I dialled the mobile number three times and hung up before it even began to ring but, pulling my nervous stomach into line, I finally allowed the ringtone to begin.

Speed, accuracy and love were my goals. Would I ever get another chance?

The phone was answered.

'Hello Iddin, it's Mum. I'm sorry to intrude and I really don't want to make you feel uncomfortable, but I really, really wanted to hear your voice. I love you and I really miss you and I am so sorry that I couldn't get you home and I tried, I really tried, but it was so impossible.'

(Quick gasp for breath.)

'I sent you presents and cards and letters and I don't know if you ever got them. I just wanted you to know that I am really proud that I have you as my son and I will love you no matter what you choose to do in your life.'

(Gasp and sob from me.)

'OK, I'll go now, I'm sorry that I've intruded. I love you so very much—'

'Hey, Mum, don't go! I'm really sorry I didn't email you or ring after Shah got the numbers but, Mum, I just didn't know what to say or how to write it. I'm scared, Mum, and I love you too!'

It was the best ham-fisted, needy and garbled phone call I have ever made. A wave of profound peace swept over me as I heard my son tell me I was loved and remembered. For now, that was enough.

Twenty-Nine

Lysander the Magnificent

The importance of finding out who my children were as grown-up individuals was foremost in my mind. Because they had been kidnapped in a pair, it was far too easy to lump them together. I had to make a conscious effort to allow them each true individuality. Their experiences over the intervening years — according to their gender, scholastic achievement, obedience and adaptability — would have varied enormously. Little by little, as we talked and corresponded, I was to discover more about each of these two beloved people.

And all the while I watched Verity grow and thrive, developing into a funny little individual full of unself-conscious smiles and the utter security of being loved by Bill and me. She took to bathing the baby doll we had bought her to ease her into the concept of a little brother, and would press her mouth up against my belly and talk to the baby about painting and food and whatever else came into her head. She had watched a birth video with me and wasn't at all perturbed; rather, she was enthralled with the whole process. She loved the knowledge that she had grown inside my tummy and could still remember being breastfed.

Shah, too, via long distance, had a real fascination with descriptions of the baby's movements inside me and the photographs I sent her via email of my condition and of Verity too. My pregnancy led to lots of talks with Shah about my feelings for her, her birth and what she had been like as a little person. It was obviously important for her to hear the mothering in my voice. Verity and Shah even began to develop a relationship of their own. They would have small chats on the phone and Shah began to call Verity 'V' – her special pet name for her little sister.

The pain came in concentric circles from my lower back. Leaning my forearms over the edge of the bed, I rocked as Bill rubbed my back. It was 21 April 2003, a Monday, and I was in labour for the birth of my fourth child.

Verity was safely ensconced with her grandparents, Bill's mum and dad, and would stay with them until her baby brother was born. They would spoil her to death, I knew, as they were utterly devoted to their granddaughter, the first grandchild in the family. Bill would laughingly complain that all the Greek strictness he had been brought up with had completely evaporated when it came to Verity.

The hours went by and I paced and rocked, trying to speed the delivery along. Then I phoned Shah in Malaysia.

'Mum! Have you had the baby yet?' she squealed before I had even said hello. She was completely in the moment and wanted a description of how I was feeling. It was an amazing situation to be in, whispering secretly to my daughter, while she encouraged me to hurry up and give birth to her little brother!

Things don't always go to plan with babies, and so it was with the birth of Lysander. Instinctively, I knew that all was not right – even when the pains increased marginally in strength, they weren't nearly painful enough. Twelve hours of labour had passed, the contractions were ninety seconds apart and I could still talk and joke and walk around. I should have been almost speechless with pain by this stage and approaching the need to push, but the weight in my pelvis felt wrong.

The doctor did another pelvic exam, and the news was not good. The baby had cocked his head backwards and jammed it just above the birth canal. His heartbeat was still strong, but my heart was showing signs of fatigue. To have a successful and safe vaginal birth with a strange head presentation such as this was an impossibility, given my weakened heart muscle. It was going to be an emergency Caesarean section, my biggest dread about childbirth.

Less than twenty minutes later I was flat on my back in an operating theatre, numbed from the waist down and being rocked and pulled as the doctor wrestled our son through the incision in my belly. Bill sat at my left shoulder, perspiration beading his forehead. I knew he was worried he would faint at the sight of so much blood. But then he was swept up in the moment, as Lysander Antonio appeared over the top of the surgical screen spanning my belly. It was 9.21 p.m.

Bill cut the umbilical cord, and I had a moment to plant a kiss on little Lysander's forehead as he gave a lusty yell.

Groggy joy and relief spilled out of me, and I wept in a slightly befuddled cloud of painkillers. But then, suddenly, things threatened to go pear-shaped – I began to haemorrhage.

Bill was hustled out with Lysander before I had got a good look at him and the surgical team set to work again.

Two hours later, all sewn up and doped to my eyeballs on morphine, I held Lysander in my arms for the first time and inspected our baby son, with Bill hovering at the edge of the bed as I could barely manage Lysander without help. Amazingly gorgeous, and enormous!

Lysander was born the largest of my four children, a whopping 3.9 kilograms (8 pounds, 6 ounces) and 62 centimetres (26 inches) long – we'd better start saving for big shoes, I thought. His head circumference was 37.5 centimetres – suddenly I was rather grateful for the C section.

Lysander had bright blue eyes and blondish hair and extraordinarily long toes and fingers. He took to my breast with gusto, emitting lots of satisfied little grunts before drifting off to sleep.

Handing me the phone, Bill said it was Shah, whom he had called with the news. This was an incredibly emotional chat; the drugs were kicking in and I was so happy I could only weep. Thousand of miles away, my daughter wept with me and I recalled the wonder I felt at the birth of all my amazing children, and hoped I would soon be introducing them to each other.

Thirty

Surges and Roller-Coasters

Now my life was filled with lightness of spirit as I threw myself into the wonderful joy of mothering my two youngest children. Verity and Zan loved each other fiercely – when they weren't clashing, as siblings do.

Verity had started kindergarten and was thrilled with it, and Lysander was a happy, relaxed little fellow with blond curls and twinkly blue eyes. Given half the chance, Verity would paint or draw for the entire day and both children would have me read them books and tales for all the waking hours.

Sometimes I couldn't help reflecting that with the wonderful experience of being able to mother children again, my entire world had begun to right itself – my life was loving and peaceful at last.

As the children grew bigger, I began doing some freelance magazine writing and started to participate regularly in the Department of Foreign Affairs and Trade (DFAT) consular training courses as a consultant. I was teaching diplomats how to deal empathically with distressed people, like the left-behind parents who might contact them for assistance and guidance.

By this time I was working only sporadically at the coalface of parental child abduction – I had just about suffered burnout on this issue – but was immensely satisfied that over the years some of my recommendations were adopted by the European Union, the Australian Attorney General's Department, British Lord Chancellor's Department, Hong Kong Family Law Association, a body of American judges specialising in family law and, most recently, DFAT.

Bill, too, had made a sea change, distancing himself from his former life as senior executive with a multinational telecommunications firm. Already holding a science degree, he returned to university to further his studies, at the same time following his passion for building and construction by starting his own firm. He also kept his hand in the field of technology and continued to consult to large corporations in need of his expertise.

We had decided that we needed more room for our growing family and to cater for the possibility that Shah and Iddin might want to visit us some day. So Bill set about renovating and extending the house we owned next door – essentially building a house atop a house and cleverly turning a single-storey Victorian terrace into a light-filled four-bedroom modern home. He did the work himself, during 2005, with a crew of employees, and me catering – hot lunch for the workers every day! My amazing father-in-law, who is in his 70s, insisted on working at the building site every day too. His grandchildren, Verity and Lysander, love their *Papoo*, and revelled in his presence.

Aid work was something I now missed, but taking off to a war or disaster zone at the drop of a hat when you have a family, especially with small children, is out of the question. After the tsunami in South East Asia in late 2004, I did some fundraising for CARE, and was pleased to be able to contribute to the relief effort in this small way. I will probably always twitch when I see places and people I could possibly assist if I were still in the field, and I don't think I will ever get that part of my life out of my blood. I doubt if I really ever would desire to, for it is something I hope my children learn from and are proud that I did.

Contact with Shah and Iddin grew more and more frequent, richer and more intimate. We went to great pains to keep it secret. The weight of keeping this wonderful news to myself in the face of well-wishers enquiring about our family was a daily strain; over and over I reminded myself that the children came first, and held my tongue.

Little by little, I had the honour of knowing that I was becoming Shah's confidante and, little by little, Iddin's friend. It was a thrill to receive a text message from Iddin, wishing me a happy Mother's Day and telling me I was the best mum in the world. A Christmas wish or just a hello was blissful. The simple and joyous pleasure of a text message, or a call on my birthday after so many years, meant the world. For so long I'd had to pretend that I hadn't experienced twinges of envy when all around me received these markers of normality and love. Now that it was returned to me, I vowed I'd never take my children's love for granted.

Shah had begun to study architecture at university. This course was not something about which she was personally passionate, and it disappointed me that she was not encouraged to follow, or even allowed to discover, her own heart's desire. But some things, like her veil and her studies, were for her father to command, it seemed.

Shah and I had by this time developed pet names for each

other. Shah had a deep love of Louisa May Alcott's *Little Women*, and long ago I had cried over the book too. We spoke of the March family often, and eventually I became her 'Marmee', and she my 'Jo Girl'.

Iddin, meanwhile, was a young man trying to find his feet and his own way in the world. I was so proud of him when, late in 2005, he finally found his voice and his passion – photography – and decided to follow his heart instead of his father's dictums. It took a lot of guts to go against those expectations of the royal family.

Thirty-One

The Incy Wincy Spider

'Mum, I'm supposed to go to London and Paris with Abah and the other kids in a week or so, what will I do? I'm going to be looking after five of them as their mothers aren't going.' Shah was referring to her step-siblings, the children of her father's numerous wives.

Goodness, what was the subtext to this statement, I wondered.

Shah's relationship with her father was quite volatile; she wasn't always the obedient daughter he required. The children had never been allowed any independent travel; certainly the passport issue was a fraught one, yet here Bahrin was offering Shah an international trip, albeit in the dead of winter and to the opposite end of the globe to where her mother lived. Apparently Bahrin staunchly avoided any mention of me to the children, they'd not been allowed a single letter or gift from me in all those long years; he probably felt that his years of indoctrination and unyielding discipline had cleansed their minds of me. He still had no notion that Shah and Iddin were in contact with me; had he known he would surely be apoplectic. After all, this was the man who insisted on choosing his wives' and children's clothes – to match his!

This offer to Shah was a first, and I ran through various scenarios in my head. Did her father mean it as a diversion because he suspected her growing disenchantment with her regimented, restricted life?

Both Shah and Iddin had said they wanted very much to come home to Australia, but the definitive break was proving harder for them emotionally than any of us had expected. To visit me would be a declaration of rebellion against their father and everything that had been drummed into them. In a culture of filial piety and unquestioning obedience, it would be viewed as disrespect of the first order and constitute a grave loss of face for Bahrin among his peers, and before the public at large.

It was also an incredible leap of faith for Shah and Iddin to contemplate leaving Malaysia – all they were familiar with as adults was in that country.

Financially, I wasn't wealthy and simply didn't have the wherewithal to open a cheque book and write Iddin and Shah a new life. I could provide money for tickets, yes; a roof over their heads and food, of course; and bottomless love and unequivocal acceptance – but not the lifestyle and diversions they were used to. Neither of them had ever worked; royals simply don't have after-school jobs at McDonald's. Shah had done a little tutoring for spare change, but that was hardly the reality of student life in Australia. Both were accustomed to a generous allowance from Bahrin, even if there were strings attached. How would they cope back home in Australia?

Two years had passed since Shah's first email, and at times first one and then the other had been ready to make the leap to freedom and Australia, but never, frustratingly, at the same time! We would get a part of the way down the track and then one wouldn't want to leave without the other – the timing was always off.

Now, trying to sound casual, I ventured to Shah that if she wanted it, I could arrange for help to get her home from Paris or London – all she had to do was get to the Australian Embassy and they would assist her. Under Australian law, I reminded her, she was an adult and legally able to do as she pleased. 'Heavens, you can even tell me to take a flying leap and there is nothing I can or would want to do about it,' I assured her.

Tentatively, she began to ask what she would have to do. She worried that she wouldn't be able to find her way around Paris or London alone, so I gave her the telephone numbers of some friends who lived close by. Both of them could be trusted implicitly, and either of them would drop anything at her call and take her under their wing.

Shah and I put a plan in place over a couple of days of intense phone calls. If she felt confident enough, she would attempt to leave the hotel in London or Paris on her own, without her father being aware she was missing. Or perhaps she would simply wander into a fitting room at Harrods or Printemps and disappear.

The next thing I did was call the Department of Foreign Affairs. I blessed the fact that I could speak directly to the officer in charge of consular affairs, because of my work with the Department. They swung into action, notifying the various overseas stations and smoothing the way.

I had my fingers crossed and was praying for a miracle. But I pushed my excitement to the background and pretended to myself there was nothing unusual going on.

We moved into the newly renovated house in the middle of Shah's trip to Europe. It was complete except for the kitchen – I had to limit my cooking to barbecues, barbecues and the added flavour of stir-fries cooked on, you guessed it, the barbecue. Thank goodness it was summer.

Setting up the Christmas tree with Zan and Verity, I fastened our bedraggled fairy to the top of the tree and wondered if Shah would see it in place over the New Year.

Christmas drew near. Two days before the holiday, the phone rang – I held my breath expectantly. Shah had been in touch with one of my friends in Paris on her mobile, a number of times – but then silence had fallen.

I rationed my tears to ten minutes alone in the bathroom. I'd had years of disappointment, I joked to my reflection in the mirror. Time to get on with it again.

Although there was still a chance Shah would activate the plan, I felt instinctively that this was not the time when I would hold one of my older children in my arms. I brought my attention back to the little ones, who had been in a flurry of Christmas wrappings and sticky tape when the phone rang.

Shah would later tell me that she simply couldn't leave her little sisters unchaperoned, marooned and distressed in a large, unfamiliar department store, and that she was too frightened to make the leap. I reassured her that it was OK, it was her decision to make – I wasn't cross, I told her. I loved her whether she was near or far – no ifs or buts and it wasn't dependent on her turning up in my living room. I would see her if and when the time was right for her.

Thirty-Two

Down Came the Rain

Tuesday, 14 February 2006, began ordinarily enough.

Verity had started primary school a few days earlier, at Bill's old school just around the corner from our house. It was a point of pride to her that she was following in her dad's footsteps, as she delighted in announcing to all and sundry. I was still coming to terms with the rapid passage of time! Verity was now almost five and was suddenly a tiny schoolgirl.

Lysander was less than his exuberant self that day, having had a general anaesthetic and three hours of surgery on his mouth and jaw, for a dental problem, a few days earlier. I was negotiating a play with his train set instead of television when the telephone rang.

'Mummy,' cried the sobbing voice, 'I want to come home now! Now, Mum, I've had enough. I can't do this any more.'

'Shah, what's happened, darling? What's wrong? Are you hurt?' I was in a panic.

'No, Mum, I just can't keep doing architecture – I hate it and I want to come home and see you *now*!'

Gradually I calmed her, and we started to consider how she might come home.

'Shah, have you still got the Malaysian passport you used for the trip to Europe?'

'I've got it, Mum, but what happens if Abah has a security flag on it and I get stopped when I try to leave the country?' Her father could do this, as Shah was still not of legal age in Malaysia.

I tried to think of the right words to say. All I could come out with was, 'Darling, if you want to come home, then we'll make it happen.'

She was still upset, but adamant that was what she wanted; now all I needed was to come up with a plan.

'Give me until tomorrow morning to put all the things in place, but I want you to start getting ready now. If we don't want your father to find out what you're doing ...'

'I can't tell him,' she wailed. 'He'll stop me for sure and I'll be sent back to Terengganu and I won't be able to see you or even talk to you. He doesn't understand,' she went on. 'I'm not happy here and I can't do architecture just because he wants me to be like him. I need to see you, Mum' – huge gasp for breath and hacking sobs – 'I want to come home. I want to be myself.'

'OK, darling,' I gentled her. 'The first thing is to understand that the best way for you to leave, if you really think that Abah may have an alert attached to you, is to get to the Causeway.'

The Causeway is the bridge that connects the peninsula of Malaysia with the Republic of Singapore. It was a few hours' drive from where Shah was living. Scores of buses and cars crossed the border at this point daily, bringing cheap labour from Malaysia into affluent Singapore. Shahirah would have a better chance of leaving Malaysia at this point than any other. It was normal for Malaysians to drive over to Singapore for a day of shopping; it would appear as if Shah was going on an innocent shopping trip. If she was caught, it would seem less sinister if she was without luggage – it would simply look like she was being a bit naughty and going for a jaunt to buy some trinkets without her father's permission. That she actually needed his permission at the age of twenty greatly angered me. She was an adult; even I shouldn't have control over her.

'You'll have to go across really early one morning,' I told Shah. 'Do you still have a bodyguard following you around?'

'No, not any more, not that I've noticed, not since I've been in uni, but then Abah has arranged for lots of people to keep an eye on me.'

'OK, you're going to have to be very brave and organised and do exactly as I tell you, Jo Girl. You can't tell anyone you're going and you won't be able to take anything with you except a small backpack, like a day bag.'

'My friend thinks I should tell Abah that I'm dropping out of uni. She says she'll come with me, but I'm afraid.'

'Do you think that's a good idea, darling? What do you think might happen if you tell your father?' I cursed this naive friend in whom Shah had already confided, then wondered if the friend perhaps knew which side their bread was buttered on.

'I don't want to speak to Abah, but I do want to tell Iddin what I'm planning and see if he will come as well.'

'OK, that's your decision, but you have to do it quickly, and I'll ring your brother as well.'

Taking a big gulp of air, I outlined more of the plan that was working itself out in my brain.

'You're going to have to find out the bus schedules from Kuala Lumpur to Johore or Singapore and give me the time of the one you think you can catch. Do you have any money?'

'I think I have enough for the bus fare, but that's all,

Marmee.' She was starting to sound calmer again, which made me worry less.

'Don't worry about anything else, I'll arrange the ticket out of Singapore to Melbourne,' I assured Shah. 'I'm going to contact the Australian authorities and see what they can do to help us.'

Thinking about the different times zones, I made rapid calculations about whom I would need to call first.

'I'm going to go now. You keep your phone on and I'll call you back later.'

What happened next was an amazing flurry of phone calls, right at the end of the business day, to the Department of Foreign Affairs in Canberra, and some intense conversations. Diplomatic cables flew off to the mission in Singapore, though I was careful to make it clear that this could all disappear in a split-second and that Shah was highly emotional.

Within hours I was able to ring Shah back with a solid plan and a contact number at the Australian consulate in Singapore. Speaking at length to the Consul, Ross Tysoe, I was struck by how level-headed and unflappably sensible he was – and how compassionate.

Fortunately, according to Shah, my former husband was in Dubai on business and so the prospect of him confronting her and physically stopping her departure seemed less likely than I'd feared.

'Mum, my friend wants to drive me to Singapore to say goodbye,' Shah announced, and I bit down my irritation with this friend once more. In any case, it was Shah's choice, and I'd agree to anything to see her safely to the Causeway and her rendezvous in Singapore.

It had been determined that a dawn crossing would be best. The Australian High Commission staff had been put on alert, as had Qantas, that they might have a special passenger in the next few days for one of their flights to Australia. We had made the call that any flight to Australia would do; the imperative was to get my daughter out of the region. If there were no seats available, Shah would travel in the cockpit of a Qantas aircraft, as this was considered Australian territory and not subject to the laws of another country.

'No more mobile calls about the package, Ms Pascarl,' said my final official contact in his best 'M' voice. 'There's always a lot of interest around,' he added cryptically.

'Do you still want to do this, darling?' I asked Shah in our next phone conversation, holding my breath for her answer.

'Yes, Mum,' she answered without hesitation. 'I need to come home. I want to be free.'

'OK, if you are sure. Now I want you to buy a prepaid SIM card for later. When you are safely clear of Kuala Lumpur, you'll have to take your old SIM card out of your phone and toss it away.'

Surely we'd covered all instructions now?

I hardly slept a wink that night: it was only hours until we knew if this plan would work, and erase fourteen years of yearning.

The next day, 15 February, was Iddin's twenty-third birthday. I resolved to call him later in the day when I knew he would probably be alone. I feared putting him in the position of knowing too much if he wasn't coming too. The last thing I wanted was for him to be blamed for Shah's departure. In Bahrin's book, non-disclosure was as bad as outright lying. Grey areas of behaviour were strictly reserved for him.

The following day, Shah and I spoke every three hours from 11 a.m. Melbourne summer time. Malaysia was three hours behind us, and I could barely function that whole long day watching the clock tick over the minutes and the hours. Bill kept Verity and Lysander occupied, leaving me free to fixate. Jumping out of my skin every time the phone rang, I remained in front of the computer taking care of final details with Foreign Affairs.

Whenever Shahirah and I spoke she swung between utter determination and nervous anxiety. I tried to calm her when she started to panic: 'Darling Jo Girl, it will be fine, you just have to be very brave and remember what to do. It will all be fine, sweetie. You're an intelligent grown woman, this is your decision to make as an adult. I love you sweetheart, and so do Verity and Zan — they can't wait to see you. Just hang on, darling, and we'll soon be able to give each other a huge hug. You can do this, darling, just be brave.'

Eventually, I put the little ones to bed and pushed down my gnawing anxiety as I read them story after story. Lying between them both, I listened to their peaceful breathing and occasional snuffles and began to let down my guard and wonder what it would be like if Shahirah arrived in Melbourne the very next night. I wondered what a hug with her would feel like or if she would be too shy to want that. I dreamed of laying the palms of my hands on her face and learning its contours.

Rising from the bed, I walked downstairs to phone Iddin for his birthday, and a very serious chat.

Iddin told me he felt it wasn't time for him to come home just yet. He was also rather worried about Shah's departure.

'Abah is going to be so pissed off, Mum. I don't want to get the blame.'

What could I say to him? All I could ask was that he not obstruct what his sister was about to do.

'I really love you, Mum. Thanks for the birthday call – I'm really sorry I can't come right now, but I will come soon, I promise.'

Hours later, my stomach was churning, as if I was on some unhinged amusement park ride and my nerve endings were uncomfortably electrified. The departure time was scheduled: midnight Malaysian time, 3 a.m. Melbourne time.

Shah's last call had come an hour earlier, at 10.30 p.m., and I was beginning to get worried. The friend who was supposed to drive her to Singapore was trying to persuade Shah to say goodbye to the friend's family, with whom Shah was close. Were we never to have peace from outsiders meddling in our family life?

At 1 a.m., the telephone rang. It was Shah and she was completely distraught. Her friend had persuaded her that it was wrong to run off without telling her father, and she was losing her nerve. The friend had refused to drive her to Singapore and had taken a detour and the opportunity to browbeat her. I was furious! This so-called friend, I felt, was being utterly self-serving and ignoring Shah's wishes. For so many years, people had been telling Shah what to do and here was another example of her powerlessness over her existence and her opinions.

In the middle of a devastatingly emotional discussion, Shah's mobile phone rang.

'It's Abah,' she began to scream hysterically. 'He's coming to see me now! I can't do it – he's back early and I can't do it now – it's too late, Mummy. Oh, Mummy, I'm sorry, so sorry, I love you so, I can't get to you now.'

I heard loud hammering on a door, voices in the background, the sounds of a scuffle.

'Oh, Mummy, I'm sorry I waited too long, I lo–' and the line went dead.

Shredded by fear and worry I began to sob, and dialled and redialled Shah's phone with no answer. Frantic with anxiety at what had happened to my daughter, I tried to recall exactly what I'd heard in the background during the call. Someone had obviously alerted her father to what was going on and he had hotfooted it back from the Persian Gulf. I had my suspicions, but it was too late for me to do anything about it. Shah had been stalled, worn down and manipulated, until time simply ran out.

Gutted beyond belief, I stared into the darkness, waiting for the sun to come up. It was akin to having her kidnapped all over again. That we'd come so close was no consolation.

This waiting game, and always having to pick myself up and keep going, was getting to be too much. I was seriously pissed off at any higher power that was floating around out there pulling the strings of my life.

Thirty-Three

On Tenterhooks

It was 2 a.m. in Belgium, and Patsy's voice was toneless. Her amazing and extraordinary Walter, her husband, had suddenly collapsed and died without regaining consciousness.

Walter had been a sturdy bull of a man in his early 40s. Patsy wept, and said he'd just returned from a trekking trip that weekend. He had caught a terrible bug that had attacked most of his organs.

I wanted to jump on the next flight to Belgium, but Patsy insisted I not come yet.

'Come later, when I'm really alone. You're the first person I've told: I knew you and I could understand each other. I've just driven back from the hospital, and soon everyone will be here. After the funeral, when they've gone, then you may come to Ambly.'

Bill and I had both spoken to Walter a few weeks earlier. Now, listening, Bill was ashen; he and Walter had become friends over the Internet. They had very similar personalities and had ribbed each other endlessly.

Melbourne was gripped in a sports-mad fever; the

Commonwealth Games had rolled into town, bringing with it elite athletes from around the globe and an arts festival that was a moving feast of activity and colour. The city glowed in the early autumn sunshine and the weather held, bringing the mercury to thirty-five degrees and the people to the river and the beach and all the places Melbourne offered in between.

So I was pulling myself out of all the doldrums, taking Verity and Lysander to the fun activities put on during the school holidays against the backdrop of the Commonwealth Games.

The city crowd on this glorious day was raucous; roving minstrels added to the cacophony, and the strains of a jazz band competed with the laughter and shouting of children building sandcastles on the artificial beach temporarily lying outside the art gallery. The sky was blue and cloudless, the sun hot and bright.

We had joined Verity's best friend and her big sister for this outing. Lysander and the girls were digging delightedly in the sand. I sat together watching the fun. The girls had spent two years at kindergarten joined at the hip and were now attending the same school.

I felt a strange vibration in my trouser pocket, and it took me a while to realise it was my mobile phone. Drawing it out at a fumble, I saw Shah's number pop up on the screen.

We'd had very limited contact since the abortive flight to Singapore. It had been several days before I learned that she was unhurt, but very fragile. Weeks had now gone by, and my emotions had evened out and found a safe plateau.

Somehow, Shahirah had managed to keep the full truth from her father, and he still had no idea that she and Iddin had developed a secret relationship with me. Therefore, the recriminations had been limited. Bahrin viewed Shah's planned 'shopping' trip to Singapore as a caprice, a whim of fancy by a silly and rebellious girl. He hadn't a clue about who our daughter was and what she needed. I wondered if he had ever really looked at her and seen anything other than his own reflection.

'Hi, Mum! When's Verity's birthday party and Lysander's? Oh, and Easter too, when's that?' came Shah's questions out of the blue.

Rising to my feet, I moved away slightly. Giving the dates, and glancing back at Zan and Verity as I answered, I asked her how she was.

'I'm great, Marmee! I'll be coming to see you next Saturday – Abah's buying me a ticket!'

It was now Wednesday. Fasten your seatbelt, I warned myself, here we go again.

'Mum, are you still there? I'm really coming this time. I've told Abah I want to see you and he's given me permission to come for a short holiday.'

How I wanted to scream now, at that patronising word 'permission' – she was twenty years old. She didn't need permission, particularly to visit the mother from whom she'd been kidnapped. The visit, if indeed it went ahead, would take place just three months short of her twenty-first birthday – and her legal majority under Malaysian law too.

Somehow I mustered a semblance of cautious enthusiasm, not wishing to deflate Shah when she sounded so happy, but feeling very dubious about this storybook chapter unfolding – it was just too good to be true, unless Bahrin planned to bring Shah right up to the wire and then pull the pin on the whole plan.

'Are you pleased? I'm going to be there for Verity's birthday party!' Shah said again.

'Absolutely, darling, but how did all this come about? How much does your father know about us?'

'Not that much. He thinks I've only just spoken to you in the last couple of weeks.'

'Well, this is amazing news, darling, thank your father for me!' And with just a little more bewildering chat, she rang off.

I couldn't help but note that Saturday's date would be 1 April – April Fools' Day – was this Bahrin's idea of a cruel joke?

The next day, I went through the rigmarole of contacting Foreign Affairs again and putting a game plan together. Worried that this would also prove to be a false alarm, I explained the maze of difficulties and apologised in advance – just in case.

If Shah really did arrive in two days' time, the last thing we wanted was a media feeding-frenzy. Immigration flagged Shah's arrival and ensured it would not be necessary for her to be processed in the public arrivals hall. The manager of Melbourne Airport was brought into the loop; he organised for me to park at the rear of the terminal, out of public view. I could wait for Shah in the government's VIP room, where there was little chance of bumping into anyone who would catch on to what was happening. Customs officers would escort Shahirah off the plane and directly to the room. To avoid my being seen, it was decided I should arrive two hours prior to Shah's flight and bunker down in the VIP room to wait.

I would have to leave home at 4.30 a.m. to get to the airport, and we had decided we wouldn't rouse Verity and Zan. Bill would stay at home with them, and a friend, Peter Wallace, would go to the airport with me. It was best for Verity and Lysander to remain in ignorance of Shah's possible arrival. Saturday was the day of Verity's fifth birthday party and an early start would be too much for her on such an exciting, busy day. There was also this: if Shah didn't turn up, Verity would be devastated and it would ruin her birthday. So we strove to keep the lead-up to the big day as normal as possible.

Our family friends would be at the party early, sworn to secrecy; and later arrivals would be introduced to Shah as a non-English-speaking exchange student. So with twenty-four hours to go, and a birthday party for twenty-five children to cater for, I rolled up my sleeves and began a baking frenzy. If Shah really did walk off that flight, then I wouldn't have any time for party preparations and it was vital that Verity's big day go ahead as planned. Psychologically, the cancellation of her birthday party should not be linked with a big sister she had never met and who nevertheless promised to change the family dynamic forever. As few waves on the sibling rivalry front, the better.

I finally managed to wrangle an excited Verity and Zan into bed on Friday night. Then I phoned Shah. It was 7.30 p.m. I almost wept when she said she had her ticket in her hand.

At 7.45 p.m. Australian immigration authorities confirmed Shah had an active travel visa in their system.

At 8.30 p.m. I spoke again to Shah: she was still packing and couldn't decide what to bring.

At 8.45 p.m. our friends began to telephone to check if we were on track. I promised to ring with an update before I went to bed.

At 9 p.m. Judith Curran was on the line – she was anxious and doing some of the worrying for me.

At 9.10 p.m. another call. Was Shah was at the airport yet? No, I said, we're still waiting.

With a nervous chuckle I reflected that it felt a bit like being pregnant and all your friends knowing the due date: everyone calls to find out if Mother Nature is running to schedule. In this case we were all hostage to Shah's father, and whether or not at the final hour he would allow her to board the aircraft and let it take off.

By 9.30 p.m. Shah had finished packing and was about to leave for the airport. I told her I wouldn't call again until 11 p.m. my time.

At 9.47 p.m. I talked to Iddin: 'Don't worry, Mum, Shah is going tonight. Love you a lot, Mum, I'm going to come soon too, promise.'

At 10 p.m. the airport duty manager phoned, to go over security details and arrangements for my vehicle. He was incredibly helpful and also excited for us.

I moved to the computer and began to send out thank-you messages to all those who were helping with delivery of the 'package'. I wanted to ensure that they knew I was grateful for all their thoughtful assistance, regardless of the outcome.

An email I sent to a close friend in London that night says it all.

> Well, it may just be on for Saturday ... I won't know until midnight Melbourne time. Proof of the pudding at 8 a.m. on Saturday!!!!!!!!!!!!! Feel alternately nauseous and paralysed with excitement.
>
> Meanwhile, I'm catering for Verity's fifth birthday party on the same day at 2 p.m. – am up to my armpits tonight in honey joys and chocolate crackles! I also have to bake a mermaid cake!
>
> – Will keep you posted.
>
> Love
>
> Jack xxxx

My feelings and thoughts were a whirl of confusion. I told Bill over and over again: 'She won't come, you know, she's not going to be allowed to get on the plane.' My coping mechanism had flicked onto self-protection mode.

Bill played things very close to his chest, but he spoke of Walter. 'I always thought that when this moment came and the big kids came back, I would talk it through with Walter and ask him what to do – he was the one person I knew who had experienced something like this.'

When I rang her, Patsy had said that Walter was 'up there' watching over us, orchestrating a positive outcome. But still the manic words continued: 'She's not going to come, she's not going to be on the plane.'

The clock ticked around to 11.30 p.m. and I ventured another call to Shah.

'Hi, Mum, I've just checked in! It's happening!'

'Quick,' I said, 'give me your seat number. I need to notify the people at the airport. You have to stay on board the plane and not get off until a Customs and Immigration officer comes to fetch you. OK darling?'

I scribbled down the seat number, and told her I loved her very much.

'Oh, I love you too,' said her joyous voice. 'I'll be with you soon, Mummy darling, I'll see you in the morning! Verity doesn't know, does she? I really want it to be a surprise for her birthday!'

Assuring Shah it would be and hanging up the phone, I realised that I was trembling. Surprise it would be for Zan and Verity, but would my nervous heart make it through to morning?

I called the special telephone number I had been given by Foreign Affairs. 'The package is in seat 7C and will await collection.' I rang off after an acknowledgement from an unknown voice.

Bill and I sat up to watch a movie, then, bizarrely, unable to relax, I got it into my head to wax my legs. I perched on the kitchen bench slopping burning wax about then ripping it off as Bill winced at my grunts of pain. All the while I muttered under my breath, 'She's not going to be on the plane, she's not really coming, he's going to drag her off at the last minute.'

Just after midnight, I received a text message:

See you in the morning, Love Jo xxx

Bill and I trundled upstairs wearily; tomorrow would either be a very good day, or a very bad one. In any case we would have a birthday party overflowing with five year olds rampaging around the house. It was going to be a very busy day, come what may.

Placing a kiss on Verity, and Zan's brow, I straightened their covers and gently closed the door. If all went well in the morning, their lives would change forever as well. The family dynamic would shift – adjustments would be made by all of us and we'd absorb the changes with love and with each other's help. I said a silent prayer that I would finally have the opportunity to rise to the challenge.

But first, just like a child on Christmas Eve, I had to chase some sleep before I could see what Santa would bring me in the morning.

Thirty-Four

The Incy Wincy Spider Climbed up the Spout Again

A sharp rap sounded on the door of the VIP lounge and it swung open. Two uniformed Customs and Immigration inspectors were there, and the airport duty manager was hovering solicitously and protectively in the background.

'G'day, Jacqueline, my name is Paul and this is Mick,' said the taller of the two officers. 'You won't remember, but you went to primary school with my brother.'

'Of course I remember your brother; what's he up to these days?' I replied with a nervous smile. I could hardly remember my own name at this stage.

'Anyway,' Paul continued, 'I just wanted to say that I've followed your story for years and really felt for you and the kids. We both have' – with a jerk of his head he indicated his partner – 'and we really hope that it turns out all right for you this morning. I just wanted to let you know that the flight has touched down and we'll be heading down to the gate, and then we'll see. Fingers crossed, eh?' He finished with an encouraging smile.

I nodded tremulously, then sincerely thanked them. Until I

saw Shah for myself, I wouldn't believe it was true. There was still a possibility it was all another cruel hoax.

The door swung closed and Peter and I sat together in silence. I suddenly thought it was a good thing that Peter was a trauma surgeon – if my heart stopped with grief or joy, he'd know what to do.

'Cheer up,' said Peter, 'we'll know in a little while.' He reached over and gave me a bear hug, then turned to look up at the arrivals monitor. 'It says offloading,' he told me. Peter had been my friend since I was fourteen, had known Bahrin and watched Iddin and Shahirah grow in the years preceding the kidnap.

'By the way, what's with the get-up?' he quizzed, jabbing a finger at my hair and make-up. 'Bit dressed up, aren't you?'

'Well, you don't get many chances to meet your own child all over again and I wanted to make a good impression,' I explained with a tense and embarrassed grin.

Minutes dragged by. I could hear the steady tick of the clock on the opposite wall. I was tortured with anticipation and nerves. 'She's not on the flight, she didn't get on,' I kept telling myself over and over again.

And then a loud knock on the double doors. Peter and I leapt to our feet.

I was halfway across the room when the door opened wide and a whirling blur of brown flung itself towards me as I opened my arms.

A huge wail like a stab of pain echoed round the room. 'Muuummmyyy!' came the anguished cry.

I didn't even see her face, just felt the arms clinging around my waist as we both let out a sob at exactly the same time. Somehow we had staggered across the room and were standing in the doorway, blocking it. Peter gave us a gentle push backwards and firmly closed the door, leaving us alone.

Our embrace did not falter; we couldn't let go as fourteen years of tears began to fall. From a distance I registered the keening sounds of long pent-up grief, and realised Shah and I were the source. We howled like banshees; I had not thought it possible to chorus such a wave of emotion and grief in audible tandem and survive.

No words were spoken, except, over and over again: 'Mummy.' And my reply, 'Shah-shah.'

Sobs and tears caught in our throats and still we clung together not moving a muscle. Shah's head had burrowed itself into the right side of my neck and I grasped her furiously to me, afraid to let go.

We had taken up a kind of rocking sway – a dance of comfort and of grief and comfort again. I was her mother once more, and she my child to be rocked and cradled.

We wept and wept, till surely we could weep no more, but still the tears came.

'Sore neck, change,' I half laughed, half cried, and automatically we switched the sides of our embrace: no talk needed and still no drawing away.

At some point I think the door opened a crack and was rapidly closed again.

'I don't even know what you look like,' I finally murmured when our howls had subsided to occasional gulps of air and big snotty snivels. 'On three, we'll look at each other,' I ventured.

'No, no, not yet,' protested Shah, 'Just a bit longer.'

And so I rocked her some more. Her shoulders shook and her hair was saturated with my tears.

'One–two–three,' I counted then, and drew back to look at my child, the girl I had given birth to all those long years ago.

She was amazing.

She was beautiful.

Dark-brown almond-shaped eyes, red-rimmed from all the crying, looked back into mine. Slim, delicate features and slender wrists. Masses of tousled, brown-black hair and a shy smile.

I cupped her face in both my hands and gently kissed every inch of it in wonder. I ran my fingers through her hair and rubbed them across her ears – they were the same little ears I had played with as she dozed off to sleep as a child.

She had taken off the traditional veil on the plane, she said, running her fingers through her hair. I wanted to ask more, but those sort of questions would wait.

The door opened again. Peter poked his head in and said we'd better leave. He'd already put Shah's suitcase in the car. We hugged each other once more and turned for the door, arms entwined. In the corridor, the two Customs officials, Paul and Mick, beamed at us with tears in their eyes. I hugged them both and Shahirah followed suit. We walked from the terminal to the waiting car within a cordon of protective people. Shah, enveloped in my giant quilted coat, was insulated from the cold. I kept my head down and walked fast. Peter packed us gently into the back seat and we sped away, the tinted windows protecting us. No one saw us; the route we took was deserted.

Shah and I snuggled close and held hands on the drive home. She immediately pulled a stack of photographs from her bag and began to show me a record of some of the missing years. We grinned at each other continuously and I registered that my face was beginning to ache.

It was still hard to absorb the reality of her presence.

'You're really here,' I kept saying inanely. 'Oh, I've missed you so.'

Then I remembered to tell Shah about the birthday guests who would be coming this afternoon.

Shah laughed at the prospect of impersonating an exchange student who couldn't speak English and turned her attention to the passing scenery.

'This looks so right, the colour of the trees and the sky; Malaysia's always looked weird to me. *This* is what I remember home looked like.'

I knew what she meant. When I lived in Malaysia I found the green lushness both stifling and overwhelming; I suspect lots of travellers feel that way and can't put their finger on what's wrong. That's probably why those who go away to work overseas eventually come home. In Australia, our sky is different and our trees.

When we pulled up outside the house, Shah shot me a nervous and uncertain look. My children were about to meet each other.

She hid behind the front fence pillar as I rang the bell.

'Mummy!' came the excited cry over the intercom. Then Shah and I could hear Bill talking to the kids.

'Mum has a surprise for you. Why don't you go and see?' he suggested.

The gate popped open and Verity and Lysander came running towards me expectantly.

'Where's the surprise?' they demanded as Shah popped into view, crouching down low to say hello.

'Hi, Verity! Hi, Zan! It's me, Shah-shah, I've come for your birthday party.'

'Yay,' squealed Verity, leaping into Shah's arms and almost knocking her over. 'Did you bring me a present too?'

'Tar-tar,' said Zan. He came forward and grabbed her hand.

'Hi, Shah. Welcome,' Bill greeted her. 'This has been a long time coming!' he ended with a quick hug.

We tumbled through the door, a jumble of rowdy children and luggage. There was hardly time to take Shah to her room before the little ones were pulling her away to show her all their favourite things.

Exhausted and elated, I leaned into Bill's arms and let out a sigh of relief. 'I'll give them five minutes and then go and rescue Shah,' I told him.

Eventually, I dragged Shah away from Verity and Lysander and bundled her into her room, after a quick tour of the house. She hadn't slept on the plane, so I hugged her again, showed her the snugly green robe I had bought her and the nightie.

'You just have time for a couple of hours' rest before your godparents arrive.'

Once she had changed, I tucked her up beneath her fluffy white duvet for a nap. Kissing her forehead and stroking her cheek, I savoured the moment, still doubting its reality. Whispering the bedtime blessing from her childhood into her ear for the first time in fourteen years, tears filled my eyes.

'Sweet dreams, God bless. I love you millions, billions, trillions and infinities.'

The rest of the day passed in a blur of joyous happiness: extended hugs; balloons; teary-eyed 'aunts' and friends; Shah's delight at finding the party food included chocolate crackles and honey joys – favourites from her own birthday parties; Lysander earnestly trying to take photographs of the event with his biggest sister, Shah, squatting beside him; Verity's sighs of sheer bliss as she unwrapped the fairy dress and pink accessories Shah had given her; a mermaid-shaped birthday cake.

There was peace and contentment too. Amid a flurry of

running and jumping five year olds, a shy Shah beamed at me, at her little brother and sister, at all her friends.

Uncle Eric, Shah's eighty-three-year-old godfather, had wept at the surprise appearance of Shah, and his warm embrace seemed to go on forever. One friend spoke discreet and private words with Shah and her eyes glistened all afternoon afterwards, while another let her matter-of-fact exterior dissolve into a long squeeze punctuated by more tears. Tissues were at a premium in our home that day.

I seemed to hover outside my own body, observing and revelling in the jubilation.

A few friends whom I hadn't had the chance to warn pulled me aside and sceptically quizzed me. That Japanese student of yours looks a lot like you, they said as realisation began to dawn, grins of joy lighting their faces.

We couldn't cope with media, I said over and over, but most importantly, I felt instinctively that for all Shahirah's upbeat bravado, beneath the surface I had a very traumatised girl on my hands. Time and space to get to know each other, and for the family and children to work through the dynamics, was vital. A media circus would impede that and make it much harder to do with natural timing and exploration.

Twenty-eight days was the time limit that had already begun to count down in my head. That was the supposed duration of Shahirah's stay with us – how would I ever let her go.

I decided to push the timeline to the back of my mind and just enjoy the next few days. We would cross that bridge when we came to it.

The guests had all departed, Verity's big day had been a success, the cleaning up had been done and now it was time for bed.

Lysander and Verity climbed into Verity's double bed for their evening story. I lay between them, and Shahirah found room to nestle at my feet across the width of the bed, wrapped in a rug. I read *Possum Magic*, a book as much a part of Shah's early childhood as it was her little brother's and sister's. Afterwards, Shah and I crept out when the small ones were asleep. Going down the stairs, Shah ventured a question.

'Mum, can I have a really deep bath? We don't have hot water over there and I've *really* missed baths.'

'Of course, darling, this is your home too,' I replied.

And then, very shyly, she followed with a rather confronting question.

'Mummy,' she said, her heart-shaped face tilted downwards, 'will you have a bath with me?'

Swallowing my panic at the prospect of revealing my forty-something body to a 'stranger', I answered yes. It wasn't that I had a problem with nudity – the little kids took showers and baths with me all the time, and I'd done the same with Shahirah and Iddin all those years ago. I was just a bit taken aback that Shah was feeling comfortable enough to suggest it, considering her recent religious upbringing. In my mind, there was also an element of worry that I might disappoint or even scare her with my body. Had she grown up with me, she would be used to my body getting older, losing some of its youthful elasticity and ageing as it should. This would have given Shah some perspective on her own physicality and body image. I could already see that we shared an almost identical body type – it was just that my 'gear' was ten inches wider or lower than it had been. After all, I had breastfed four children. But if Shahirah wanted to have a bath with me, then so be it.

In the bathroom I lit candles and brought out my most delicious perfumed bubbles. Turning on the tap at full bore, I ran us a steaming hot bath, blessing the fact the tub was huge and luxurious.

We sank into the water, settling down amongst the foamy bubbles. After a while in the warm water, Shah began to pour out her heart. She filled in the blanks of the stolen years, the treatment she'd endured at the hands of her first stepmother. To break down a little girl, over the years this woman had systematically taken every opportunity to tell my beautiful daughter that she was ugly, deformed and useless. My child had been snatched from a foreign country and her real mother; why couldn't she have shown Shah compassion and love in an alien land? We touched on the abduction, about which Shahirah was reluctant to speak, so traumatised was she fourteen years later. We talked about her life in Malaysia. Although her father had gone to the trouble of abducting her and Iddin, he'd left it to others to rear the children: Shahirah and Iddin hadn't even lived with him at his house, they'd been put in spare rooms at their grandmother's home next door.

When I heard about her father's brand of discipline for small children I was devastated. Shah gave a chilling account of the punishment for talking back to her stepmother. Bundling Shah into his car in the dark of night, Bahrin would regularly drive her to the cemetery, remove our daughter from the vehicle and leave her to spend the night alone in the deserted graveyard in the pitch black. Iddin had apparently been spared this punishment but was regularly caned.

'Sometimes,' Shah told me in a flat voice, 'I tried to run after his car, and I remember clawing at the tyres as he left.'

It was a small comment at the end of Shah's story that

upset me the most. 'I probably deserved it for disagreeing with my stepmother,' said Shah. My poor daughter didn't realise that no child, especially one who was already traumatised by a kidnapping, deserves to be left in the dark in a cemetery. What was done to her was very wrong, and in most countries a parent would go to jail for treating a child that way.

On the fingers of one hand, Shahirah could count the people who had been truly kind and loving towards her during all her time in Malaysia. Only three had ever said anything positive to her about me, and even they had spoken in whispers out of Bahrin's earshot.

It turned out I had been right: the kidnap was all about possession, not love. The vindication was hollow – I would have infinitely preferred to wave a magic wand and erase all those years of pain my children had suffered.

As the water in the bath chilled, we replenished it again and again, spending nearly three hours in its warmth, so that by the time we emerged we had begun to resemble wrinkled prunes.

For Shahirah and me, that bath was a rebirth of another kind. We once again became mother and daughter; but we also became women connected by more than genetics and circumstance.

'Stay with me, Mum, I'm too scared to sleep alone,' pleaded Shah. We'd talked for hours more propped up on a mountain of pillows in Shahirah's bed. We talked more, and finally my voice went hoarse and I had to beg to be allowed to sleep.

As I laid my head down next to Shah's sleepy head in the wee hours of the morning, the words of the child's nursery rhyme came back to me.

The incy wincy spider climbed up the water spout
Down came the rain and washed poor incy out
Out came the sunshine and dried up all the rain,
And the incy wincy spider climbed up the spout again.

It just went to show, I reflected, that if you hold on long enough, the sun will come out and the rain will go away.

Thirty-Five

The Clamouring Hoards

The next two days were blissfully normal in a strangely abnormal way. Shah's wish list had nothing to do with sightseeing, for she didn't consider herself to be a tourist. She wanted to reconnect with places and things that were familiar. So we drove to our old houses, her school and kindergarten; we stopped whenever she got a prickle of recognition down her spine and she would peer intently at whatever it was that had caught her eye and try to remember why. I had to drag story after story from my memory bank to illuminate the particular incidents and places Shah remembered.

One afternoon we trundled down to the Royal Botanic Gardens to feed the ducks and swans, much to the delight of the younger children. This was an activity chiselled into the stone of Shah's deepest memories, for we had spent many afternoons there when she was little.

Lying on the grass, I felt almost as if I was watching a six year old again, as Shah luxuriated in the mild sunshine and the wide open spaces. Swans and ducks swam to the children and were fearlessly fed titbits by all three of them.

Monday, we had time for a girlie expedition, heading over

to my hairdresser, whom I had known for more than twelve years. When I introduced Shahirah, the floodgates opened and couldn't be closed. But this was more than I had expected: she sobbed and blubbed for an entire hour at the revelation that Shah and I we were reunited.

But our peace was not to remain undisturbed for long. When Shah spoke with her father by phone on Monday, Bahrin let drop that he might have spoken to the media about Shahirah's trip to Melbourne. A couple of hours later, a friend rang to say that speculation of Shah's return was being discussed on the radio.

The phone began to ring, until it was ringing incessantly. It was already too late for most of the media to make print or broadcast deadlines, but I knew what this meant. Taking Bill aside, I told him we'd better pack some bags and leave the house until it all blew over, but he was adamant — we should stay put amidst familiar surroundings.

'You have no idea what it will be like,' I argued, but he remained firm and so I resigned myself to making the best of a very bad situation. I was particularly worried for the younger two children. Shah certainly had some idea about the media, but for the little ones, being trapped inside a house was not a very healthy thing — physically or mentally.

We went to bed with the bell on the phone turned down low.

But by seven next morning, the extent of media interest was clear. Our doorbell was ringing over and over again — as were those of our neighbours, by reporters seeking information and gossip. The house next door was peered into and our telephone quietly rang off the hook — the message machine filled in just an hour. We kept all the curtains drawn and hid inside.

Shah was horrified and burst into tears, then retreated to her room, lying on her bed and staring sightlessly at the ceiling. The distress of all she had suffered during the years of abduction was very deep, and now this media attention traumatised her.

Cars and camera crews choked the street and by, 9.30 a.m., it was almost impossible for passers-by or residents to enter or leave, either on foot or in a vehicle. The police were called and began to issue traffic fines to all and sundry. It proved no deterrent; the reporters and photographers knew their employers would pay and refused to move on.

The only funny thing was that all the camera crews were waiting outside the empty house next door, their long lenses trained in the wrong direction. However, that didn't last long as a police officer wanting to speak to us rang our bell and we were forced to answer the door.

That was when I knew for sure that Bahrin had purposely put out the story. He was the only one who had the incorrect number for our street address. At the last minute before Shah's departure he had asked her for the address and she had inadvertently given him the wrong number.

In the absence of comments at our end, the media began to chase and broadcast interviews with Bahrin. Shah telephoned him and asked him to desist, describing the rowdy siege outside our house, but he went on fuelling the media fire. I believe that Bahrin wanted to ruin Shah's trip home to Australia, to make it look as if I was media-hungry and willing to exploit her.

In desperation we asked the police again for assistance and they tried to clear the street. Still, Verity was forced to go to school with a blanket covering her head, and so, too, Lysander.

At night, the paparazzi showed terrible persistence. Donning balaclavas against the cold, they threw stones against our windows in the hope they would tempt us to open the curtains and peer outside, affording them a blurry picture. My two youngest children were terrified by this behaviour and I was hard pressed to get them off to sleep. Friends who visited in the evening had to run the gauntlet of photographers just to drop off food, as we couldn't leave the house to shop.

Shahirah was a mess and I was rapidly turning into an unpleasant manic mother lioness. Lysander was so frightened that I found him sticking plasters along the length of his bedroom door to 'keep the naughty people out'. Verity was confused and needy; she just wanted her normal life back. Her school had to put guards on the door, as reporters attempted to find an angle to the story there as well.

It had to stop. It was evident that the press would not leave us alone until we gave them part of what they wanted. I understood that they bore us no malice, and that the majority were overwhelmingly pleased for our happiness, but they were ravenous for a picture.

Right smack in the middle of all this insanity, Judith flew in from New Zealand to meet Shah and share in our joy. She was like a bright light being flicked on.

We decided to pull ourselves together and allow the release of video footage and one photograph of Shahirah and me together. We were not interested in exclusives or payments, although we did pause for a while aghast at the huge sums being bandied around. But ultimately we decided that it would be best if the pictures were distributed to every media outlet in Australia and any other interested media around the world. For over fourteen years, people had been so kind and supportive, this was our family's way of saying thank you.

We left the house for the first time in five days.

A couple of paparazzi attempted to snatch a picture. But in general, at last, we were left alone.

One thing that really heartened us was the goodwill shown by people who recognised us. Strangers ran across the street to hug us and burst into tears. When we went shopping, we were hugged and congratulated repeatedly. Many of those parents from our local kindergarten and school whom I had thought aloof in the past expressed their happiness for us, and said that for so many years they had avoided speaking to me as they simply hadn't known what to say or how to deal with our tragedy.

This was behaviour Shah had not experienced before. In general, she explained, Malaysian people had treated her like a royal oddity and, over the years, had been quite rude with their personal and insensitive questions. Kindness was such a revelation to Shahirah it made me want to weep all over again.

We managed a wonderful family holiday over the Easter break, hiding out at the foot of the Victorian snowfields in a log cabin and enjoying a wonderful Easter-egg hunt with friends at their pub. The children ran around like wild things and we paddled in the river and generally had a great time. If we were recognised, people limited their contact to expressions of congratulations and then left us alone.

My two girls, even though separated by sixteen years, sometimes bristled with sibling rivalry. It was difficult for them to come to terms with each other's existence; on a deeply loving level they did not falter, but when it came to engaging my attention they were competitors. As Verity and Shahirah jostled, I tried to dispel any jealousy, and to give them the tools to sort things out themselves. They were still learning that my love is elastic, adaptable, squishy and big enough to go around all four children. Instant families are very hard for any child to slip into.

Eventually, life found a nice rhythm, and I watched Shah gain confidence and begin to blossom. It was wonderful.

The ordinariness of our daily activities was so elating that I refused to see this precious time through the lens of a camera and only took a minimal number of pictures. For me mundanity was the key and the most extraordinary gift. If I had spent the entire time with a camera in my hand, I would never have experienced the little and intense moments of love, the glue that holds a family together.

One night towards the end of her twenty-eight-day visit, Shah, Bill and I were watching an action movie on television. During a scene in which one of the protagonists fired a pistol, Shah casually remarked, 'That's like the one I use,' gesturing to the gun onscreen.

'What do you mean?' I was amazed.

Shah explained that she and Iddin were taught how to shoot a few days after they were kidnapped. When they arrived in Indonesia on the way to Malaysia, they were given rifles and taught to shoot tin cans. They were told they had to learn to protect themselves from me if I came to get them. After that, Bahrin made sure they trained with pistols, in case I turned up. Iddin and Shah still sometimes went to the firing range to relax.

Great, I muttered in my head, my children not only use weapons, they're taught to shoot their mother!

It was horrifying to learn that Shahirah took guns and shooting so nonchalantly.

'Abah always carries a pistol and all our bodyguards too,' she told us.

I quite literally began to bang my head against the sofa.

What else would the years uncover about my children's upbringing in Malaysia?

The day of Shah's departure drew nearer, and finally arrived.

'Mummy, please believe me, I *will* come back soon,' she said as I tried to smile.

Verity and Lysander clung to Shah's legs as she lay on the floor of the VIP lounge with her head cradled in my lap.

Yes, she did have to leave; she had given her word to her father, and Iddin would suffer the consequences if she failed to return. But the boarding call sounded terribly final, somehow.

'I'll see you all again soon – I love you all so much!' She was sobbing now. And then the airport duty manager took her away to the departure gate.

I felt a profound emptiness and wept as she disappeared from view. Bill and the little ones did their best to comfort me, and together we went home.

Thirty-Six

Row, Row, Row Your Boat

Then, eight days after Shah left, the phone rang.

'Mummy, I don't belong here, I know that now. I want to come home for good. Can you get me out?'

So, twenty-four hours later, Shahirah walked off that plane again – to begin a new life in Australia. She was just in time for Mother's Day.

The decision as to where she lives and what she does was rightly hers: she is an adult and has a right to a life of her own making. She needs to find out what she wants to bring to the world and how she can do that herself. She needs to discover her own tastes and passions, without moral blackmail, without manipulation. She needs to simply live, surrounded by our love and encouragement. Make her own mistakes and learn from them, knowing we will love her no matter what.

We had the great privilege of sharing Shah's twenty-first birthday here in our home – with a cake of her choice baked and iced by me! It was our traditional family birthday cake, double chocolate mocha rum cake. For presents, her list was specifically non-acquisitory and gave some hint of her interests: she requested piano and guitar lessons, reasoning she had a lot of catching up to do on things most Australian children would have experienced by her age. She is exploring exactly who she is and how to nurture and enrich her soul.

I always smile to myself when I hear her singing in her room, for music has been only a partially explored passion until now.

As a mother of an adult woman, I am learning too: learning to fight my protective instincts and not second-guess Shah too often. We are all finding our way in our new family, and that includes the young children as well.

It can be quite amusing when Verity and Shahirah rummage through my wardrobe and openly covet my collection of shoes and evening bags or particular items of clothing – each vying with the other about who will have first dibs on certain pieces now or when, in Verity's case, she is grown up. It's sometimes all sequins and Manolo's at twenty paces between the girls, but I truly relish these 'normal' mother and her daughters episodes. I've also gotten to fulfil at least one motherly milestone with Shah – I taught her how to walk steadily in sky-high heels and not wobble all over the place. A small and trifling moment to most people – definitely a vacuous fashionista moment – but a small maternal triumph after having missed so many.

Sometimes it is frustrating having our own real princess in the house: there is a distinct lack of domestic nous in Shahirah. We had to have a go at domestic boot camp, for Shah had never had to worry about the nuts and bolts of living, or boring chores. But I am incredibly proud that she has dived in head first, having a go at waitressing and reception work in an attempt to find a niche for herself. I have great faith that when she does find her path, she will throw herself into it wholeheartedly, and I will support her in that.

A loud kerfuffle had broken out downstairs. I was nearly dressed but we were perilously close to being late that morning. It was time to leave on the short walk to Verity's school. Tuesday, 22 August 2006, would shape up to be a whirlwind of a day.

The little ones were calling out with great excitement. I dashed out of the bedroom – and saw a burly figure climbing the stairs towards me.

Behind him came Verity dancing, Lysander jumping, and Shah.

'Mum,' the man said to me.

'Iddin!' I shrieked, and he caught me as I teetered on the top step.

I burst into tears, sinking to the floor and being kissed by him and crushed in a strong and wonderful hold.

Flummoxed, shocked, completely at a loss for a sensible thing to say, I couldn't stop touching his face and grasping and regrasping his fingers.

Iddin was trying to halt his own tears, saying over and over, 'It's all right, Mum, I'm here now, I'm home. It's really me, Mum, I'm home. Don't cry, Mum, it's going to be all right. I'm home, Mum, I'm really home.'

I nestled in this fully grown man's arms like a small child, our roles reversed.

Dozens of questions ricocheted around my brain. 'How? When?' was all I could utter.

'Shah helped me, Mum. I wanted to surprise you – did I?' he asked hopefully. The answer must have been clear in my gobsmacked face.

Bill strolled in at that moment, straight from the shower. And he didn't miss a beat – extending his hand and saying, 'Welcome,' then laughing and shaking his head.

Verity presented a freshly created drawing to her big brother, one she had just whipped up in honour of the occasion.

'This is for you, Iddin,' she said shyly and sat down to observe him.

'WELCOME HOME IDDIN', the caption read, and the picture showed her brother and our house and the sun shining down on us all.

Zan just stared in awe at Iddin; I suspect he thought his brother would be the size of a photograph, but here he was sporting a beard. From that moment, my littlest boy imprinted on my biggest boy like a duckling and followed his big brother around with adoration in his eyes.

As I gazed at him, Iddin laughed and volunteered, 'I'm going to shave it off, Mum, but I wanted you to see it.'

I loved it, a young bull showing his manliness to his mum.

After a while Iddin said, 'Mum, if the media comes, let's just give them what they want straightaway; I don't want to waste any of my time with you at all.'

It was sad that Iddin had come to think so pragmatically. I went back for another enormous hug.

How in heaven's name had my small frame produced such a bear of a man? It was utterly befuddling and amazing.

Then I roused everyone. 'Come on, all of you, I want to walk to school at least once with *all* my children around me.'

And so in the bright spring morning we walked hand in hand to drop Verity at school – Bill, Zan, Verity, Iddin, Shah and me. It was absolutely glorious – it surpassed any daydream I had ever conjured up.

Within hours, the first media outlet had made contact. Fortunately, this time we had an experienced publicist poised to help and a game plan that the media outlets accepted and respected. Iddin's break from university was so short, only ten days — not a second would we waste of family time together.

Bahrin had called a press conference to announce he had magnanimously allowed the children to visit me for a short time. It was a pathetic stab at saving face, but his lack of respect for their independence distressed Shah enormously.

We resolved that the two eldest children and I would appear at our front gates for a photo session and a brief comment the next day. And indeed the media left us alone afterwards, even though we declined all requests for further interviews.

Together we talked an enormous amount, again filling in some of the blanks of the lost years, but for the most part Iddin was more keen on living in the present than the past. He knew without a shadow of a doubt that I had never given up my fight for him and his sister; the lengths to which his father had gone to obliterate me from their minds only confirmed my devotion, he said.

Iddin had a list of wishes for his time in Melbourne. Many involved me cooking his remembered favourite foods! Catching up with his old school friends was also high on his agenda. He also wanted to find some surf clothing and, like Shah, visit old haunts and familiar places.

The timing was a bit awkward as I was due to have minor surgery that Friday, but we managed to fit in an amazing shopping trip the day before I had to go to hospital. Iddin had a great time. After fourteen years to be able to give my eldest child a treat after so many missed birthdays and Christmases was such a thrilling thing to do.

As well, Iddin and I often found quiet times together after everyone else was fast asleep. Cuddling up on the couch, we talked of his love of photography and scuba diving. Watching his face illuminated with enthusiasm made me thank heaven that he had discovered his passions. He was determined to complete his course in photography and wanted to focus on underwater shots – that would marry his two passions.

On the day before his departure, I organised for Iddin to dive with the sharks at the Melbourne Aquarium. Lysander and Verity were mesmerised by the sight of their big brother swimming with stingrays and sharks inside the massive glass tank. I was transfixed by Iddin's body language: he placed himself on the bottom of the tank as colourful fish swam around him and nibbled at the bubbles from his mouthpiece. He looked completely chilled out, like an underwater Buddha.

Being a typical male, Iddin waited until the last moment to express his emotions to me. Four hours before his flight was due to take off, he seemed suddenly aware of all he had left unsaid. Holding my hand, he made sure he had my attention before beginning.

'Mum, I really love you, I want you to know that. I want to finish my course and then come back and live here, but I want to be able to support myself and work. *I am coming back*,' he stressed emphatically. 'Mum, I want you to know that I am really proud of all the work you've done overseas helping people. I'm proud that you're my mum. And I really love you. I know that you never gave up on us, Mum, you never quit. I know you tried everything to get us back.'

'I did, I did,' I said from behind the tears that had started to well up in my eyes.

'Mum, promise me you believe me when I say I'm coming back, that you'll see me next holidays. None of what happened to us was your fault, Mum, I know that, OK? None of it, and I love you, Mum.'

We hugged each other crushingly – I still felt oddly little in my son's arms. How fiercely I loved him and how much I wanted to ask him to stay. But later, as I watched him go through the departure gates, I was proud that I had refrained from doing so.

I was now a parent of adult children, and part of me had to get used to letting go; allowing Iddin and Shah to go their own ways – so they could come back of their own free will.

My greatest wish had been to one day introduce all my children to each other, to reach out my hand and be able to touch their cheeks and not have them disappear in a puff of smoke as they did in my dreams. Blessedly, that day had arrived – and it was truly wonderful.

As to what I want now, not much. I would like to be allowed the grace to raise Verity and Lysander and watch them grow and help them to flourish. My biggest dream had come true when I stood in my kitchen and watched all four of my amazing, unique, beautiful and individual children sitting together around the dining table, joking and smiling, waiting for me to serve them food I had just prepared. There's not anything else that can surpass what I consider life's greatest and most amazing bonus – my children.

My children Iddin and Shah have always deserved to have both of their parents as a constant presence in their lives. Yes, I suffered over the years, but my main concern was always for my abducted children, and how they were coping. The relationship they have with their father is complex, but I don't begrudge them the validity of the love or allegiance they feel for him. And as hard as it is, as unpalatable as I may find it, my role is to accept and respect their feelings. Bahrin is their father, just as I am and will always be their mother. As adults, the setting of parameters and boundaries is their decision, and we, as their parents, must accept their choices, even if sometimes we may not agree with them. For me, it's always been about love, not power.

In the future, I will tell any mother or father who comes to me after they have lost their child to abduction, that if they have always seen their child as an individual, not a possession, and loved them with respect for *their* needs and not the parent's own, then love will someday override borders and prejudices and indoctrination and their children will return.

One must always live in hope.

Epilogue

I hope this book and its precursor, *Once I Was a Princess,* serve as a cautionary tale that will encourage parents going through a relationship break-up, or a difficult time with their former partners, to realise that revenge, anger and retaliation are futile and damaging actions. To use children as a weapon against a partner will hurt them terribly, but not their relationship with the left-behind parent. So many years on, my conviction was correct: stolen children always come home when they can. But the relationships they will have with the abducting parent, once they are mature and informed adults, will reflect what was done to them as children.

Anger and revenge are motivations that eat away at one's inner core, and taint any future happiness on the horizon.

Family law is such a complex and emotional minefield; it can mark one's life, and that of one's children, for decades to come. A knee-jerk response to certain situations is not always the most rational or the best long-term plan when dealing with a family or a relationship – even a relationship that has devolved into something alien and bitter. Dignity and commonality are strong principles which will hold a person in good stead when putting down the foundations of a new life after divorce or separation.

Physical control only lasts over one's child while they remain young. How one, as a parent, behaves in the here and now will determine if you are a chore to be 'tended', or a welcome guest and participant at the major milestones of their adult lives.

During the fourteen long years I was without Iddin and Shahirah, I discovered the worst and the best in other people – but most of all, I've found a commonality of humanity around the world which gives me hope that our very ordinariness will be our salvation. For all the turmoil in the world, there is a calm place deep within each of us that –regardless of race, creed or nationality– carries our dreams, hopes and expectations for our children and our children's children. My belief is that at the very core of all humans there is a fundamental desire to nurture and to value the simpler things in life and that through this collective sanity it is possible to celebrate our sameness, and not our differences.

I've learned many important lessons during my fourteen years of stubbornness, reinvention, battling and lobbying, but three, in particular, have special resonance. First, we must never take anyone or anything for granted – especially our children. We simply can't count on tomorrow to say 'I love you'. Secondly, I've learned to never give up, and thirdly I now know always to turn a negative into a positive.

Life is simply a work in progress; the trick is to make sure you apply yourself to the job well.

Acknowledgements

Over the years, I have been fortunate to accrue an amazing host of friends without whom this book would not have been possible. During the years when my children Iddin and Shahirah were withheld from me, my friends are what kept me going. It is to them I proffer my deepest and most sincere gratitude and love.

As well, my love and thanks go to my eldest children Shahirah and Iddin for trusting in my love for them and our memories to make their leap of faith. Verity, you are my sunshine miracle girl and you have been so patient, allowing me to write this new book, thank you with lots of squishy love. Lysander, although you aren't quite four, there is a wise old man behind those eyes and I love you very much. Bill, what a light at the end of the tunnel; you so detest publicity I can't go into more detail HBMMGSLA – thank you!

In no particular order, each of you have been on this rocky journey with me: Sue MacArthur, Deb Gribble, Auntie Connie and Uncle Kevin Coverdale, Gavin McDougall, Dean White, Heather Brown, Sally Nicholes, Mike Fudge, Barry Goodman, Patsy Heymans, Judith Curran, Chris 'Geeb' Allen for being the braun and the brain who kept me out of harm's way in sticky situations, Sarah Beard, Andrew and Caroline Blackman, Charles Tapp, Dawn and Martyn Bradley, Jane Allen (now McLean) and Jason McLean, Valerie Hardy, Maria Balinska and John Udorovic (who always said the sun would come out again).

Special thanks to my extraordinary friend and literary agent, Deborah Callaghan, for chanting, *I think I can, I think I can* during the home-stretch insanity.

Appreciation and thanks to James Fraser, Sonny Mehta, Miss Jackie Collins, Tracey Chapman, John Judge, Shakira Caine, Steven Candries, Uncle Eric Waller, Richard and Joanne Waller, Ingrid Butters, Sonia Patterson, Anthony Blair, Martin Grant, Jocelyn Mitchell, Drewe Balmain, Jane Hill, Sophie Daou and Neil Milne. My thanks to Rove McManus for allowing me to hear Belinda Emmett's music, which motivated me and reminded me to be frank and less than perfect. Our dear Marianne 'Mim' Henneveldt, who helped to wrangle Lysander as I wrote much of this book, and Elizabeth Lew for her sixteen years of 'back-up'. Rob and Janine Goldstein, Lyn and Harold Jossel and all your clan, when the times have called for it, you've been my South African back-up team.

Thanks for the wonderful support and the unwavering commitment I have received from Fiona Brownlee and Bill Campbell of Mainstream Publishing, and the sterling work of Deborah Warner, my editor.

Appreciation to the people from CARE International past and present: Antony Robbins, Chloe Bayram, Stephen Gwynne-Vaughan, Guy Toussignant and Geoffrey Dennis.

To the people I have had the privilege to meet through aid work, my writing and travels, I owe you a debt that I can't sufficiently repay. You have allowed me to listen to your thoughts and record your stories, reminding my readers that life is so much bigger and broader than our living rooms and the television screens that flicker in the corner.

Sincere thanks must also go to those people who have wished my family well and worried on our behalf about the outcome of this gruelling experience. Your kindness ticking over in the background kept me going.

Thank you, *merci, danku, hvala, tack, grazie, obrigado, danke, assantisana, pakka per fyrir, falemnderit.*

Contacts

Jacqueline Pascarl
www.jacquelinepascarl.com
Email: info@jacquelinepascarl.com
PO Box 282
Hawthorn Vic 3122
Australia

International Parental Child Abduction

Australia
Nicholes Family Lawyers
Specialists in Parental Child Abduction Issues and Hague
Convention Law
Level 3, 224 Queen Street
Melbourne Vic 3000, Australia
Tel: +61 (0)3 9670 4122
www.nicholeslaw.com.au
Email: sally@nicholeslaw.com.au

Attorney General's Department
Canberra, Australia
Tel: +61 (0)2 6250 6666
www.ag.gov.au

Department of Foreign Affairs and Trade
Canberra, Australia
1300 555 135 (24 hr hotline)
www.dfat.gov.au

Belgium
Missing Children International Network
Tel: +32 (02) 534 5631 or +32 84 211 461
Fax: +21 84 221 1394

European Union
Child Focus
European Centre for Missing and Sexually Exploited
Children
Tel: +32 2 475 44 99 (24 hr hotline)
www.childfocus.org

Canada
Missing Children Society of Canada
Suite 219, 3501–23 NE
Calgary, Alberta T2E 6V8,
Canada
Tel: +1 (403) 291 0705
Fax: +1 (403) 291 9728
www.mcsc.ca
Email: rmorgan@mcsc.ca

France
Collectif de Solidarite aux Meres D'Enfants Enlevees
9 Rue des Chaillots 92190
Meudon, France
Tel: +33 (1) 4534 4910
Fax: +33 (1) 4623 1164
Email: csmee@wanadoo.fr

United Kingdom
Reunite – International Child Abduction Centre
PO Box 7124
Leicester LE1 7 XX,
United Kingdom
Advice Line:
Tel: +44 (0) 116 2556 234
General Enquiries:
Tel: +44 (0) 116 2555 345
Fax: +44 (0) 116 2556 370
www.reunite.org
Email: reunite@dircon.co.uk

PACT

Parents and Abducted Children Together
PO Box 31389
London SW11 4WY
United Kingdom
Tel/fax: +44 (0) 20 7627 3699
www.pact-online.org
Email: support@pact-online.org

United States of America
The National Center for Missing and Exploited Children
(US Central Authority for Incoming Cases)
Charles B Wang International Children's Building
699 Prince Street
Alexandria, VA 22314–3175,
USA
Tel: +1 703 274 3900 (24 hr hotline)
Fax: +1 703 274 2200
www.missingkids.com

Can anyone help locate Audrey Leinoff?
She was abducted in 1988, aged four.
www.audreyleinoff.com

Humanitarian Aid and Development

CARE International
www.careinternational.org
'Click' on the country site most appropriate for you.

JACQUELINE PASCARL has worked in radio and television, and as a documentary film-maker. Her work includes the award-winning documentary *Empty Arms – Broken Hearts*, which investigates the issue of child abduction. In 1995 she became involved in the area of child literacy and established Operation Book Power, a project operating in Kenya and South Africa. In 1998, she was appointed Special Ambassador for CARE International and worked as an emergency aid worker in the war zones of Bosnia, Kosovo and East Timor.

Recognised internationally as an expert on the Hague Convention and International Parental Child Abduction, Jacqueline has lectured at the US State Department and the Australian Department of Foreign Affairs and Trade, as well as to the European Union and the Hong Kong Family Law Association. Awarded the United Nations Special Commendation for the International Year of the Family, and two recognition awards from the National Center for Missing and Exploited Children, USA, Jacqueline has been a high-profile international lobbyist on human rights and refugee issues. In recognition of her humanitarian work, Jacqueline was appointed to a new role as a patron of CARE International in January 2007.

Jacqueline is the author of the bestselling *Once I Was a Princess*. She has four children, and now resides in Melbourne, where she is concentrating on her writing.